"It's about time a book like this hit the market! No caricatures of 'them,' no hackneyed stereotypes of 'the other side,' this is an honest assessment of where the debate lies. Although an expert himself, Dr. Rau shows his seasoned pedagogical skills and does not lose nonspecialist readers in unnecessary technical jargon. If you've suspected that there are more options than just creationism or philosophical materialism, this book is for you."

NICHOLAS G. PIOTROWSKI, Crossroads Bible College

"Eminently qualified with advanced degrees in genetics and science education from top universities, Dr. Gerald Rau not only aims to present the arguments for each position as neutrally as possible, he actually succeeds where angels, let alone countless other scholars, have feared or failed to tread. His thoughtful Christian voice rings clearly in the midst of an often shrill debate where too many are unwilling to acknowledge how their respective worldviews shape their interpretations of scientific data."

ROBERT OSBURN, executive director, Wilberforce Academy

MAPPING THE ORIGINS DEBATE

Six Models
of the Beginning
of Everything

Gerald Rau

IVP Academic

An imprint of InterVarsity Press
Downers Grove, Illinois

Inter-Varsity Press
Nottingham, England

InterVarsity Press, USA
P.O. Box 1400
Downers Grove, IL 60515-1426, USA
World Wide Web: www.ivpress.com
Email: email@ivpress.com

Inter-Varsity Press, England
Norton Street
Nottingham NG7 3HR, England
Website: www.ivpbooks.com
Email: ivp@ivpbooks.com

InterVarsity Press®, USA, is the book-publishing division of InterVarsity Christian Fellowship/USA® <www .intervarsity.org> and a member movement of the International Fellowship of Evangelical Students.

Inter-Varsity Press, England, is closely linked with the Universities and Colleges Christian Fellowship, a student movement connecting Christian Unions in universities and colleges throughout Great Britain, and a member movement of the International Fellowship of Evangelical Students. Website: www.uccf.org.uk.

While all stories in this book are true, some names and identifying information in this book have been changed to protect the privacy of the individuals involved.

Cover design: Cindy Kiple
Images: Shunyu Fan/iStockphoto
Interior design: Beth Hagenberg

USA ISBN 978-0-8308-3987-2
UK ISBN 978-1-84474-616-3

Printed in the United States of America ∞

Library of Congress Cataloging-in-Publication Data has been requested.

British Library Cataloguing in Publication Data
A catalogue record for this book is available from the British Library.

P	20	19	18	17	16	15	14	13	12	11	10	9	8	7	6	5	4	3	2	1
Y	29	28	27	26	25	24	23	22	21	20	19	18	17	16	15	14	13	12		

To my beloved wife, D. Victoria Rau,
without whose encouragement this
book would not have been possible

Contents

Abbreviations 9

Preface 11

Acknowledgments 15

1 WORLDVIEWS, PHILOSOPHY AND SCIENCE 19
  1.1 What Is Eternal? 20
  1.2 What Is Science? 23
  1.3 What Questions Need to Be Addressed? 28

2 A SPECTRUM OF MODELS 31
  2.1 What Is a Model? 31
  2.2 What Is the Spectrum of Opinion? 35
  2.3 What Are the Models? 38
  2.4 What About Intelligent Design? 52

3 ORIGIN OF THE UNIVERSE 57
  3.1 What Is the Evidence? 59
  3.2 How Does Each Model Interpret the Evidence? 73
  3.3 What Difference Does It Make? 80

4 ORIGIN OF LIFE 82
  4.1 What Is the Evidence? 83
  4.2 How Does Each Model Interpret the Evidence? 94
  4.3 What Difference Does It Make? 99

5 ORIGIN OF SPECIES 101
  5.1 What Is the Evidence? 102
  5.2 How Does Each Model Interpret the Evidence? 119
  5.3 What Difference Does It Make? 127

6 ORIGIN OF HUMANS 129

6.1 What Is the Evidence? 130
6.2 How Does Each Model Interpret the Evidence? 142
6.3 What Difference Does It Make? 148

7 WHAT WE CAN LEARN FROM EACH 153

7.1 What Evidence Needs an Explanation? 154
7.2 What Contribution Has Each Made? 155
7.3 What Does Each Need to Address? 162
7.4 Seeing the Big Picture 170

8 THE DEFINITION AT THE HEART OF THE DEBATE 175

8.1 Whose Definition of Science? 176
8.2 The Heart of the Debate 183

Epilogue 191

Appendix 1: *Tables Comparing Six Models of Origins* 193

Appendix 2: *Comparison of Various Interpretations of Genesis 1* . . . 206

Glossary 209

Bibliography 223

Subject Index 233

Person and Organization Index 237

Abbreviations

AAAS	American Association for the Advancement of Science
BSCS	Biological Sciences Curriculum Study
CMBR	cosmic microwave background radiation
COBE	Cosmic Background Explorer
DE	directed evolution
DNA	deoxyribonucleic acid
HGT	horizontal gene transfer
ID	intelligent design
MN	methodological naturalism
NAS	National Academy of Sciences
NE	naturalistic evolution
NOMA	nonoverlapping magisteria
NRC	National Research Council
NTE	nonteleological evolution
OEC	old-earth creation
PE	planned evolution
RNA	ribonucleic acid
SETI	Search for Extraterrestrial Intelligence
YEC	young-earth creation

Preface

The first to present his case seems right,
till another comes forward and questions him.

PROVERBS 18:17 NIV 1984

• • •

Thousands of books have been written on evolution and creation, so how is this one different and why should you read it? Most authors try to convince readers that their position is correct. A few books present a dialogue between proponents of two or more views. Many attack another position without presenting a comprehensive scientific model with better explanatory power. The diversity of approaches and failure to state axiomatic assumptions makes it difficult for the novice reader to understand, much less evaluate, the arguments. This book presents the full range of possible models and demonstrates how our religious and philosophical presuppositions, rather than the evidence, dictate our preference.

Currently there are at least six major classes of models explaining the origin of the universe, life, species and humans, but few people can clearly describe more than two or three of them. In this book you will find (1) an overview of the models, (2) the evidence that each uses to justify its position, and (3) what data each refuses to allow as evidence and why. As much as humanly possible, I will try to present each of the positions objectively, using neutral language, in order to give the reader a chance to evaluate the arguments in the absence of rhetoric, positive or negative. I will also argue that each, viewing the evidence from a different perspective, sheds important light on the subject.

When I was in high school, a speaker came to our church youth group to talk about how the biblical flood explained all the fossil evidence, disproving evolution. I was convinced. When I got to college, evolution was rigorously defended. I was confused. I had been told that this was a scheme of the devil, yet the evidence seemed to point to gradual change in life forms over a long period of time. I read a number of books, each with a convincing argument, but none that for me resolved the apparent conflict between science and religion. Eventually I set the issue aside to be examined later. Many in the church today can undoubtedly relate to my dilemma.

Although I intuitively knew there must be a middle position that reconciled the two, I did not know where to find it. Not until after I had completed my doctorate in plant breeding from Cornell University and moved to Taiwan did I begin to find an answer. There I was introduced to David Newquist, a professor of physics at Tunghai University, who taught a course on faith and science. He pointed me to a number of resources that confirmed others had followed the same path I had, coming to similar conclusions, and had sound evidence and arguments to back up their ideas.

About that time I began teaching at Lincoln American School, later renamed the American School in Taichung. I struggled with how to teach evolution, and read eagerly about old-earth creation and theistic evolution positions. Gradually I developed a table outlining four, five and eventually six models of origins and what they believed. At the same time I began thinking about the nature of science, how science is actually done, and realized the shortcomings of what I had been taught about the scientific method. This gradually became the unifying focus of the science curriculum, and the basis for teaching origins.

In my naiveté I thought I had stumbled on something unique, only to find when I tried to publish that there was a whole literature on the nature of science in science teaching which I was not familiar with. This reflects the problem in the field of origins as well. The question is so broad, with so many aspects and evidence from so many disciplines that no one can be familiar with all the literature, let alone be an expert in every area. Religion and philosophy come head to head with geology, astronomy, biochemistry and genetics, to name a few, but in the research world today a generalist is hard to find. My background of research in applied genetics, followed by teaching every branch of science in the middle and high school curriculum, along with freelance editing of journal articles from many disciplines, and finally going back for a master's degree in science education, focusing on the philosophy of science, has given me a unique perspective from which to write this book.

Those who are specialists in one area or have read widely in this field will undoubtedly feel this book is too simplistic, overlooking important distinctions, missing vital nuances or not presenting enough details. Please forgive me, but this book is not intended for you. It is a simple map to help high school or college students find their way through hotly disputed territory, to guide their journey from the one-sided and greatly oversimplified arguments they have heard in science textbooks or church sermons to the depth of scientific, theological and philosophical literature that exists. It will also be useful for adults who want to understand the issues but have forgotten the science they studied many years ago and are confused by the many techniques developed since then. It is a scaffold to support learning, not a research work to advance knowledge.

It is my hope that this book will provide a good introduction to the topic for some, a clarification for others, and perhaps a challenge for those embroiled in the battle. I am not so naive as to think that this will resolve the issue, but I hope it will at least help the audience notice when participants use unfair tactics in the eternal debate.

Acknowledgments

• • •

As with any author, I am indebted to more people than I could possibly remember or list. Nevertheless, some individuals deserve special mention.

The first and arguably one of the most important is Jim Hoover, my former InterVarsity staff member from college, now the associate editorial director of InterVarsity Press, who was willing to review and comment on the first version of this book in 2004. Although he rejected it (when it was half-written), saying it would run six hundred pages, covering too many different topics for too diverse an audience, his comments showed me how to proceed. When I sent another version over the transom in 2010, he again took time from his busy schedule to consider it and show it to others.

Thanks go next to Gary Deddo, senior editor at InterVarsity Press, for being willing to pick up an unknown author and give him a chance. Where criticism was warranted, he was direct but gracious, but what I remember most was the encouragement. Other staff at InterVarsity Press, many of whom I have never met, have done a wonderful job helping to bring this project to fruition. I am in their debt.

One of my students at Wheaton College, Ed Meadors, took time to have lunch with me and ask why Christians cannot agree about origins. Many other students helped sharpen my ideas, but it was during that conversation that the focus of this book became clear and the desire to write it burst again into flame. His "Dine with a Mind" ticket paid off handsomely.

As I was completing the first draft, four men, Raymond Lewis, Kenneth Lundgren, Eric Norregaard and James Orme, took time to read the entire draft and meet once a week for eight weeks to give me feedback. Not only did their comments contribute substantially to the accuracy of my presentation of each model, they also modeled how believers holding young earth, old earth and evolutionary creation positions can talk productively about this question, really listening to one another and wrestling with the issues. It was a great experience that I fervently hope others will replicate.

Along the way many others also read and commented on all or part of the manuscript. The two anonymous reviewers pointed out errors and potential pitfalls, and made numerous suggestions that immeasurably improved the final product. Robert Bishop looked over an early version of the first chapter and told me everything that was wrong with it (which was considerably more than what was right), instead of giving it a pocket veto as two other philosophers of science had, and pointed me to the book by Hugh Gauch that now plays a key role in both the first and last chapter, tying the scientific debate to the social debate.

Other professors at Wheaton College also contributed time or encouragement to this effort, including Pattle Pun, Jennifer Busch and John Walton, among others. Pastor Jeff Holwerda and Nicholas Piotrowski asked me to speak at the Fox Valley Theological Society in the early days of the project, which provided feedback from a broad audience, as did a talk sponsored by the Wesleyan Christian Fellowship at my alma mater. I would be remiss not to also mention all of my students over the years, both high school and college, whose questions helped clarify the organization and wording in many previous versions of the tables found in appendix one.

Throughout the course of my research I cannot count the number of times I came up with a new insight, a revelation that would change the world, only to discover six months later that someone else had already written essentially the same thing. Although this is humbling, it is also encouraging, and I have noted their work. It is entirely possible that other authors have previously expressed other ideas I have presented as original. If so, the omission is unintentional, and if such are called to my attention I will be glad to rectify the situation in future editions, if there are any. Truly, as Solomon realized, there is nothing new under the sun, but maybe there are still new ways of putting old ideas together.

Finally, I must thank my wife for her constant support. For nearly ten years, from the time this book was conceived until it reached the form you have in your hands, she never stopped believing that it would one day be completed.

None of the people mentioned above will agree with everything I have written. They have contributed greatly to this work, but the opinions expressed and any errors that remain are mine alone.

Worldviews, Philosophy and Science

• • •

What is eternal? Various opinions have been offered by science or religion throughout human history, but at the most foundational level there are only two possible answers: the natural world, or something supernatural. Thus the debate about origins is eternal and interminable, because at its core lies a conflict between two diametrically opposed, fundamentally irreconcilable viewpoints: naturalistic and supernaturalistic. Yet within those two basic viewpoints are multiple ways of interpreting both the empirical and documentary evidence about origins, leading to a spectrum of opinions on the issue. This book is an attempt to present that spectrum in a way that is comprehensible to those with little background in either science or theology, as objectively as possible, to promote understanding of the presuppositions and logic of each position. In doing so I must necessarily make generalizations and will not do full justice to any particular argument, but notes will lead interested readers to literature representing each position.

Before we can discuss what each position holds, the subject of the second chapter, it is important to think briefly about how we know anything.[1] Much of what we know is based on ideas we pick up from

---

[1] This is the subject of a branch of philosophy called epistemology. A full study of the question is beyond the scope of this book.

those around us, often without conscious thought or evaluation. These deeply held but often unrecognized convictions affect our answer to the question at the heart of the debate: what is eternal?[2] In this book I will attempt to distinguish two components that affect the way we look at the world: the worldview we absorb as part of our culture, and the personal philosophy we choose.

The focus of the book, however, is not the worldviews or personal philosophies themselves, but how these affect our interpretation of the scientific evidence. The fundamental thesis of this book is that although everyone has access to the same evidence, the presuppositions implicit in a person's philosophy determine the perspective from which he or she views the data, leading to different logical conclusions about which explanation best fits the evidence.

In this first chapter I will examine briefly the connection between science and philosophy. This will be followed by a functional definition of science, showing the interaction between evidence, logical inferences and presupposition in natural science. Those who want to jump into the debate itself can read the first paragraph of each section of this chapter for now, then come back to it before reading chapter eight to see the broader perspective.

1.1 What Is Eternal?

When looking for answers to a question, a logical place to start is to list all possible alternatives. Rarely is this easy, because although we list all the alternatives we can think of, there may be others we have not considered. Usually, however, it is relatively easy to list all possible *classes* of alternatives; that is the case with the question of origins. Since the universe is present, it either always was present or came into existence at some point. If it came into existence, something external to the universe must have been present—either another source of the matter and energy it comprises or something with the ability to create matter and energy. Put more simply, there are only two logical choices for what is eternal— natural or supernatural.

---

[2]"[F]or many of the combatants on both sides the dispute really is worldview-driven" (Ratzsch, 1996: 182).

Within each of these two major classes of alternatives are more specific proposals, sometimes called worldviews, related to a particular religion or set of beliefs. But worldviews include elements drawn from culture and society as well as religious texts, so there may be many variations within a single religion, just as denominations often reflect the culture (both ethnic and temporal) in which that particular group originated or developed. Beyond culturally shared views there are ideas we hold personally, which make up our personal philosophy.

Worldviews and personal philosophy. Much has been written recently on worldviews, a word largely unknown to previous generations. James Sire (2004) has defined a worldview as

> a commitment, a fundamental orientation of the heart, that can be expressed as a story or in a set of presuppositions (assumptions which may be true, partially true or entirely false) which we hold (consciously or subconsciously, consistently or inconsistently) about the basic constitution of reality, and that provides the foundation on which we live and move and have our being. (p. 122)

According to Sire, a worldview is an individual commitment, and his definition has had a strong impact on evangelical Christian thought in America over the last few decades. But many elements of our worldview are picked up wholesale or piecemeal from the culture around us, often without conscious thought, because the ideas are deeply embedded in the language and fabric of the culture, and other authors claim the term *worldview* should be restricted to this cultural level. Because I must use some term, but do not want to be embroiled in this debate, in this book I will use worldview when referring to a general cultural phenomenon, and personal philosophy to refer to the set of philosophical presuppositions and commitments that affect the way we individually see the world.[3] Although a person may change his or her personal philosophy as a result of some experience, the worldview formed in childhood has a strong influence on a person throughout life and often remains largely unquestioned.

---

[3] I am indebted to one of the anonymous reviewers for making me aware of this issue, and clarifying the distinction between the two components.

Part of our personal philosophy includes what we consider to be true, or whether we can in fact know something to be true. In recent years a philosophy known as relativism has been gaining prominence, especially in intellectual circles. According to this view there is no absolute truth; each person must decide what is true for him- or herself. This stands in stark contrast to most traditional religions and the basic premise of most scientists. A basic premise of this book is that truth exists independently of the observer, and it is our responsibility to seek and, to the best of our ability, live by that truth, even if our knowledge of it is imperfect.

How worldviews and personal philosophy affect science. Worldviews form early because they are embedded in the language. Words and ideas are grouped together, forming the ontology of the language. Certain words are given positive or negative connotations. Word choice by parents also affects the way a child views different concepts. Accordingly, every child develops a personal philosophy long before he or she is exposed to science in any form, certainly before being exposed to any direct scientific evidence about origins. Thus our worldview and philosophy shape the way we view that evidence from the first time we hear it.

Those who hold to a naturalistic, materialistic, atheistic perspective must of necessity postulate a way for matter and energy to be eternally self-existent. They must also find some sort of self-organizing principle or principles to account for the increasing complexity of the universe and life, based either on necessity or probability. According to this perspective, it should be theoretically possible to find a natural explanation for every event, past, present or future, and there is nothing that cannot be studied by science.

Those working from a theistic perspective may have various views of science, depending on how they believe God interacts with the world. Since the theistic side of the debate about origins in America is dominated by various Christian positions, that will be the focus of this book, but as each model is described in chapter two I will show how similar interpretations of the scientific evidence are expected from other monotheistic, polytheistic or pantheistic perspectives. Frequently more than one Christian interpretation of the scientific evidence is possible, being closely related to the interpretive framework used to understand the Bible, especially the early chapters of Genesis (Poythress, 2006: 82-85).[4]

1.2 WHAT IS SCIENCE?

We all have an intuitive sense of what science is, yet when it comes to a formal definition, science is remarkably difficult to define. At its root, science is the quest to understand the natural world. But there are many different types of science, each with its own methods and techniques, including theoretical science, experimental science, observational science and historical science, making it hard to delineate where science ends and some other way of knowing begins.

Nevertheless, attempts have been made to define the basic characteristics of science. One of the more successful, by a working scientist with extensive training in philosophy, is *Scientific Method in Practice* by Hugh Gauch (2003), who contends that, "Every conclusion of science, once fully disclosed, involves components of three kinds: presuppositions, evidence, and logic" (p. xv). All other ways of knowing also involve presuppositions and logic, so we will begin by considering the component unique to natural science, empirical evidence.

Empirical evidence. *Empirical evidence (terms with an asterisk are defined in the glossary) is anything that can be observed with our five senses, with or without assistance. Things we can see, hear, feel, taste or smell can be sensed directly. Sometimes we use instruments to assist in extending or quantifying our senses. For example, a microscope or telescope extends our vision, while a spectrophotometer helps quantify our sense of color, and a compass helps us observe magnetic fields that we cannot sense directly at all, although we see their effects.

There is a difference in the way empirical evidence is collected in different types of science. *Experimental science examines phenomena that are repeatable, regular occurrences, by manipulating a variable to determine its effect. This is the type of science most people currently think of as prototypical science. Although typically associated with laboratory science, experiments can also be conducted in agriculture or

---

[4]A brief summary of different interpretations of Genesis is presented in appendix two.

ecology by applying treatments to different plots of land. Phenomena that are too large, time consuming or where there are ethical constraints on experimentation must be studied observationally. Examples of *observational science include investigation of stars, earthquakes or disease spread. *Historical science is the study of nonrepeatable physical events, including the ice ages or origins. *Theoretical science makes predictions, often based on mathematical calculations, that can be tested by one of the three empirical approaches.[5] A famous example is the prediction made by the theory of relativity, and later confirmed, that gravity could bend light.

As we will see in subsequent chapters, empirical evidence from every branch of natural science contributes to the debate about origins, making it difficult for anyone to have a full command of all the various lines of evidence. Beyond the strictly empirical, theoretical sciences like cosmology and population genetics with strong mathematical components and mathematical tools like statistics have also long been part of the debate, and arguments from other branches of mathematics, including probability and information theory, are increasingly being entered as evidence as well.

Logical inferences. But empirical evidence by itself is not enough. The process of science involves making logical *inferences. An inference is a conclusion, explanation or judgment based on the evidence. The difference between evidence and inference is essential to the question of origins, as indeed it is in every area of science, so we must learn to clearly differentiate the two.[6] This will be a major emphasis of chapters three through six.

There are two basic types of logical inference: deductive and inductive. In natural science deduction typically involves reasoning from the general to the specific, from a model to the expected data, while induction typically involves reasoning from specific cases to general con-

---

[5]Experimental, observational and historical methodologies each have a different way of forming and testing hypotheses (Haarsma & Haarsma, 2007: chap. 3; Cleland, 2002).

[6]In science education, philosophy of science is discussed under the term "nature of science." One widely cited author in this field says the most important thing for students to understand about science is "First, students should be aware of the crucial distinction between observation and inference" (Lederman, 2006: 304).

clusions, or from actual data to an inferred model (Gauch, 2003: 157-59). Because of the difference between the two types of logic, a deductive argument is either valid or invalid, but an inductive argument cannot be absolutely valid or invalid, only strong or weak.[7]

This distinction is important in the study of origins, because models are created by inductive logic and therefore cannot be shown to be true or false. On the other hand, specific predictions made by the models, which involve deductive logic, can be useful in testing their veracity. Failure of a prediction does not immediately disqualify a model, however, because the failure could be due to failure of ancillary assumptions, not the basic model.

A third type of inference mentioned by some authors, abductive, is sometimes called inference to the best explanation. It involves drawing on multiple lines of evidence to reach a conclusion, but it cannot be formalized mathematically as deduction and induction can. Almost every statement we take to be true and almost every decision we make depends to some degree on abductive inference.

Logic must be carefully distinguished from rhetoric, although both are used in argumentation, in the origins debate as well as elsewhere.[8] Court cases provide an instructive example: in court, neither the evidence nor the inferences stand on their own—they must be combined into a coherent argument. Often it is the rhetorical skill of the presenter, rather than the weight of the evidence itself, that convinces a jury to view the evidence a certain way. The same is true in the study of origins.[9]

Necessary presuppositions. At the beginning of the twentieth century, the logical empiricists, also known as positivists, claimed that science depended only on evidence and logic, without any *presuppositions. This idea has since been debunked by philosophers and historians of

---

[7]"Given the truth of all of its premises, the conclusion of a valid deductive argument is true with certainty, whereas even given the truth of all its premises, the conclusion of an inductive argument is true with, at most, high probability, but not absolute certainty" (Gauch, 2003: 158).

[8]Logic and rhetoric, along with grammar, were the three components of the trivium, the foundational liberal arts in ancient Greece, on which all other knowledge (*scientia*) was based. On the vital role of argumentation in science, including how argumentation is used to support both deductive and inductive inferences, see Duschl & Grandy (2008).

[9]Decisions of what can be admitted as evidence are also important, as we will discuss in chaps. 4, 5 and 7.

science. Hugh Gauch (2003: 112) asserts that science cannot be done without some philosophical assumptions or presuppositions, but that the necessary presuppositions are normally not disclosed because they are commonsense and therefore taken for granted.

Gauch (2003) describes a presupposition as "a belief that is necessary in order for any of the hypotheses to be meaningful and true but that is non-differential regarding the credibilities of the individual hypotheses" (p. 127). Within science there are both global presuppositions and local presuppositions related to the particular field of inquiry. Necessary global presuppositions include a belief that the physical world is real and that we can trust our senses (Gauch, 2003: 128). Almost all philosophical positions accept this, apart from radical skepticism. Thus, the necessary presuppositions are (nearly) independent of philosophical perspective, a necessary criterion for the objectivity of science. Local presuppositions "emerge mechanically as beliefs held in common by all of the hypotheses in the hypothesis set," so that they too are nondiscriminatory with regard to the veracity of the various hypotheses, which is then determined based on the evidence alone (Gauch, 2003: 131-32).

It must be emphasized here that the objectivity of science, its independence from particular worldviews, may be true of science as a whole, but is not when it comes to individual scientists. Certainly in the area of origins, which deals with what Gauch calls "deep answers," objectivity of individual scientists is not possible. It is widely accepted that the data "underdetermine" theory, that is, there are any number of theories that could explain any particular set of data. Each scientist is working from the perspective of one particular theory, which affects both data collection and interpretation. It is also likely that objectivity and consensus will be easier to obtain in the experimental sciences than in the historical sciences, particularly those like origins that are closely connected with our philosophical commitments.[10]

There are many intriguing aspects of the question of what science is and how it interacts with philosophy that we will not be able to explore in this book, including presuppositions about the nature of reality. In twenty-

---

[10]Historical science does, after all, involve an element of history, and very few believe that history is objective.

first-century America most of us take a *mechanistic perspective of the world for granted, but this has not always been the case, nor is it necessarily so in other parts of the world. I must simply note here that there are deeper issues related to this for the interested student to explore.[11]

Is science the only way of knowing? E. O. Wilson divides all human intellectual activity into science and the creative arts, the former representing transmissible knowledge, the latter personal ideas (Wilson, 1998: 12). This reflects his view that all knowledge will ultimately be subsumed under the umbrella of science. Others have distinguished the natural sciences, which study universal events caused by natural regularities, from the social sciences, which study unique events caused by human vagaries, arguing the two use different methodologies (Pearcey & Thaxton, 1994: 50). It could certainly be argued that mathematics, depending only on logical inference from certain axioms without any reference to empirical evidence, represents a different way of knowing. But the boundaries between the different ways of knowing are vague, with one merging into the next.

One of the presuppositions of this book is that ultimately there is a unity of knowledge—a reality that can be known—but we use multiple approaches to seek that knowledge. Mathematics and philosophy, building logical arguments on basic premises, contribute to that knowledge. Natural and social science, building logical arguments on empirical or artifactual evidence, contribute to that knowledge. And religion, building logical arguments on sacred texts, also contributes to that knowledge.

Like all presuppositions, this cannot be proven or disproven. It must simply be accepted or rejected, based on one's philosophical position.[12] But like the presuppositions of science, it emerges from the set of hypotheses under consideration. All fields of study feel they have something to contribute to the study of origins. Whether that contribution turns out to be large or small, it is only fair to allow each to have its say.

---

[11]For a brief analysis of how neo-Platonic, Aristotelian and mechanistic views of nature have interacted throughout Western history see Pearcey & Thaxton (1994).

[12]Gauch (2003: 152) notes that "there are exactly two faith choices: by faith to accept science's presuppositions, or by faith to reject science's presuppositions. The choice is not between faith and non-faith, but between one faith and another faith."

1.3 WHAT QUESTIONS NEED TO BE ADDRESSED?

The topic of origins is very broad in scope, both in the range of questions addressed and the number of disciplines contributing evidence in an attempt to answer those questions, so it is impossible for anyone to be an expert in every area. Since everyone tends to view his or her own specialty favorably, it is inevitable that differences exist in what is considered to be the most compelling evidence.

The dual assertions of this book are that none of the evidence is unimportant, and that it is important to seek a position that is both internally consistent and logically defensible in light of all the evidence from every applicable area of study.[13] These assertions cannot be defended scientifically, based on empirical evidence. Like all other assertions of value, they fall in the realm of the nonempirical. The assertion that none of the evidence is unimportant, coupled with the fact that no one can be an expert in every area, implies that we need to trust that experts in each area are doing their best to ensure that the evidence they provide is as accurate as possible. Thus, we must deal with that evidence rather than brush it aside as unimportant, even if we feel the inferences they have drawn are incorrect or incomplete based on what we know about evidence from a different field.

Four origins. There are at least four major origins that need to be explained: the origin of the universe, of life, of species and of humans. Any coherent model needs to explain all four in a way that is logically consistent.

In chapter two I will define the term *model*, distinguishing it from other related terms used in the literature, then show how six different models represent sections of a continuum of possible interpretations of the evidence, how each flows logically from its philosophical underpinnings and how each seeks to provide a complete explanation of the beginning of everything. In the following four chapters we will explore each of the origins in turn.

The origin of the universe is the question of cosmology. How did the basic stuff of the universe, matter and energy (and whatever else might

---

[13]Philosophers call the idea that you should take everything you know into account "the principle of total evidence."

be out there that we have not detected), get here in the first place? In some sense this is the ultimate and most basic question, for it gets at the root of the issue of what is eternal—the material world or something immaterial. We will examine how different models answer this question in chapter three. Evidence for this comes from various branches of astronomy and theoretical physics.

It is entirely possible that a universe could be filled with nonliving matter. In fact, as we will find in chapter four, this seems to be far more probable than that there is life of any sort. The question of how life originated is primarily the realm of biochemistry, with contributions from geology and other fields.

Once life existed, by whatever means, it diversified over time. How did this occur? This is the question of origin of species, with much of the evidence drawn from paleontology and genetics, as well as other branches of biology. It is the area in which the public debate is most obvious, partially since the evidence is somewhat more visible and tractable to the general public than the former two, and partially due to the fact that this was the first of the four questions brought to the forefront of the debate. This will be the focus of chapter five.

The question of how humans originated is perhaps a subset of the previous question, but it is included as a separate question because of the number of traits that seem to separate humans from other living things, and its importance to us as a species. Because the origin of language, culture and religion deal more with the social sciences than the natural sciences, I will limit our discussion to the origin of the human form. Most of the evidence here is again from paleontology and genetics, as we will discuss in chapter six, but the broader question of human origins also draws from anthropology, psychology and linguistics.

In chapter seven I will evaluate what scientists from different perspectives have contributed to the debate. I will argue that each of the models has contributed to our understanding in some way, and each still has unanswered questions that it needs to address.

Finally, in chapter eight we will return to some of the ideas of this chapter, looking again at the importance of the definition of *science* to the debate, and the question of whether science can provide evidence for the existence of God or the veracity of the Christian faith.

Evaluating the models. For whatever reason, our brains seem to be programmed to favor explanations that are logically consistent. Philosophers may debate why this is, but scientists take it for granted that the best explanation is one that is both internally coherent and consistent with the available evidence from various fields, possibly including areas outside the realm of science. Science is built on the principle of logical consistency, making logical inferences based on the available evidence. Yet we will find that, based on different assumptions made about the presence or absence of God, or how and how often he interacts with the natural world, several different positions are all internally consistent (Sober, 2008: 13), and all can be considered to be consistent with the evidence.

Many people evaluate *others'* models based on their *own* personal convictions, and find them to be logically untenable. In this they are correct. Each model rests on and is inextricably connected with particular philosophical presuppositions. Apart from that, it is nonsense. Thus, when passing judgment on a particular model, we are usually not judging its logical consistency or ability to explain the evidence as much as its philosophical or religious roots.

This leads us back to the purpose of this book. I do not expect to convince anyone that his or her model for understanding origins is incorrect. In fact, I will not attempt to do so. Instead, my purpose is to map out the different models, showing where they are similar or different and how each is logically consistent and tenable, based on certain underlying assumptions. In the process of discussing each model, I hope to cause you as a reader to examine your own philosophical perspective, the assumptions it makes and its logical consequences, as well as help you understand, if not appreciate, why others hold different views. Having laid the foundation, we are now ready to examine the various models of origins.

A Spectrum of Models

• • •

The first chapter laid the necessary foundation for the book, sketching out very quickly the importance of philosophy to the debate and defining science as the process of drawing logical inferences from empirical evidence. When it comes to the issue of origins, those inferences are strongly colored, often to the point of being determined, by the underlying philosophical presuppositions of those making them. In this chapter we will examine six major classes of models of origins and see how each is indeed directly and causally related to an underlying philosophy.

Before I can describe the six classes of models, however, I need to explain the scientific concept of models, especially since a scientific model is quite different from the common definition of a *model*. To do this I will compare the term *model* with several other terms used in the literature to describe scientific explanations, many of which also have common meanings at odds with their scientific use.

2.1 WHAT IS A MODEL?

There are two common meanings of the word *model*: a small-scale replica or perfect example of some category. When we talk about a model train or model car, we are using the first sense of the word. When we talk about a model citizen or a supermodel, we are referring to the second.

The scientific is yet a third, although related, meaning.

Scientifically, a *model (sometimes called a conceptual model) refers to an idealized and often simplified representation of a situation or phenomenon that tells us something about how or why the real object works. There are many different types of conceptual models, including physical models (such as a model car), representational models (such as a diagram) and computer models (such as climate-change models) (Gilbert & Ireton, 2003). The key difference from the common definition is that a scientific model helps us understand how or why a particular phenomenon occurs—its purpose is explanatory. As scientists gain greater understanding of a particular topic or phenomenon, they move from a vaguely defined mental model to a more carefully defined conceptual model.[1]

Hypothesis, theory, law, model. Four terms—*hypothesis, theory, law* and *model*—are used by scientists when talking about scientific explanations of the data, and it is important to distinguish how each is used, although it is beyond the scope of this book to provide a full discussion of the relationship between them. Unfortunately, in popular science writing they are often used interchangeably or incorrectly, making it very hard for the inexperienced reader to sort out what the author intends. Even scientists use the same term differently in different branches of science, increasing confusion in the study of origins, which involves so many different fields of study. Although three of the four have a similar denotation, differences in connotation lead to rhetorical choice of one over another in the debate, making it even more important to clarify various ways they *are* used, and how they *should* be used.[2]

*Hypothesis is commonly viewed as the most tentative of these terms. It is used in statistical testing to refer to the proposed explanation being tested by a particular experiment, which may be supported or questioned by the data. Since this type of hypothesis is easily falsified, the

---

[1]"Conceptual models are in some senses the external articulation of the mental model that scientists hold and are strongly interrelated with mental models" (National Research Council, 2012: 56).
[2]The following definitions are both descriptive (showing how the terms are actually used, based on the author's reading of journal articles in various fields over many decades, popular science, textbooks, and science teaching literature) as well as prescriptive (how they ought to be used, according to current consensus in the nature of science literature).

term in general has the connotation of something quite tentative. Nevertheless, since a hypothesis is based on past research that provides some understanding of the system being studied, it is not just a wild guess or speculation.[3]

*Theory is perhaps the most difficult of the four terms to define, as the common meaning is very different from the scientific, and it is used quite differently in different branches of science. In nonscientific speech, theory is often used to refer to a vaguely supported guess, as in "I have a theory about that." In science, the term *theory* commonly refers to a unifying idea tying together a large body of related knowledge statements, including tested hypotheses, laws, definitions and a broad range of empirical data. Biologists arguing for the strength of the theory of evolution often assert that this is the only proper scientific meaning of the term, but that is not the case. In modern theoretical physics, theory frequently means a mathematically plausible explanation that has not been empirically tested. Nevertheless, for most areas of science the term *theory* tends to imply a greater degree of support than *hypothesis*. This leads to situations in which advocates of a particular explanation will refer to it as a theory, while detractors will refer to the same explanation as a hypothesis.[4] Although theories, like all of science, are provisional and may be revised in the light of later discoveries, the term is typically reserved for explanations for which there is a good deal of empirical or mathematical support.

One of the most widespread misconceptions in science is the idea that an explanation starts as a hypothesis, but as more evidence is gathered it may become a theory and eventually a law.[5] Even practicing scientists and textbooks have been known to publish this error. The

---

[3]Nor is a hypothesis the same as a prediction, although the two are often used interchangeably in science laboratory guides. A prediction is a statement of what should be observed if the hypothesis under consideration is correct.

[4]So opponents of evolution will speak of the evolutionary *hypothesis* instead of evolutionary *theory*, and some use the term *intelligent design* (ID) *theory* while others discuss the *ID hypothesis*.

[5]In a list of fifteen "myths of science" propagated by science education, the first one listed is "Hypotheses become theories that in turn become laws." The author goes on to explain that "Laws are generalizations, principles or patterns in nature and theories are the explanations of those generalizations" (McComas, 1998: 54). "Laws are *statements or descriptions of the relationships* among observable phenomena. . . . Theories, by contrast, *are inferred explanations* for observable phenomena" (Lederman, 2006: 305).

truth is that law and theory are two entirely different entities.[6] One never becomes the other, and a law usually precedes the associated theory. A *law is a pattern in the data, often expressed mathematically. A law explains and predicts *what* happens, but does not provide an explanation of *how* or *why* it happens, which is the role of a theory. Obviously a pattern is usually recognized (law) before it is explained (theory), and the existence of a pattern (law) will always have greater certainty than the explanation of why it exists (theory).[7]

In recent years philosophers of science have increasingly noted the importance of models in all areas of science.[8] A model provides a framework for understanding a phenomenon. For example, a geocentric model of the solar system views the moon and stars as actually moving around the earth, while in a heliocentric model the motion is considered to be apparent, caused by the rotation of the earth. Models may be explicitly stated or implicitly held, but they direct our research in the same way our worldview and philosophy subtly shape our thoughts. They have been shown to affect both the choice of what data to collect and how the data are interpreted. Because this term has a neutral connotation (as opposed to theory or hypothesis), and because it is currently the preferred term in philosophy of science literature for the paradigm guiding a research group, I have chosen to use this term to describe different perspectives for viewing the evidence about origins.

Why terminology is important. Language both reflects and influences our perception. One group will call a suicide bomber a terrorist, while another will call that same person a martyr. The terms refer to the same individual, but reveal and reinforce two very different notions of what is

---

[6]The concept of distinction is clear, even when the terminology used is different. One philosopher of science differentiates "empirical or phenomenological" theories from "explanatory" theories, but the examples he cites for the former are all known as "laws," such as the gas laws (Ratzsch, 1996: 121).

[7]Examples of law preceding theory include the laws of definite and multiple proportion preceding Dalton's atomic theory, and Mendel's laws of segregation and independent assortment being explained by chromosomal theory.

[8]Over the last century there has been a shift from a view of science as experimentation to one of science as model building and revision, from being based on sensory perception to being theory driven (Duschl & Grandy, 2008: 1-2) so that now "it is all but impossible to consider a scientific problem without some implicit or explicit model as a frame of reference" (Windschitl & Thompson, 2006: 786).

acceptable or even laudable behavior. In the same way language is often used in the origins debate to denigrate specific positions and individuals who hold them. Needless to say, calling someone a terrorist or an infidel does not foster good communication about the underlying issues. Similarly, use of pejorative terms does not promote scientific exchange. Thus, throughout the book I will strive to use neutral terms in describing each model, both to help the reader evaluate them more objectively and to provide an example of how fruitful discussion can be fostered between proponents of different positions.

The same situation presents itself when looking at the data. A fossil may be viewed as transitional or merely intermediate, the choice being more dependent on the perspective of the viewer than the characteristics of the fossil. Thus, sometimes I will choose not to use terminology employed by a particular scientific or religious community.[9] This should not be taken to imply that I necessarily disagree with it, rather that I am striving not to use terminology that prejudges an issue and would thus block further dialogue.

2.2 WHAT IS THE SPECTRUM OF OPINION?

Use of antagonistic terminology has led to polarization of the question of origins. When any group feels attacked and disrespected, this naturally leads to a hardening of their position as they become defensive and seek to promote their cause. This is certainly the case with the two dominant positions in the public debate about origins, each of which vilifies the other.

Yet in almost every matter of public opinion there are not only two extremes but a range, a gradient, a spectrum of views between those extremes. For most issues there is a relatively large group in the middle, but the ends dominate public awareness because of the easily recognizable rhetoric. Those who try to defend a middle position or promote discussion between the extremes often find themselves being attacked by both ends.

---

[9]Every model, and even every research group, has its own preferred terminology. Anyone with experience in a specialty can tell at a glance which research group, or even which author, produced a paper submitted for "blind" review, based on word choice.

Ends dominate public opinion. It serves the self-interest of those at the extremes of any debate to polarize the issue, because if people feel those are the only options, they must gravitate toward one or the other. No matter what the conflict, this has always been the strategy of the extremists, who are usually the ones to initiate and perpetuate a conflict.

In the case of the question of origins, the extremes are naturalistic evolution, often simply called "evolution," and recent creation in six days according to what proponents consider a straightforward reading of the first two chapters of Genesis, commonly called "creation."[10] For many years these two dominated the public debate to the point that all intermediate positions have been grouped by both the legal system and the press into one category or the other, perpetuating in the public eye the myth of the dichotomy.

Intermediate positions. Between those two extremes there are a spectrum of opinions, each of which is logically consistent based on a specific set of philosophical presuppositions. In a light spectrum it is relatively easy to distinguish the middle of one color from the middle of the next—it is easy to distinguish green from yellow. Yet as one approaches the boundary it is much harder to know where to draw the line—it is hard to distinguish yellowish green from greenish yellow. The same will be true in our distinguishing models of origins. In truth there is a continuous gradient, just as there is in the electromagnetic spectrum, but it is useful to break it up into discrete segments to facilitate naming and discussion. Another characteristic of light is that if we mix red and green light (not red and green paint) it will appear yellow to an observer. Similarly, some authors may be placed in a category not because they agree with all the tenets of that category, but because their mix of ideas gives the overall impression of a particular model. With that as a caveat, it is now time to divide the spectrum of opinions on origin into discrete models.

---

[10]Creation supporters currently prefer to use the term *straightforward*, meaning the most obvious meaning in the context, rather than the term *literal*, since some sections are obviously intended to be read nonliterally, for example, metaphors (Ham, 2006: 202). Opponents counter that what is the most straightforward reading to us may not have been the most straightforward reading to the original audience, who were used to different genres, and thus had different ideas of how to interpret stories.

For a long time, those close to the debate have recognized two intermediate categories between naturalistic evolution and young-earth creation: theistic evolution and old-earth creation.[11] However, within theistic evolution is a very wide range of interpretations of both the
scriptural and empirical evidence. Based on several distinguishing features, I propose breaking this category into three distinct models: nonteleological evolution, planned evolution and directed evolution. Some
will argue for more, others for less. The same happens in the naming of
biological species, when facing the question, How different does something have to be to be called a new species? It also happens in grading
of fruit—how many size or quality categories is enough to differentiate
important characteristics without being too many to keep track of?
Placing specific authors together does not indicate they all agree with
one another in all aspects, merely that they share enough characteristics
to distinguish them from other models.

Relation to presuppositions. Our philosophical stance is very closely
connected to our choice of model of origins. The question is, which is
primary, which influences the other? Although it seems obvious that to
some degree the influence goes both ways, I contend that in most cases
our philosophy determines choice of model rather than the opposite.

My first argument for this is based on cultural identity. A person
grows up in a particular culture, including the specific culture of the
family, using language that is not neutral with regard to origins.[12] He or
she will subconsciously assume the values of the culture, including beliefs about whether there is a supernatural world, and if so how that
interacts with the natural world. Sometimes a person will decide to
modify or discard the values he or she grew up with, but normally when
this happens the person has chosen to join a different community with
different beliefs, often as a result of some sort of conversion experience,
religious or secular, following a time of crisis.

A related argument is based on time of formation. Based on his or her

---

[11] Three previous attempts to be more complete in delineating various models include Scott (1999)
(also available on the NCSE website), Wise (2002) and M. R. Ross (2005).
[12] Creation is often spoken of as a pseudoscience by those at one extreme, while any reading of
Genesis 1 other than six twenty-four-hour days is called a "compromise that undermines the
gospel" by those at the other extreme.

upbringing, everyone develops a commitment to a particular set of personal philosophical presuppositions long before being exposed to any direct evidence about origins.[13] In fact, someone who looks no further than school textbooks or the popular scientific press may never be exposed to any direct evidence. Rather, both textbooks and the popular press report inferences as if they were truth, without recognizing the distinction between evidence and inference; almost always, in modern society, those inferences represent an evolutionary perspective. Those who have no prior exposure to an opposing viewpoint will typically accept the position presented in these textbooks without question. Those raised in a home where evolution is not accepted will challenge it the first time it is mentioned, as many teachers can attest.

The gradient I am proposing, which determines the model of origins chosen, is *the degree of interaction between the supernatural and natural worlds.* Obviously, if there is nothing supernatural, a naturalistic position, there can be no interaction, so we must seek a naturalistic explanation for every phenomenon, including the origin of the universe. On the other end of the spectrum is the view that God not only exists but has supernaturally revealed both his method and timing of creation in the first chapters of the Bible. This leads to a position that takes the creation story as literal twenty-four-hour days. Between these two extremes lie the remaining positions.

2.3 WHAT ARE THE MODELS?

To separate any continuous gradient into discrete units one needs to determine how many units there should be and reasonable boundaries for each. As mentioned earlier, four different classes of models of origins have been recognized for many years: naturalistic evolution (NE), theistic evolution (TE), old-earth creation (OEC) and young-earth creation (YEC), each with many variants. Theistic evolution, however, is a very diverse class, both in terms of interpretation of the scientific evidence and underlying theological differences. The first difference is between effectively *deistic and truly *theistic models. The former allow a

---

[13]"America's cultural conversation on origins is profoundly complicated by the various religious commitments made by people long before they have ever contemplated the question of origins" (Giberson & Yerxa, 2002: 181).

role for God only at the moment of the creation of the universe, after which the universe is allowed to unfold in accordance with the laws established at creation. There is also a fairly sharp divide among theists with regard to the degree of intervention in the process of speciation, leading me to propose a further split in that group.[14] To avoid confusion with the established term *theistic evolution*, I am proposing the three categories be called nonteleological evolution (NTE), planned evolution (PE) and directed evolution (DE), for reasons that will be spelled out later.

Like any division of a continuous variable, the choice of categories is somewhat arbitrary, depending on the intent of the division. Thus any such categorization should be viewed as a utilitarian tool, rather than something that can be considered true or false. There will inevitably be some who fall at the edge of two categories who will feel they do not fit well in either. This is especially the case where more than one variable is being considered at the same time. In this case, there is a philosophical gradient, a theological gradient and a gradient of interpretation of the scientific evidence. Although the three tend to follow the same pattern, the correspondence is not absolute, so there inevitably will be some that do not feel comfortable with the proposed division. Since my main concern is with different interpretations of the scientific evidence for origins, in some cases widely divergent religious views resulting in similar scientific views will be grouped in the same category.

Overview of the models. An overview of the factors that distinguish the six models is presented in table 2.1. It will become apparent as we examine the evidence in the following chapters that these varied philosophical convictions result in different interpretations of the evidence related to the four different origins: the origin of the universe, life on earth, different species and humans.

The first model, naturalistic evolution, asserts that there is no super-

---

[14]A similar three-way split of theistic evolution was proposed in Giberson & Yerxa (2002: chap. 8), based on Ian Barbour's *Religion in an Age of Science*, using slightly different criteria for the discrimination. Since I did not read this until after the manuscript of the present book had been submitted, the similarity of ideas gives greater credence to the suggested split. Other similarities between the two books include an attempt to present the whole continuum of ideas objectively and the connection noted between a person's choice of position and prior philosophical or religious commitments.

natural, or that it cannot be known. The other five models admit the existence of the supernatural, but they differ greatly from one another based on their interpretation of the Bible or other religious documents. The focus of this book will be on various Christian viewpoints, but in the following sections I will also describe how other religions arrive at similar perspectives on the scientific evidence.[15]

The term *evolution*, used in the name of four of the models, is sometimes restricted to origin of species, by which definition *abiogenesis (origin of life) and *cosmology (origin of the universe) are not considered evolution.[16] Nevertheless, in addition to evolution being at the heart of the public debate, the concept has been extended beyond biological evolution to biochemical evolution and stellar evolution, so evolution is an appropriate term for models of origins as a whole.

It is also important to comment on my choice of the use of *evolution* or *creation* as a descriptor for different models, especially since many proponents of what I call planned evolution (PE) prefer the name "evolutionary creation." They choose this name to show that creation, the noun, is the major idea, whereas evolutionary as an adjective explains the mechanism of creation (Lamoureux, 2008: 30). Rhetorically, this places the group more firmly in the theistic camp, which is their intent. In some sense all of the models except naturalistic evolution could by the same logic be called creation models, in that they are based on the existence of a Creator. On the other hand, I have chosen to call planned evolution and directed evolution evolutionary views, since *my primary focus is on the interpretation of the scientific evidence, and the theological position is secondary.* In terms of mechanism proposed to explain the evidence, the greatest difference is between those models that propose descent with change from a common ancestor (evolution) and those that propose discontinuous origin of diverse organisms (creation); the names chosen highlight this major break point in the spectrum.[17] Thus I

---

[15]For a summary of the views of different Christian positions, endorsed by the American Scientific Affiliation, a Christian scientific association, see "Commission on Creation" (2003), *American Scientific Affiliation*, www.asa3.org/ASA/topics/Evolution/commission_on_creation.html.

[16]Specific definitions of evolution will be discussed in chap. 5.

[17]The distinction between evolutionary and creation positions has sometimes been referred to as biological continuity or discontinuity (M. R. Ross, 2005).

Table 2.1. Distinguishing features of the six models of origins

Model	Naturalistic Evolution (NE)	Nonteleological Evolution (NTE)	Planned Evolution (PE)	Directed Evolution (DE)	Old-Earth Creation (OEC)	Young-Earth Creation (YEC)
Theology	no supernatural	Creator	Creator	Creator	Creator	Creator
Teleology	no purpose	no purpose	purpose	purpose	purpose	purpose
Intervention	no intervention	no intervention	no intervention	intervention	intervention	intervention
Genealogy	common descent	common descent	common descent	common descent	de novo creation	de novo creation
Cosmology	old universe	old universe	old universe	old universe	old universe	recent creation
Process	spontaneous natural processes only	conditions necessary for life established at creation	perfect creation naturally fulfills God's purposes	changes in universe and life subtly directed over time	major body plans created over millions of years	each "kind" created in one week, within the last 10,000 years

will sometimes refer to the first four models as evolutionary and the latter two as creationary, when this distinction is relevant.

With this brief introduction, we will now turn our attention to each of the six in more detail. In addition to describing the basic position, I will mention common variations within the model, citing authors where possible, based on evidence from their writings. I will also very briefly lay out the theological basis for each position. A summary of the six models in table form can be found in table A1.1. Some of the well-known modern proponents of each model are listed in table A1.6.

Naturalistic evolution. When most people use the term *evolution*, what they are referring to is *naturalistic evolution (NE), based on philosophical *naturalism, the conviction that everything can be explained by natural causes. Naturalism is closely related to *materialism, the idea that there is no reality apart from the material world, so naturalistic evolution could also be called materialistic evolution, but *naturalistic* is preferred since evolution is an explanation of a process rather than the underlying substance.

The connection between NE and its underlying worldview is very clear. If there is no supernatural (the assertion of *atheism) or if nothing can be known about the existence of the supernatural (the assertion of *agnosticism) it follows logically that every process from the beginning of time must have been naturalistic. The position that science must only admit naturalistic explanations makes absolute sense based on the philosophical assertion that the natural world is the only thing that is real or knowable. It also follows logically that there can be no revelation, therefore religious writings are the works of men and the creation stories are treated as myths.

Although atheists and agnostics take the same naturalistic approach to the scientific evidence, they hold different opinions of the value of religious belief. Staunch atheists, such as Richard Dawkins (1996, 2006) and Daniel Dennett (1995), view religion as an evil to be overcome by the liberating truth of science. Agnostics, such as Stephen Jay Gould (1999, 2002), are willing to allow a social role for religion, but hold science and religion to be *nonoverlapping magisteria (NOMA), *complementary domains of knowledge answering distinct questions with no overlap. A few, like Edward O. Wilson (1998), view all areas of knowledge as unified, and look forward to the day that religion is subsumed under science. Other prominent proponents of NE, including Ernst Mayr (2001), who wrote mostly about the scientific aspects of evolution, and Eugenie Scott, whose goal is defending the teaching of evolution in public schools, are less direct about expressing their religious views, although their atheistic beliefs come through in their writing.[18] Many of the writers of science textbooks also hold a naturalistic position, whether this is directly stated or not.[19]

The distinctive ideas of the naturalistic evolution model can be summarized as follows:

- *Philosophical axiom.* There is no supernatural, or nothing can be known about the supernatural.

- *Inferences.* Evidence from the natural world, empirical evidence, is the only basis for knowledge, so science is the only way of knowing and only explanations based on natural processes are allowed.

- *Logical conclusion.* Since the only things we can know are natural, anything else is mere speculation or pure falsehood.

Nonteleological evolution. *Nonteleological evolution (NTE) posits that there is no intervention of the supernatural after the foundation of the universe. Thus it is basically a deistic perspective, although many proponents would not willingly accept that moniker. Many authors who support NTE espouse a liberal Christian theology, such as process theology. Scientists who come from a pantheistic worldview, whether Buddhist, Hindu or New Age, in which the supernatural and natural are one and the same, would also logically favor a position similar to NTE.[20]

---

[18]Eugenie Scott has for many years been the executive director of the National Center for Science Education, http://ncse.com.

[19]Many high school textbooks throw a bone to theists by stating that although evolution is well enough established to be considered a fact, science can say nothing about whether there is a God directing it. Many college texts, on the other hand, drop all semblance of objectivity, stating clearly that evolution is undirected, with clear philosophical implications (Rau, unpublished data).

[20]Normally, Eastern and pantheistic religions do not enter the debate, since they view the physical world as illusory or temporary. Scientists in these religions would probably hold a view similar to NTE, that the two domains of knowledge answer different questions, while devotees would be more likely to say, similar to YEC, that the only important answers are provided by religion.

The term *nonteleological* is chosen to convey that although the universe was created with the ability to evolve, there was no specific end or direction (*telos*) in mind at the beginning.[21]

Nonteleological evolution is almost identical to naturalistic evolution in interpretation of the scientific evidence, with the exception of the origin of the universe, because it also seeks to identify a natural cause for all natural phenomena subsequent to that point. Thus this form of theistic evolution is considered acceptable by the major scientific and science teaching organizations, whose policy statements limit science to a search for natural causes, and naturalists have no quarrel with NTE because they agree that the laws of nature, and therefore science as we know it, breaks down at the moment of the origin of the universe.[22]

Nonteleological evolution accepts the idea that science and religion are separate and complementary domains of knowledge, but, unlike naturalistic evolution, thinks that the two are equal in value or that religion is superior. Therefore the only point of contention is in the religion, not the science, and most of the identifiable proponents of NTE write to support their theological position at least as much as the scientific. These include Christian de Duve (1995), Ian Barbour (2000) and John Haught (2010).

The distinctive ideas of the NTE model can be summarized as follows:

- *Philosophical axiom.* There is a supernatural, but whatever the nature of that force, it has no plan for the universe and therefore does not intervene in it.

- *Inferences.* Only natural forces have influenced the universe since its beginning.

- *Logical conclusion.* Since the supernatural does not direct the natural, naturalistic explanations are sufficient to explain any natural phenomenon.

---

[21]Lamoureux (2008) uses a similar term, *dysteleological evolution*, which is preferable in terms of language purity since *nonteleological* mixes a Latin negation with a Greek root, but English is replete with such mixing and I believe this will be an easier term for the general public. His dysteleological evolution includes NE and NTE.

[22]Statements from the NSTA, NABT and AAAS can be found in Appendix C of National Academy of Science 1998. NABT dropped the words *impersonal* and *unsupervised* from their statement in 1997 (Chapman, 1998).

Planned evolution. The difference between *planned evolution (PE) and the two models just described is again more theological than scientific. It is nevertheless important to list it as a separate model since the question of *teleology, which separates them, plays a prominent role in the debate and has important ramifications. According to this view God had a definite *plan* in mind, which was set into motion at the moment of creation. Planned evolution could be called teleological evolution, but this would not differentiate it from the next model, another variant of teleological evolution. Unlike the many theological variants of NTE, planned evolution is essentially a monotheistic position. As with the other three monotheistic models, the main proponents in America write from a Christian perspective, but similar positions are possible from Jewish and Islamic perspectives.

Theologically, PE would be considered by most who hold it to be a moderate position, although strong religious conservatives would certainly label it liberal (the terms being chosen for their rhetorical value). Proponents typically employ an interpretation of the early chapters of Genesis in which the creation story is treated as an ancient genre wherein the emphasis is placed on the actor rather than the action, on God as the Creator rather than on the process of creation. The most common reading of Genesis 1 is that in the beginning the earth was *without form* and *void of life*. During the first three days of creation God *formed* the air, sea and land, and during the second three days he *filled each with life*. Views on Adam and Eve vary, but many view them as a group of individuals or symbols of humanity, rather than single progenitors of all humans (Lamoureaux, 2008: 290). A brief summary of this model of understanding Genesis is presented in appendix two, in comparison with other models of biblical interpretation.

According to PE, God has the capacity to intervene in nature but does not need to do so because of the perfection of the original creation, what Howard Van Till (1999) calls "the fully gifted creation," which is able to bring forth life in various forms over time in response to the changing conditions, ultimately leading to humankind. This model has recently gained prominence due to the work of Francis Collins (2006) and the BioLogos Foundation (biologos.org), but has been represented for many years in court cases by Kenneth Miller (1999), who has argued that evolution and theism are not mutually exclusive.

Scientifically, this results in a position almost identical to naturalistic evolution (NE) and nonteleological evolution (NTE), since God does not regularly intervene in the development of life or species, and therefore natural processes are thought to be sufficient to explain the evidence. The difference lies in the fact that PE asserts the mechanisms for change were built into creation and established for the specific purpose of bringing about God's plan of creating a sentient being who could worship him.

Since this model also seeks only natural causes after the moment of creation, the scientific inferences made are in many cases indistinguishable from NE and NTE. The theological underpinnings, however, are a matter of contention for atheists, who find no need for a Creator in a system that can run perfectly by itself, and the teleological aspect bothers both NE and NTE, which view evolution as a fundamentally undirected process. Like the first two models discussed, PE views science and religion as separate and complementary domains of knowledge (they accept the idea of NOMA), but they tend to see each as important and each superior in its own area of study.

The distinctive ideas of the PE model can be summarized as follows:

- *Philosophical axiom.* God created the universe with a plan and created it perfectly to bring that plan to fruition without further intervention.

- *Inferences.* The natural laws and processes created by God are sufficient to account for all natural events since the moment of creation.[23]

- *Logical conclusion.* Since God did not intervene in natural processes after creation, science can always find natural explanations for natural phenomena.

Directed evolution. *Directed evolution (DE) and planned evolution share a similar overall interpretation of Genesis 1, although proponents of DE are more likely to view Adam and Eve as single individuals, pro-

---

[23]The question of whether God's plan is deterministic, the theological question of predestination or free will, is separate from the scientific debate, but many from a Calvinistic tradition favor PE or DE positions.

genitors of the entire human race. Directed evolution asserts that God not only brought the universe into being but continues to act in it, not only in the lives of individuals in response to prayer but also in creative events, to bring about his plans. In many cases this does not involve superseding natural law as much as *direction* of low probability events, hence the name of the model.

Since DE assumes God can and sometimes does intervene in natural events, it makes sense to ask whether God's intervention is scientifically detectable. Some proponents of DE expect to be able to detect evidence of God's work, while others do not.[24] For those who think that God's intervention is scientifically detectable, it makes sense to ask whether a particular event has a natural or supernatural cause. Although natural causation is expected for most events, the large number of low probability events that have occurred at each level of origins is taken by this group as evidence of God's direction.

From a DE perspective, science and religion are not viewed as distinct or complementary domains of knowledge, but as *interacting domains of knowledge.[25] This is a crucial difference. Complementary domains have no overlap. They deal with a separate set of questions and answer those questions based on disparate methodologies. Interacting domains do intersect. According to this view at least some questions are best addressed using evidence from both domains. In the case of DE, the only evidence admitted from Scripture about origins is the existence of a deity who intervenes from time to time in miraculous ways, with science providing the evidence for mechanism. The two creationary models, described next, assert that Scripture also tells us something about the method of creation, which DE denies.

Most of the authors who embrace this position seem to write either to convince conservative Christians of the viability of an evolutionary

---

[24]Those who think God's intervention is detectable generally support ID, while others do not. B. B. Warfield, who had a strong influence on the fundamentalist movement and the current evangelical view of biblical inerrancy, thought that God's continual work in nature might appear mechanistic, apart from things such as the human soul that show direct intervention (Livingstone, 1984: 115-22).

[25]The terminology of complementary versus interacting domains follows Moreland & Reynolds (1999: 9-10). Other possible ways of viewing the interaction between science and theology are discussed in Dembski (1999: chap. 7).

position or to convince methodological naturalists of the improbability of undirected evolution. Examples of the former include Henry Schaefer (2003) and Deborah Haarsma and Loren Haarsma (2007). Examples of the latter include Michael Behe (1996, 2007). Since none of these provide a full description and justification of their model, it is impossible to say for sure that they would espouse DE, but inferences from their writings or opposition to their position by authors representing models on both sides seem to place them in this category. At this point I am not aware of any author who gives a complete scientific and religious justification of this model.[26]

The distinctive ideas of the DE model can be summarized as follows:

- *Philosophical axiom.* God has a predetermined purpose for the world, and the Bible shows that he intervenes in the natural world as necessary to accomplish that plan.

- *Inferences.* Miracles are recorded in the Bible to show that God intervenes occasionally in redemptive history,[27] so it is reasonable to think the same might be true for natural history.

- *Logical conclusion.* Since we see a large number of low-probability events that seem to be directed toward a goal (teleological), these would be best explained as interventions.

Old-earth creation. In contrast to the four evolutionary models just described, which claim there are no gaps in natural processes where God's creative hand is evident, the two creationary models claim that empirical evidence of direct creative acts can be found in the creation. The two models in this group are called *old-earth creation (OEC) and young-earth creation (YEC), both terms well established in the literature, based on their claims about the age of the earth. The creationary models assert that the Bible explains not only the purpose of creation but also something about its mechanism.

---

[26]The closest I have seen is Poe & Davis (2012). Although the authors are exploring a question rather than presenting a position, they advance an evolutionary model that involves God's continuous interaction with the universe, mainly at the level of quantum and chaotic effects.

[27]Miracles happen throughout the Bible but are most prevalent at the time of the establishing of the old covenant under Moses and the new covenant under Christ (including the greatest miracle, the incarnation of Christ).

Old-earth creation agrees with DE that science and religion are interacting domains of knowledge, but OEC further asserts that the Genesis account has explicit scientific value, that the order of events in Genesis 1 accurately reflects the order of what happened. This is viewed as an accurate prediction of later scientific discovery and often taken as evidence for the supernatural inspiration of Scripture (Ross, 2009).

At least four different models—PE, DE, OEC and YEC—believe that the Bible and the world are equally important revelations of God, and that the two, properly interpreted, will not conflict with each other.[28] The difference arises in how the Bible is interpreted. Reflecting this tension between two sources of knowledge, empirical evidence and religious texts, OEC sometimes chooses to interpret the Bible in the light of scientific evidence, but other times chooses to interpret science in light of the Bible. An example of the former is the age of the earth, where OEC accepts the standard geological chronology that the earth is billions of years old, by taking the term *day* in Genesis 1 to mean an unspecified period of time. On the other hand, adherence to the idea that God created in distinct phases (days) leads to the interpretation of periods of rapid appearance of species in the fossil record as creative events.

Over the years there have been numerous variants of OEC models, including progressive creation, day-age creation and gap models.[29] Currently the most prolific proponent of OEC is Hugh Ross and the staff at Reasons to Believe (reasons.org). Stephen Meyer (2009) and many others at the Discovery Institute Center for Science and Culture (discovery.org/csc) also follow an OEC model.

The distinctive ideas of the OEC model can be summarized as follows:

- *Philosophical axiom.* God chooses to reveal himself through the Bible and creation, both of which clearly disclose his existence and identity.

---

[28]The idea that scientific evidence will not conflict with the Bible when each are properly interpreted goes back at least as far as St. Augustine.

[29]Briefly, gap models, popularized by the Scofield Bible, translated Genesis 1:2 as "the earth *became* formless and void," proposing the destruction of an earlier creation to explain both the fossil record and the old age of the earth, while retaining a young age for the present creation. Day-age and progressive creation models both propose that creation followed the order given in the days of Genesis, but that those days represent long time periods. The term *day-age* was more common before the middle of the twentieth century, and progressive creation after that, so the arguments differ based on what evidence was available, but the basic underlying idea is similar.

- *Inferences.* We must find the most straightforward interpretations that allow us to harmonize the biblical statement that God created in six days with the empirical evidence that the universe and earth appear to be billions of years old.

- *Logical conclusion.* Since God wants his actions to be clear, the earth must indeed be billions of years old, and his work in creation will be clearly discernible as discrete creative acts over time, in the same order as revealed in the Bible.

Young-earth creation. *Young-earth creation is referred to by its advocates as "scientific creation" and by its detractors as "creationism," using what E. O. Wilson (1998) refers to as the "hissing suffix," a jab returned in the use of "Darwinism" and other variants.[30] Many court cases ruling against teaching creation in the schools refer specifically to YEC, but this has led to the designation "creationist" being used indiscriminately in the debate as a rhetorical way of discrediting other models that are quite distinct from YEC.[31]

Young-earth creation is based on a philosophy I will call *overlapping domains of knowledge. As opposed to the complementary or interacting domains envisioned by other models, overlapping domains refers to the idea that where evidence from another domain, particularly natural science, appears to conflict with what the Bible says, it is the latter that comes out on top and we are to trust. This is based on the joint assertions that Scripture is trustworthy because it is the inerrant Word of God and that science is constantly changing and therefore not to be trusted, and is a perfectly logical conclusion based on those premises.[32]

The idea of overlapping domains of knowledge explains the strong animosity between YEC and naturalistic evolution (NE). In discussing NE, I said it was built on the idea of distinct but complementary domains of knowledge, an idea popularized by Gould, an agnostic. Athe-

---

[30]Wilson talks about "other sins made official by the hissing suffix," a reference to the action of labeling any position we do not agree with as an "ism" as a way of discrediting it (Wilson 1998: 11).

[31]The rhetorical use of *creationist* is documented by Beckwith (2003: 67-68).

[32]"When a scientist's interpretation of data does not match the clear meaning of the text in the Bible, we should never reinterpret the Bible." "Skeptics often claim, 'The Bible is not a science textbook.' This, of course, is true—because science textbooks change every year, whereas the Bible is the unchanging Word of God—the God who cannot lie" (Ham, 2006: 78, 141).

istic proponents of NE may nominally accept this idea, but in practice they act as if the two were overlapping domains, with science on top, claiming that science holds the ultimate authority and answers to every question, including ones about the afterlife, ethics and other areas claimed by religion.[33] Thus, YEC and NE are polar opposites, the former claiming that the Bible overrules scientific evidence, the latter that scientific evidence disproves the Bible.

Christianity is of course not the only religion with a recent creation story. Every traditional culture had some story of creation. In discussing YEC in the following chapters, I will be primarily referring to the Christian views common in America, but conservative elements of Islam and Judaism may voice similar views. Most traditional religions of other cultures make no effort to harmonize their creation stories with modern science, but if they did the arguments made would logically have to be similar to those of YEC.

The Christian YEC model claims that the Bible clearly teaches that God created the world and everything in it in six literal twenty-four-hour days about six thousand years ago, and that any other view involves "reinterpreting the Word of God on the basis of the fallible theories of sinful people" (Ham, 2006: 88). Other key tenets of YEC include Adam and Eve, two individuals created *de novo* by God, being the progenitors of all humans, one act of sin leading to the fall of humankind, no death of any sort before the fall, a worldwide flood and separation of human language groups at the tower of Babel. Well-known proponents include Ken Ham and others at Answers in Genesis (answersingenesis.org),[34] Jonathan Sarfati and others of Creation Ministries International (creation.com), John D. Morris of the Institute for Creation Research (icr.org), Walt Brown (2001) of the Center for Scientific Creation (creationscience.com/onlinebook), Paul Nelson and John Mark Reynolds of the Discovery Institute (discovery.org/csc), Steven Austin, Jerry Bergman, D. Russell Humphreys, Michael Oard, John Sanford and Kurt Wise.

---

[33]Some of the more forthright, such as Dawkins, are very clear in their support of the overlapping domains model. This view is also known as "scientism."

[34]Other authors associated with AIG include John Baumgardner, Gary Parker and Andrew Snelling.

The distinctive ideas of the YEC model can be summarized as follows:

- *Philosophical axiom.* The Bible is the inerrant Word of God, and each word should be understood in accord with its normal, common meaning, unless there is clear evidence to the contrary within the Bible text itself.

- *Inferences.* When the Bible says God created everything in six days, it means six sequential twenty-four-hour days. When it says he created each kind of animal, or that he created man (male and female), it means each was created separately and fully formed.

- *Logical conclusion.* Since the Bible says God created everything in six days, and each kind of creature individually, only interpretations of scientific observations which are consistent with those revealed truths can be correct.

2.4 WHAT ABOUT INTELLIGENT DESIGN?

Those who have followed the origins debate at all will have noticed that one influential position has not yet been mentioned: *intelligent design (ID). Some readers may have noticed the names of authors associated with the ID movement listed in connection with three different models. This requires clarification, but first we must separate the idea of design from the ID movement.

An idea and a movement. Design is both an ancient idea and a modern social movement, but not all who accept the former are comfortable with the latter. The idea of design has been part of the origins debate from the beginning, being rooted in the natural theology that was common in the early church and still popular at the time of Darwin.[35] The modern intelligent design movement, on the other hand, is usually traced back to the work of Charles Thaxton (Thaxton, Bradley & Olsen, 1984), was popularized by Phillip Johnson (1991, 1995, 1997) and is closely connected with the Discovery Institute's Center for Science and Culture (discovery.org/csc).

At its root, design is a teleological concept. Thus all four models

---

[35]Some authors have traced the history of natural theology from William Paley back to Thomas Aquinas and St. Augustine (Ruse, 2004).

that accept teleology (PE, DE, OEC, YEC) also affirm the basic idea of design.[36] They disagree on how that design was manifested, through slow natural processes or direct *de novo* creation, but all agree that the natural world reflects the intended design of the Creator. This stands in sharp contrast to the two nonteleological models (NE, NTE), which contend that natural processes produced order, giving the appearance of design, but without the intentionality that characterizes true design.

The ID movement characterizes itself as "an evidence-based scientific theory about life's origins that challenges strictly materialistic views of evolution" (Meyer, 2009: 4). The focal point that binds the movement together is commitment to the tenet that design in nature is empirically detectable—not only detectable in principle but also that empirical evidence of design exists. Based on that evidence it asserts that new biological forms could not have arisen by the *neo-Darwinian model of gradual accumulation of small random mutations, although this does not necessarily mean total rejection of evolution, as will be explained in chapter five. In the bigger picture, ID employs a combination of scientific, philosophical, theological and social components to combat what it sees as the negative effects of naturalism on society.[37]

The distinctive ideas of the ID movement can be summarized as follows:

- *Philosophical axiom.* Design in nature is empirically detectable, and provides evidence for the existence of the supernatural.

- *Inferences.* Natural structures that could not have been built in a

---

[36]For example, Denis Lamoureux (2008), writing in *Evolutionary Creation* to support a model herein classified as PE, frequently talks about the intelligent design of creation, although he and most others who embrace this model reject the goals of the ID movement.

[37]"Mere creation is a four-pronged approach to defeating naturalism. The prongs are as follows:

  1. A scientific and philosophical critique of naturalism, where the scientific critique identifies the empirical inadequacies of naturalistic evolutionary theories and the philosophical critique demonstrates how naturalism subverts every area of inquiry it touches;

  2. A positive scientific research program, known as intelligent design, for investigating the effects of intelligent causes;

  3. A cultural movement for systematically rethinking every field of inquiry that has been infected by naturalism, reconceptualizing it in terms of design; and

  4. A sustained theological investigation that connects the intelligence inferred by intelligent design with the God of Scripture and therewith formulates a coherent theology of nature" (Dembski, 1998: 28-29).

stepwise manner, with each step having a positive selective value, are empirical evidence against Darwinism and for design.

- *Logical conclusion.* Design provides a better explanation than undirected processes for the complexity we observe in nature. Since this is based on empirical evidence, it deserves to be called a scientific explanation.

Relation to the models. The ID movement has from its inception been dedicated to a "big tent." Proponents include members of old earth and young earth, creationary and evolutionary models. Although the bulk of its constituency is drawn from old-earth creation (OEC), some proponents of young-earth creation (YEC) on one side and directed evolution (DE) on the other are also found in its ranks. Thus it is true, as detractors claim, that intelligent design does not present a single explanatory mechanism for origins, and in that sense cannot be called a scientific model. It is also true that many of its claims are philosophical rather than scientific, and that the concept of detectable design has obvious theological implications for the existence of a designer. On the other hand, ID is not primarily a religious model, as some opponents have charged.

There are distinct limits on what models will be able to espouse the ID movement. As noted earlier, its central assertion is that design is scientifically detectable. This philosophical assertion leads ID to oppose both naturalism and *methodological naturalism (MN), which it says are functionally equivalent in modern society.[38] In response, naturalistic evolution (NE), rooted in philosophical naturalism, and nonteleological evolution (NTE) and planned evolution (PE), which embrace MN as essential to science, strongly oppose ID.[39]

Methodological naturalism is based on the philosophical claim that although God created the cosmos, he does not normally intervene in its

---

[38]"But once science is taken as the only universally valid form of knowledge within a culture, it follows that methodological and metaphysical naturalism become functionally equivalent" (Dembski, 1998: 28).

[39]"Intelligent design is logically compatible with everything from utterly discontinuous creation . . . to the most far-reaching evolution. . . . That said, intelligent design is incompatible with what typically is meant by theistic evolution" (Dembski, 1998: 19-20).

function, and therefore all natural phenomena should be explainable in terms of physical causation. This idea was an important factor in the development of modern science, at a time when Christianity was the dominant religious and social force in the Western world. In this context the rationality of God was taken as a foundation for belief in the rationality of creation, which therefore could be studied to discover its regularities. Scientists in that era considered that in finding scientific mechanisms they were explicating the works of God; scientists in NTE and PE still believe they are doing that. The ID movement, on the other hand, claims that methodological naturalism *a priori* excludes the possibility that God's work might be detectable scientifically, rather than examining the empirical evidence to see whether it is or not.

Methodological naturalism in its modern form is closely tied to the philosophical contention that science and religion are *complementary* (separate and distinct) domains of knowledge, as advocated by NTE and PE. Intelligent design, on the other hand, views truth as indivisible, with science and religion, or more broadly empirical and nonempirical ways of knowing, as *interacting* domains of knowledge.[40] This philosophical commitment also explains why the majority of ID proponents come from OEC, which is also based on this philosophical presupposition, but relatively few who subscribe to YEC are active in the ID movement, since the dominant underlying philosophical viewpoint for that model is *overlapping* domains of knowledge, rather than interacting ones. Although directed evolution accepts the philosophical underpinning of interacting domains of knowledge, it also is split in regard to ID since some within that model agree that God's direction is empirically detectable, while others do not. The ID movement also draws support from a few nontheists who oppose methodological naturalism on philosophical grounds.[41]

Opponents of ID frequently claim that it is not science because it rejects the principle of methodological naturalism. It must be noted,

---

[40]"ID theory—like natural theology more generally—nicely points to one of the fundamental problems in our intellectual life: the all too uncritical compartmentalization of knowledge in academic disciplines" (Nord, 2003: 57).

[41]For example David Berlinski, an agnostic who is a senior fellow at the Discovery Institute.

however, that both opposition to MN and commitment to MN are philosophical positions, so the two are equivalent in this regard. A related criticism leveled against ID is that many of its proponents do not follow the principles of scientific argumentation. Although several of the key spokesmen of the ID movement are scientists by training (e.g., Michael Behe, Paul Chien, Guillermo Gonzalez, Dean Kenyon, Charles Thaxton, Jonathan Wells), many others are philosophers (e.g., Stephen C. Meyer, David Berlinski), mathematicians (e.g., William A. Dembski), lawyers (e.g., Phillip E. Johnson, David DeWolf) or historians (e.g., Thomas Woodward). Thus the charge made by natural scientists that they do not follow the rules of scientific argumentation may be correct, as they are following the rules of their respective fields. The charge, however, begs the question of whether natural science can be completely separated from other ways of knowing, which is the central question raised by ID.

Intelligent design may be as much a philosophical argument as it is scientific, but it is certainly not, as opponents have often claimed, "closet creationism." It is true that the ID movement uses many of the same arguments that are used by young-earth creation, but this is due to the common goals of challenging Darwinian gradualism and the commonly used definition of science, rather than support of any particular model of origins or religious position.[42] Neither does ID promote the teaching of religion or theology, or even any particular model of origins, in schools.

Although both religion and philosophy are nonempirical, there is a difference. Philosophy underlies all ways of knowing, defining what is and is not an acceptable argument in any field. As such it is impossible to teach science without implicitly promoting one philosophy, but it is certainly possible to teach science without promoting a particular religious belief (including atheistic belief). The ID movement seeks to level the playing field for all religions by promoting a philosophy of science that does not exclude certain explanations a priori. We will return to this idea in chapter eight.

---

[42]Many of the arguments used by ID are also found in YEC literature, for example the idea of "irreducible properties of organization," (very similar to ID's "irreducible complexity") and an emphasis on the Cambrian explosion. See Morris & Parker (1987: 34, 129).

Origin of the Universe

• • •

Any successful model of origins must provide a consistent explanation for four separate events: the origin of the universe, life, species and humans. Having described the philosophical and theological assertions underlying six different classes of models, it is now time to examine how each of those models explains the relevant evidence. In the next four chapters we will examine each of the origins in turn; for each we will first summarize the evidence, then the different ways various models interpret it.

It is impossible in a book of any reasonable size to describe all the evidence or interpretations comprehensively.[1] Whole books have been devoted to a single model's interpretation of the evidence relating to a single origin. The intent of this book is to provide an overview of the breadth of the topic, to see the big picture. So, for each origin I have tried to summarize two or three main classes of evidence, with examples of each, followed by a summary of the main lines of interpretation. Those who wish more detail are referred to the notes and the references in them, with the hope that this book has provided enough scaffolding that the reader will feel confident in approaching more detailed explanations.[2]

---

[1]It is important to note the difference between data and evidence. Data that do not fit the pattern expected by a certain model may be considered outliers or errors, thus excluded from evidence as irrelevant. We will return to this issue in chap. 5.

[2]In some cases the references in the notes are intended to document a point, in which case I will

I am making every effort to present both the evidence and interpretations from as objective a position as possible. One of the difficulties encountered in this approach to writing is that it is difficult to present evidence in a way that makes sense without simultaneously showing why that evidence is important and how it points toward a given conclusion. Hopefully you will see from this what contortions one must go through in order to not view evidence through the lens of a particular interpretation and recognize the importance of identifying an author's viewpoint and attendant presuppositions.

The first, and in many ways ultimate, question that any model must explain is why the universe exists at all, and why it exists as it does, in a way that supports life. An overview of the arguments is presented in table A1.2. The six models of origins fall into three categories, based on their interpretation of the evidence. Five of the models agree about the age of the earth and universe. Four of those also agree in substantial measure as to the cause behind it.

Of the four areas of origins, the origin of the universe plays a relatively minor role in the public debate, which tends to focus instead on evolution and the origin of species. Perhaps this is because astronomy is not taught in most high schools and is not a common course in college. Perhaps it is because the evidence in cosmology is too technical for most nonspecialists to understand or effectively question. Yet it is here that many find the greatest support for the existence of a Creator, and here that there is the greatest agreement among a wide range of models about the basic mechanism underlying the evidence. It is also interesting that some of the strongest support for *big bang cosmology from a Christian perspective is provided by an organization supporting an old-earth creation model, which is theologically closest to the only model, young-earth creation, that does not accept the big bang explanation. But before we look at explanations, we need to consider the evidence.[3]

---

try to cite authoritative references. In other cases online sources are cited for ease of access.
[3]Edwards (2001) looks at both the scientific evidence and the philosophical questions, being careful to distinguish between them. Written from the perspective of modified process theology (NTE), the author provides a good summary of the evidence for the big bang, fine-tuning of various constants, the philosophical claims of naturalism and a detailed analysis of the strengths

3.1 WHAT IS THE EVIDENCE?

Many people feel there is a distinction between the physical sciences, like physics and chemistry, which depend on mathematics, and the life sciences, like biology and ecology, which do not. I disagree. But it is true that traditionally the two tend to use different branches of mathematics, and they still do at the level taught in high school and lower level college courses. Until the middle of the twentieth century, physics and chemistry were based on algebra, geometry and calculus, all of which are nonprobabilistic.[4] Thus many problems in the physical sciences have fixed solutions, and proposed theories can be tested quite rigorously according to whether observations follow the expected pattern. The life sciences, on the other hand, tend to be based more on probability, optimization theory, complexity theory, even chaos theory (none of which is normally taught in high school, giving the appearance that the life sciences do not involve math), which by nature do not allow a single fixed solution.[5] Thus the predictions made in these fields will never be as definitive as those made in the physical sciences.[6] In general the degree of predictability diminishes and the importance of historical contingency increases as we move from physics and astronomy (origin of the universe) to chemistry (origin of life), to biology (origin of species) and anthropology (origin of humans), as we will see in later chapters.

Evidence for the origin of the universe comes primarily from astronomy, which like traditional physics is deterministic. From the beginning predictability has been a very important component of astronomy, allowing ancient astronomers to foretell with great accuracy

---

and weaknesses of various naturalistic models, including steady state, oscillating universe, and several versions of the big bang. Proponents of other models of origins would have no trouble agreeing with his summary of the scientific evidence, even if they disagree with his conclusion that process theology provides the best explanation.

[4]Quantum mechanics, fluid dynamics and other new areas of advanced physics are based on probabilistic mathematics, as is the idea of orbitals in chemistry.

[5]The maths (there is good reason for the British usage) we focus on in United States public schools are those associated with the physical sciences, since the current curriculum was greatly influenced by the Cold War need for physics and engineering. Perhaps it is time to include more probability, logic and graph theory at the high school level.

[6]Wilson (1998) contends that all knowledge will one day be able to be reduced to scientific knowledge, by extension of the methods of physics and chemistry into biology and the social sciences. But the preponderance of probabilistic mathematics in the latter means they will never be able to be reduced to total predictability as many aspects of the former can.

equinoxes, eclipses and other cosmic events. Not only the laws but in many cases the associated theories can be expressed mathematically, so that the distinction between the two is less clear than in the life sciences, with theory able to make predictive statements that can be mathematically confirmed to a high degree of accuracy. Thus in astronomy, as in the other physical sciences, research for at least a century has been very clearly theory driven, seeking empirical confirmations of, or deviations from, predictions made by a given theory.

Of necessity, astronomy is basically an observational rather than an experimental science since it is impossible to bring a star into the laboratory and manipulate some variable. Yet many things cannot be observed or measured directly, due to the distances involved. Thus indirect methods have been developed, often in order to test a certain theory. These methods are calibrated with direct observations to ensure they are accurate, but hidden assumptions make it more difficult for a non-specialist to determine whether the arguments are valid. Furthermore, calling something "evidence" that is not directly observed by our senses blurs the essential distinction between evidence and inference.[7] This is affecting all areas of science as they move away from what is directly observable with extensions of human senses into areas less directly related to traditional empirical evidence.

For most of recorded history people thought the universe was basically static and unchanging, with the earth at the center. But the earth was displaced from the hub in the seventeenth century, and the idea of an eternal static universe died in the twentieth. The current paradigm, the big bang, is not without detractors and unresolved questions, but overall the evidence for a changing universe is overwhelming. Similarly,

---

[7]Indirect evidence is used extensively in fields like astronomy and geology, where direct observation of a particular event is difficult. Although called evidence, it is inferential in that the observation of one thing is taken as proxy for another. For this to work, the two have to be causally related and there must be no other known explanation for the event actually observed, or other possible explanations must be able to be disproven. In common speech, as in science, we do this all the time. We may say "it rained last night" when we look outside in the morning, although we neither saw nor heard the rain. We cannot think of any other reasonable explanation for the lawn, driveway, street, trees and everything else in sight to be uniformly wet. The same is true, at a far more technical level, for much of the "evidence" reported here. For an excellent description of the principles of indirect evidence in the earth and space sciences, see Gonzalez & Richards (2004: chap. 2).

in the last fifty years it has become clear how exquisitely balanced many factors must be for life to exist. Although the details are very difficult for nonspecialists to understand, involving heavy use of indirect evidence, the overall picture is not hard to grasp.

A changing universe. One of the great myths in the history of science is that Galileo was persecuted by the church for removing humanity from the center of the universe, where the whole universe revolved around humans.[8] Such a view reveals a very modern idea of the center, and demonstrates that the problem of choosing between competing interpretations is not limited to natural science.

The documentary evidence shows that from the time of the ancient Greeks until the time of Copernicus, the earth was viewed as the center of the cosmos, but that was the lowest point, the point of greatest corruption. The heavens were perfect spheres, perfect both physically and metaphysically. Humans were made of the dust of the earth, heaviest and least pure of the four earthly elements (earth, water, air, fire), to which Aristotle added the pure undefiled ether of the heavens. Spirits destined for heaven rose; those bound elsewhere sank. Dante's view of Satan at the core of the earth reflected the actual, not allegorical, understanding of the day. Into this milieu stepped Copernicus and Galileo, proclaiming that the earth was not at the center of the solar system, upsetting the predominant model by lifting sinful man to the heavenly spheres, while at the same time imaging the imperfections of the heavenly bodies.[9] The component missing from Galileo's model was a mechanism for the motion. Once the mechanism, universal gravitation, was supplied by Newton at the beginning of the eighteenth century, acceptance of the heliocentric model was complete.[10]

Newton's model was not seriously challenged until the early part of the twentieth century, when Einstein propounded his theory of general

---

[8]Dennis Danielson, "Myth 6: That Copernicanism Demoted Humans from the Center of the Cosmos"; Maurice A. Finocchiaro, "Myth 8: That Galileo Was Imprisoned and Tortured for Advocating Copernicanism" in Numbers (2010).

[9]Johannes Kepler's demonstration that the orbits of the planets were ellipses rather than perfect circles, along with Galileo's observation of imperfections on the surface of the moon and other heavenly bodies, destroyed the idea of the perfect heavens.

[10]For more on the Copernican revolution see Gonzalez & Richards (2004: chap. 11). For a full analysis, including why the term *revolution* is misleading, see Howell (2003).

relativity. At that time the reigning paradigm pictured the universe as stable. In a prime example of how models shape science, Einstein added a cosmological constant to his equations, which without that term predicted that the universe should be expanding, in order to bring them into conformity with the current model. Within fifteen years Edwin Hubble would show the error of both the static model and the cosmological constant, by looking at light from distant stars, providing the first evidence that the universe appears to be expanding.[11]

Red shift. What Hubble observed, later formulated as Hubble's law, was that the farther away a star is, the more the light from it is shifted toward the red end of the spectrum, a phenomenon known as *red shift.[12] The stars Hubble examined were a class of stars known as Cepheid variable stars. These stars had been shown to pulse at regular intervals, the rate being correlated with how bright they are, their luminosity. While the actual luminosity of a star is controlled by how massive it is, the apparent luminosity is also affected by how far it is from the observer. By comparing the actual luminosity (determined by their pulsation interval) with their apparent luminosity (how bright they appear), it is possible to determine how far away the star is.[13]

Light from stars can be subjected to analysis with a spectrometer, resulting in the appearance of spectral lines. Similar spectral lines can be produced by heating elements on earth in the proper apparatus.[14] By comparing the two, astronomers can identify the component elements of a star, since these lines appear at very precise electromagnetic wavelengths. Hubble found that light from the more distant Cepheids was shifted relative to that from nearby stars, appearing at longer wavelengths. The principle behind this is similar to the Doppler effect, the

---

[11]For a more complete but still brief history, see Coles (2001).

[12]This is the only case I am familiar with where the theory (relativity) preceded the statement of a law associated with it (Hubble's law), although there are undoubtedly others.

[13]Many other factors also affect luminosity, but within a certain class of star, size and distance are two main factors. More recent analysis, using more distant objects and higher-precision measurements, has led to a reduction in the estimated value of the Hubble constant, but the principle is the same (Coles, 2001: 50).

[14]Similar spectral lines, not identical, because the two are inverse: elements on earth produce emission lines, while stars produce absorption lines, as elements in the star's atmosphere absorb energy at the same frequency.

lowering of sound frequency we hear when a siren is moving away from us. His interpretation was that, in agreement with the theory of relativity without the cosmological constant, the universe is expanding. This is analogous to what we do when driving at night. Knowing the real size, separation and intensity of taillights, we compare that with the apparent features and intuitively estimate how far we are from the car in front of us, how fast it is moving relative to us and whether the distance between us is increasing or decreasing.

Cosmic microwave background radiation. Between Isaac Newton and Albert Einstein lived another famous physicist, although less well known outside of scientific circles, James Clerk Maxwell.[15] In the second half of the nineteenth century he inferred that electricity, light and magnetism are all different expressions of a wave phenomenon, known to us now as electromagnetic radiation. Longer, less energetic waves comprise radio and microwave radiation, while shorter, higher energy waves include X-rays and gamma rays, with infrared, visible light, and ultraviolet light in the middle.[16] This discovery not only paved the way for discovery of the red shift, a change in the observed frequency of light due to the relative motion of the Cepheid and earth, but also for the discovery held by many to be the lynchpin in the argument for an expanding universe, *cosmic microwave background radiation (CMBR).

You may have had the experience of passing your hand over a stove after it was used. As it cools, it emits energy at a lower and lower wavelength until it reaches the temperature of the surrounding room. At first the burner glows red, later it emits infrared radiation we can feel but not see. With a little experience, it is possible to estimate how long it has been since the burner was turned off. This is the principle behind cosmic microwave background radiation (CMBR).[17]

The background radiation can be regarded as both the electromag-

---

[15]My favorite quote from Maxwell is one he is reputed to have said in a lecture at Marischal College on November 3, 1856: "Nowadays we have too much to teach, and too little time to teach it." I wonder what he would say now, after the explosion of information in the last 150 years.

[16]Magnetism is detected as an oscillating field at right angles to the oscillation of the electrical field.

[17]Radiation from the big bang is predicted to have cooled from wavelengths in the ultraviolet and visible part of the spectrum to the infrared and microwave portion, the latter being the source of the name (Coles, 2001: 61).

netic frequency and the temperature found in space between stars, the two being causally related. First detected in 1964, the background radiation was measured across a large portion of the sky in 1992 by the Cosmic Background Explorer (COBE) spacecraft and found to be extremely uniform on a large scale.[18] Later measurements, with greater detail, showed that on a smaller scale there are fluctuations that fit a particular pattern. The significance of this will be discussed later.

Relative abundance of light elements. When it became clear in the middle of the twentieth century that the universe was expanding, two mechanisms were proposed to account for it, which came to be known as *steady state and big bang. Note that formally neither of these theories is an account of the origin of the universe per se, which is held to be outside the realm of science. Rather, each is an attempt to explain how the universe expands.[19] Nevertheless there are implications of each model for the origin of the universe, as we will see. It should also be noted that neither is in reality a single theory but, like our six models, is a name given to a family of related models that may still show a fair degree of disparity.[20]

If the universe is currently expanding, as we look back in time it should be contracting. If we look far enough back, there should be a single origin, a beginning. This idea, the simplest interpretation, led to the model that eventually came to be known as the "big bang."[21] The name is somewhat misleading, in that it seems to imply an explosion of the type we are familiar with, where matter existing in time and space explodes to become spread over a wider area in a less organized form. In fact, the big bang postulates that as the universe expanded, time and space were created and matter became more organized.

An alternative explanation, the steady state model, proposed that new matter is created as the universe expands, so that there is no net change

---

[18]Smoot & Davidson, 1993. A brief summary can be found in Ross (1993: chap. 3).

[19]This is the astronomical equivalent of the distinction between evolution and abiogenesis. Biologists will sometimes refuse to talk about the origin of life, saying that evolution only talks about what happened after life existed. This of course begs the question, as does talking about the mechanism of the big bang without being willing to discuss where the initial singularity came from.

[20]For variants on the big bang, see Edwards (2001).

[21]The name was given sardonically by Fred Hoyle, a proponent of steady state, but it stuck.

in density even though the universe is expanding, allowing the universe to be infinite in time and space.[22] The new matter would be created by quantum flux, and the amount required is not great, on the order of one hydrogen atom per cubic meter over the course of the life of the universe (Coles 2001: 58).

One of the first lines of evidence proposed to distinguish between these two models was the relative abundance of hydrogen, helium and lithium, the three lightest elements, and deuterium, an isotope of hydrogen containing one neutron in addition to the single proton in the nucleus. Given these elements, *stellar nucleosynthesis theory predicts how all the other heavier elements could have been made in the core of stars or supernovas. Observations of the elements present in various classes of stars seems to support this proposed method of synthesis. On the other hand, there is no known or proposed mechanism by which these three elements could have been produced in their current proportions, except by the big bang.[23] According to the steady state model the three just happen to appear in that proportion. For this reason, as well as not explaining the observed pattern of cosmic microwave background radiation (CMBR), the steady state model has been rejected by all but a few die-hard advocates.

At first glance, this does not seem to have anything to do with evaluating our six models, but as we will see when talking about interpretations, the explanation given by one of the models bears great similarity to that given by steady state, while the explanation given by another seeks to solve the same metaphysical problem that led some to espouse steady state.

Consistency with theory. It is difficult to discuss many lines of evidence for the origin of the universe without relating them to the big bang

---

[22]I am indebted to one of the anonymous reviewers, who pointed out that popular accounts of the steady state model being motivated by opposition to the metaphysical implications of the big bang are inaccurate. See Hans Halvorson and Helge Kragh (2011, winter), "Cosmology and theology," in *Stanford encyclopedia of philosophy*, Edward N. Zalta (Ed.), http://plato.stanford.edu/archives/win2011/entries/cosmology-theology.

[23]The relative proportions of not only these four, but also He-3 and Li-7 are predicted accurately by a hot big bang model, but only for a particular value of the baryon to photon ratio, the one observed in our universe. Like many values discussed in the next section, there is no known reason why the ratio would have to be what it is (Coles, 2001: 62-64).

theory, since all were gathered specifically to test predictions of that theory. Suffice it to say that in the last half century there have been dozens of independent tests of various aspects of the big bang theory. Observations of galaxies distant in time as well as space using the Hubble space telescope have revealed a far more crowded universe in the distant past, but no objects beyond a certain age. Details of the background radiation reveal a structure consistent with the effects of expansion from an initial *singularity. Measurements of the proportions of subatomic particles are also consistent with theory. On the other hand, discrepancies with the theory have required the postulation of *dark matter, *dark energy and an *inflationary period, which have not yet been detected (Cornell, 1989).[24] The details are quite technical, but the more evidence that is collected, the more scientists have realized how precisely balanced many different values must be for the universe to support life, the topic we turn to next.

A fine-tuned universe. One of the surprises in science in the last fifty years has been how carefully balanced many different values must be for life to exist. Some of these characteristics have to do with properties of physics and chemistry necessary for the existence of elements, the physical constants. Others have to do with properties of the large-scale structure of the universe. Yet others involve the properties necessary in a solar system and planet to allow time for the development of life. Note that again it is not entirely possible to separate evidence from model, for if the earth were created in nearly its present form only a few thousand years ago, some of the conditions of the solar system necessary for life to exist for millions of years would not have to be met. Nonetheless, they are met, and this is the evidence that each model must explain.

Physical constants. Physicists tell us there are four fundamental forces of nature: the strong, electromagnetic, weak and gravitational. Each has

---

[24]More recent developments can be found in Coles (2001). Even this is out of date, having been printed before the Hubble space telescope was functional, which has greatly increased the precision of measurement and ability to see distant objects in space. For the most recent information, the Internet is the best source. For more details on the evidence for an expanding universe, from the perspective of two very different models (NE and OEC, respectively), see www.talkorigins .org/faqs/astronomy/bigbang.html, and www.reasons.org/rtbs-creation-model/cosmic-design/ cosmic-design-beginners-and-experts-guide-big-bang-sifting-facts-fictions.

a particular strength, is active over a different distance, and controls certain attractive or repulsive relationships. So far there is no theory that predicts why any of those should be at the levels they are, or that constrains them to a certain value, but both the levels of the values independently and their ratio to one another are necessary for the existence of atoms, compounds, stars and life. Read that last sentence again, as it is the crucial summary of the evidence. If the following discussion gets too heavy for your taste, that is all you need to know before moving to the next section, but it is impossible to fully grasp the importance of this without a little understanding of what each force does.

The strong force, sometimes called the strong nuclear force, is responsible for holding protons and neutrons together in the *nucleus, but is only active over short distances, the diameter of a relatively small nucleus. Because the protons in the nucleus are all positively charged, the strong force must be stronger than the electromagnetic force pushing them apart. If it were only slightly smaller, no elements would exist except for hydrogen, with its single proton, due to the repulsion between similarly charged objects. On the other hand, if it were much larger, hydrogen could not exist because the force attracting two protons would be too great.

The next strongest force is the electromagnetic force, which is responsible for chemical bonding. It is the only force that can either attract or repel. Remember that I said earlier that each element produces spectral lines at a particular frequency. This is because the electrons of a given element are found in *orbitals of certain patterns at certain distances from the nucleus, each of which corresponds to a certain energy level.[25] Since chemical bonding involves sharing or transfer of these electrons, it involves the electromagnetic force. If that force were just slightly different, there would be no chemical reactions. Slightly higher, the electrons would be too tightly bound to their own protons, their own nucleus, to form bonds. Slightly lower, they would not be suffi-

---

[25]Electrons do not travel in regular orbits, as the planets do. Rather, their position can be depicted by a probability diagram that has different shapes for different orbital types. Strictly speaking, the energy level is based on potential energy rather than actual distance, but this is a convenient way to look at it.

ciently attracted to other nuclei. Either way, bonds would not form.

The third force is the weak force, sometimes called the weak nuclear force. It acts at even shorter distances than the strong force, less than the diameter of a proton. Ultimately it is responsible for the rate and products of fusion in stars, in conjunction with gravity. In brief, in the first steps of fusion two hydrogen atoms combine to form deuterium, which joins with another hydrogen to form helium.[26] The key step in this process is the production of deuterium. Each hydrogen atom contains one proton. Deuterium contains one proton and one neutron. So in order for this reaction to take place, one proton must be converted into a neutron.[27] This is controlled by the weak force. If this force were different it would affect many things, from the stability of protons and neutrons, and therefore atoms, to the rate of fusion in stars, but one of the greatest impacts would have been on the original proportion of hydrogen to helium in the universe, and thus the production of heavier elements. Element formation is also related to gravitational force.

We think of gravity primarily as something that holds us to the surface of the earth, and perhaps secondarily as something that keeps the earth in orbit around the sun, but it also controls the rate of fusion in the sun and other stars. As gravity pulls the gases of stars inwards, it creates pressure and thus heat, finally leading to the initiation of fusion. If gravity were only slightly weaker, fusion would never have taken place. If slightly stronger, it would have taken place at a much faster rate, changing the characteristics of stars.

We have only discussed the levels of the four fundamental forces. There are other *physical constants as well, some even more esoteric, such as the coupling constants that relate these four forces to one another, as well as the speed of light and the masses of each of the fundamental particles. Perhaps twenty-six different constants are needed to completely describe the properties of matter, all seemingly arbitrary and noncontingent numbers.[28] In many cases both the individual level and

---

[26]Actually, the process involves another step, as two helium-3s fuse to form helium-4, but the key step still is the production of deuterium.

[27]More technically, a quark must change flavor, from up to down, but this has the effect of changing a proton into a neutron.

[28]It is difficult to determine how many of the physical constants are basic, and how many can be

the ratio of that value to others are important in producing the observed characteristics of matter. The fact that these numbers all fall at exactly the right level for life to exist, although not one seems to be required by any physical laws that we know, is evidence that each model of origins must account for.

Universe conditions. We will look next at the large-scale condition of the universe. Here again it turns out that a very precise balance of a number of seemingly disconnected and arbitrarily set values control both the expansion rate of the universe and the uniformity of the universe, creating the conditions necessary for formation of the variety of types of stars we observe, which in turn produce the different elements necessary for life. In order to show the importance of these universal values we will first take a quick detour to examine stellar nucleosynthesis theory, which predicts how various elements form, including the elements essential to life.

We take it for granted that in the sun hydrogen is being fused into helium, producing heat and light, forgetting that less than a century ago the process was totally unknown. Due to the intense gravitational force in the core of the sun, hydrogen atoms are packed so tight that they cease to exist as atoms, becoming a plasma of dissociated nuclei and electrons, allowing the nuclei themselves to interact and fuse. We might think that any two nuclei, with sufficient heat and pressure, could fuse, but it turns out that just as certain elements will react, forming bonds, only certain nuclei will fuse, forming heavier nuclei, and these interactions and the amount of energy necessary for them to occur are predictable given sufficient knowledge of atomic structure.

In stars the size of our sun, the main reaction taking place is the fusion of hydrogen into helium. In slightly larger stars, significant amounts of carbon are produced by fusing three helium nuclei. Adding another helium produces oxygen. Odd atomic number elements like nitrogen are produced by addition of a hydrogen nucleus, and occur in lesser amounts. A barrier, the Coulomb barrier, makes it increasingly

---

derived from something else, so numbers vary. See John Baez (2011, April 22), "How many fundamental constants are there?" University of California, Riverside, http://math.ucr.edu/home/baez/constants.html.

difficult to form elements with an atomic number greater than 10. Significantly, the four elements that make up 96 percent of living things
(HCNO), all have an atomic number lower than this, and thus are
present in large amounts in the universe. Heavier elements, several of
which are required for life but in far smaller amounts, are made only in
very large stars, then spread throughout the galaxy when that large star
explodes in a supernova.[29]

The last two paragraphs are of course not direct evidence but inferences and conclusions drawn from the evidence, yet they are unconten-
tious, accepted by all camps in the origins debate. Although considered
by some to be irrelevant to that debate, the significance comes in the
fact that different elements are formed in different kinds of stars, and
certain highly specific conditions are necessary for various kinds of stars
to form, conditions controlled by the expansion rate of the universe and
the uniformity of the universe. These in turn rest on other more basic
physical values that seem to be set arbitrarily, but are at points necessary
for life to exist.

As we discussed before, there is strong evidence that the universe appears to be expanding. At present that rate of expansion seems to be
controlled by three main factors: the Hubble constant, the mass density
of the universe, and the acceleration rate.[30] The Hubble constant mea-
sures the current expansion rate of the universe, based on measurements
of both Cepheid variables and supernovas. The expansion of the universe is balanced by the force of gravity, which tends to reduce that expansion, and is controlled by the density and total amount of mass in
the universe. Indirect evidence obtained by looking at distant galaxies
seems to indicate that the rate of expansion is increasing, a factor known
as the acceleration rate.

Although there have been controversies about the value of all of these
factors, recent improvements in measurement techniques have gradually
refined estimates. Yet questions remain. Exact measurement of the

---

[29]Kipp Penovich, "Formation of elements," *Astrophysics and Cosmology,* http://aether.lbl.gov/www/
tour/elements/element.html.
[30]"The age of the universe," University of Michigan, March 23, 2010, http://dept.astro.lsa.umich
.edu/ugactivities/Labs/cosmo/intro-cosmo.html.

values does not answer the question why they are at the current levels. What caused the initial expansion of the universe, and what caused it to expand at the rate it did?[31] What caused the universe to have the total mass that it does? What is causing the apparent acceleration? If the expansion rate were only slightly greater, galaxies could not have formed, because the gravitational attraction between stars would be overcome by the expansion of the universe. On the other hand, if the expansion rate were just a little slower, gravity would have won and the whole universe would have collapsed back into a singularity before stars even formed.[32]

The second major factor affecting the formation of stars is the uniformity of the universe. On a large scale, the universe appears remarkably uniform and homogeneous.[33] Yet on a smaller scale there are fluctuations in the mass density, expressed as fluctuations in the cosmic microwave background radiation (CMBR), bubbles and voids in the vastness of space, and the presence of galaxies and the stars within them. Here again it is impossible to totally separate evidence from theory. If the universe was created in the recent past, it could have been created in its present form. But if the big bang theory is correct, the current conditions reflect the initial starting conditions. Had the universe been only slightly more uniform as it began to expand, galaxies and stars would never have formed. Had it been slightly less uniform, more large stars would have formed. Since large stars have a higher heat in the core than smaller ones, they burn hydrogen faster and form more heavy elements, at the expense of the lighter ones necessary for life. Changes in uniformity would also have affected conditions in the solar system necessary for life, the topic we will examine next.

Solar system conditions. In many ways our solar system appears to be relatively unusual, perhaps unique, in having certain conditions that

---

[31]In addition to the general rate of expansion, many scientists believe there was a rapid period of inflation, caused by a phase shift, in the same way that water gradually expands as it is heated, until it reaches the boiling point, at which time it undergoes a rapid expansion, which was important in "flattening" space-time (Coles, 2001: 11, 87).

[32]Both statements of course assume that the expansion rate and age of the universe are what they appear to be, which is not accepted by YEC.

[33]YEC disagrees with this, contending that there are bands of concentric circles around the original center. Our position slightly off center leads to the appearance of homogeneity. See the later references in the section on apparent age.

make it suitable for life. The galaxy it is in, characteristics of the sun and other members of the solar system, and earth itself, all are necessary prerequisites for life to develop, so that our earth is not one in a million, but something far less probable than that. Again the evidence is very indirect, so it is easier to talk about conclusions based on the evidence than the actual observations themselves, but the assertions in this section would be acceptable to all astronomers, regardless of their model of origins, and represent only a small subset of the conditions that could be listed.

Our galaxy, the Milky Way, is a spiral galaxy. Other galaxy types are elliptical or irregular. Based on much theoretical work, it is thought that life could exist only in a spiral galaxy. Elliptical galaxies do not seem to have enough stars capable of producing the heavy elements necessary in small amounts for life, and irregular galaxies have too much radiation for life to develop. Similarly, it is thought that our position halfway out one of the spiral arms is the only place life could exist, for similar reasons. Too close to the center there would tend to be too much radiation from other stars, but too far out would not have a high enough concentration of heavy elements due to the low density of supernovae.

The solar system also has certain characteristics thought to be essential or very favorable to life. First, it has a single central star. In the Milky Way, about one-third of the stars are estimated to be binary or multiple stars. There is disagreement among astronomers about whether life would be possible in a planet orbiting a binary, with some saying it would be impossible due to unstable orbits and radiation (Ross, 1993: 126), but others saying it would be possible in 50 to 60 percent of binary systems.[34] Second, the sun is a mid-sized star, which is thought to be important to life due to the stability of luminosity and other factors. Third, it is rich in metals, like the rest of the solar system, but not so much that life would be impossible due to heavy metal toxicity. Fourth, the solar system contains large gas planets (Jupiter and Saturn in particular), the size and position of which are thought to be important both in stabi-

---

[34]Elisa V. Quintana and Jack J. Lissauer (2010), "Terrestrial planet formation in binary star systems," in *Planets in binary star systems*, ed. Nader Haghighipour (New York: Springer). Abstract at http://arxiv.org/abs/0705.3444.

lizing the orbit of smaller planets and in reducing the number of comets and asteroids hitting earth.[35]

Earth itself also has unique characteristics that foster life. The orbit lies within the habitable zone, in which water is present in liquid form, and is only slightly eccentric so annual temperature extremes are not too high. The slight tilt of the axis, combined with the speed of rotation, together also help maintain temperatures over much of the earth's surface at a level suitable for life. The size of the planet allows it to maintain an ideal atmosphere: a slightly larger planet would retain ammonia and methane, which are toxic, while a slightly smaller one would lose water vapor and other gases, becoming a dry planet like Mars. Various other factors—including the composition of the earth's core, crust and atmosphere; the amount of surface area covered by ocean; level of seismic activity; and even the tidal effects caused by the large moon—are also thought to be important in creating an environment suitable for maintenance of life.[36]

3.2 How Does Each Model Interpret the Evidence?

This then is the evidence: The universe appears to be expanding from a singularity that existed approximately 13.8 billion years ago, and conditions in the universe and solar system are exquisitely balanced to allow for the existence of life. But what, if anything, existed before the universe, and are the conditions the result of design, chance or some other factor? The answers given to these questions depend on the assumptions one makes about what, if anything, exists apart from the natural universe, and if there is something supernatural, beyond the ken of science, how that interacts with the natural.

In many ways the most obvious interpretation of the evidence is that the singularity before the big bang represents a real beginning, but that interpretation obviously only makes sense given the possible existence of something or someone able to create the universe. This is the inter-

---

[35]A certain number of asteroid impacts early in the history of earth is thought to have been important in increasing the metal content of the crust.

[36]For a more complete list, see Ross (1993). For more information see Conway Morris (2003: chap. 5), and Gonzalez & Richards (2004).

pretation chosen by four of our six models of origins. Those who, on philosophical grounds, deny this must come up with some other explanation that makes the big bang only an apparent beginning. A third interpretation, based on the assertion of a recent creation, has an altogether different explanation of the apparent age of the universe.

In the beginning. "In the beginning God created the heavens and the earth" (Gen 1:1). Nearly all Christians today take this famous statement that opens the book of Genesis to mean that there was a beginning of the universe, that it is not infinite in time.[37] Nonteleological evolution, planned evolution, directed evolution and old-earth creation, all the theistic models that do not hold to a literal six twenty-four-hour day interpretation of Genesis 1, interpret the singularity at the beginning of the big bang as the moment of creation, about 13.8 billion years ago.

If there is a Creator behind the universe, the answer to the question of why the characteristics of the universe are suited to life is also obvious, since the universe was planned and designed with life in mind. Nevertheless, as we will see more clearly in subsequent chapters, these four models do not agree on how much information was front-loaded into the creation. According to both NTE and PE, God created the universe perfectly, in a way that would inevitably lead to sapient life, so that no further intervention was needed after the point of creation. According to DE, God is in direct control of events, and chooses to intervene from time to time to direct probabilistic events, although perhaps at a level undetectable scientifically. According to OEC, God continued to intervene throughout the history of creation in ways that are not only scientifically discernible, but intended to demonstrate his existence. What is important to note is that underlying each of these are philosophical assertions based on a perception of the character of God and how he has or continues to work in the world, and that in general these spring from a specific method of interpreting the Bible, rather than from the scientific evidence.

Much of the published material interpreting the big bang from a specifically Christian perspective has been produced by Reasons to Be-

---

[37]This has not always been the case. See Halvorson & Kragh (2011).

lieve (reasons.org), whose founder, Hugh Ross, is an astronomer by training. Their OEC model is based on a *concordist interpretation of Genesis 1, according to which the events of Genesis 1 occurred in the order recorded in the Bible, but the term commonly translated "day" refers to an unspecified period of time.[38] According to this view, the Bible reveals things that could not have been known by the original authors, thus the agreement between the Bible and scientific discoveries bears testimony to both the inspiration of the Bible and the identity of the Creator.

Both DE and PE are based on a *nonconcordist interpretation of Genesis 1. The basic contention of the framework interpretation is that early Hebrew literature often employs parallelism, chiasmus and other literary structures suitable to orally transmitted languages. Thus the six days of creation are not viewed as sequential. Rather, God formed and filled the earth, which began "formless and empty," the first three days describing the forming, the second three the filling. Other interpretations treat the story overall as teaching something that was important to the ancient Hebrew worldview, rather than the days having significance individually, as shown in appendix two. Thus, according to these models the Bible reveals the identity of the Creator, but nothing is said about the method or timing of creation.

Where DE and PE differ is in the degree of intervention after the moment of creation. Directed evolution springs from a theological position that emphasizes God's immanence, and DE would prefer to say not that God is intervening but that he is continually involved in the creation, whether sustaining natural law or temporarily suspending it in what we call miracles. Planned evolution, on the other hand, emphasizes God's transcendence and distinguishes God's intervention in redemptive history, in the miracles of the Bible or by working in people's lives as a response to prayer, from his lack of intervention in natural history, in physical processes that can be investigated scientifically (Lamoureux, 2008: chap. 3).

Although nonteleological evolution agrees with PE in the assertion

---

[38]See appendix two for a summary of concordist and nonconcordist interpretations of Scripture.

that God does not intervene after the moment of creation, NTE goes further in asserting that God did not foresee exactly how the creation would unfold. Rather, he created a cosmos in which evolutionary processes made sentient beings inevitable, but the specific nature and appearance of that being was not specified. This is based on various theological perspectives, such as process theology, that treat Genesis 1 as mere symbol (Edwards, 2001). For the same reason, conditions in this particular solar system are thought to be ideal for life by chance, although the probability of life arising somewhere in the universe is high enough to make it inevitable.

Thus, although all four of these models agree that there is a Creator, that the big bang represents the point and mechanism of creation, and that the observed fine-tuning of the universe is a result of the creative intelligence of the Designer, there are still major differences between them, as will become more evident as we see how different groupings of the models appear with respect to the other three origins.

Apparent beginning. There is only one model that does not admit the presence of a Creator, and therefore must come up with some other explanation for the existence of the universe. Although naturalistic evolution accepts big bang cosmology as the mechanism by which the universe came to have its present structure, it does not view the initial singularity as the point of origin. Since, according to this model, there is no supernatural (and thus nothing that cannot ultimately be investigated and explained by science) the energy present at the beginning must have come from some other physical source. Currently, the most popular explanation is the idea of a *multiverse.

Before the discovery of the expansion of the universe, it was easy to believe that the universe was infinite and basically unchanging, but this is no longer the case. Over the last century a number of naturalistic explanations have been put forth to explain the origin of the universe, including hesitation models, steady state models, and oscillating universe models. All of these have been shown to have serious problems explaining the evidence, which has led to their relegation.[39] Currently

---

[39]For more information on problems with these three models, see Ross (1991: chaps. 7-10).

most naturalists favor some variation of the big bang model, usually one involving the idea of a multiverse.

There are several different multiverse models, including those that propose all universes have the same physical constants, others in which the various universes have different physical constants, and yet others in which even the physical laws may differ.[40] All are mathematically and logically possible, but all posit other universes for which there is no empirical evidence. Thus the existence of these multiverses is no less a matter of faith for atheists than the existence of a supernatural is for theistic models.

The multiverse idea has an additional attraction, beyond explaining the basic existence of the universe: it offers a possible explanation of the exquisite fine-tuning observed, in that other universes theoretically would not have to have the same conditions. In an infinite number of possible universes, by chance there would be one, ours, that had conditions just right for life. Just as there are fundamentally only two possible explanations for the existence of the universe—natural and supernatural—there are fundamentally only two possible explanations for the observation that the universe and solar system have conditions that are perfectly balanced for life, particularly sentient life: either it was designed that way or we were just extraordinarily lucky.

How lucky we would have to be is a matter of some contention. Everyone seeks to marshal evidence in support of their chosen model, including how likely they think it is that conditions necessary for life could have arisen by chance. Looking only at conditions within the solar system, there are many questions. How wide a range of temperatures could a planet have and still support life? How varied could the composition of the crust be? How much water is necessary? The list is endless. In every case, you will find that theists tend to give a narrow range, resulting in a very low likelihood of life existing by chance, so low that it is unlikely to have occurred even once in the history of the universe. On the other end, atheists come up with numbers that make it seem unlikely that we are the only sentient species in the universe. Who is

---

[40]Several of these models are discussed in Edwards (2001). Edwards also evaluates the assumptions of naturalism in chap. 2.

correct? Science cannot give us the answer, since so far ours is the only planet known that can support life, so we have no direct evidence of the possible range, only guesses based on discordant theories. The same situation exists with the physical constants that control the existence of elements and stars. If they are truly arbitrary, we are uncommonly lucky, but exactly how lucky is an open question.

In seeking to explain this apparent luck, naturalistic evolution often appeals to the *anthropic principle.[41] Simply stated, the naturalistic version says we must have been that lucky, otherwise we would not be here to ask the question. While it is true that had the values been different, we would not be here, this assertion eliminates a priori the possibility that the situation was planned and implemented by an intelligent being, and so it comes back again to a basic philosophical choice between a naturalistic and supernaturalistic explanation.

Apparent age. There is only one model of origins that does not accept big bang cosmology, with its explanation that the universe is about 13.8 billion years old, as the best explanation of observed conditions. Young-earth creation is based on what proponents consider a straightforward interpretation of the Bible, by which they mean taking each word literally, in its common, everyday meaning, unless there is obvious indication of figurative language in the text itself. Finding no such indication in the first few chapters of Genesis, YEC believes that creation occurred in six twenty-four-hour days. Based on the genealogies in Genesis, creation is thought to have occurred about 6,000 to 10,000 years ago. Of course there are other creation stories in other cultures, but for the most part no attempt has been made to justify those accounts with the scientific evidence, so the focus here will be on models proposed by conservative monotheism, particularly Christian YEC in the United States.

According to YEC theology, "Genesis is the record of the God who was there as history happened," and the Bible is inerrant not only in its theological but also its historical and scientific statements (Ham,

---

[41]For a very short summary of the anthropic principle, see Coles (2001: 125-27) or Gonzalez & Richards (2004: chap. 13). For more detailed references, see note 14 in the latter. As with the big bang, there are both theistic and atheistic versions of the anthropic principle argument.

2006: 76). If every word is true in this sense, it is logical that the scientific evidence, which is continuously changing, should be interpreted in the light of the Bible, which is unchanging. Accordingly, if God says he made the world in six days in the recent past, but some evidence makes it appear to be older, our interpretation of that scientific evidence must be incorrect. Two different interpretations have been common in the YEC community in recent years.

According to the older apparent-age explanation, a painter can paint a picture with a tree that appears to be hundreds of years old, a person sitting under it who appears to be a few decades old, and a flower nearby that appears to be less than a year old. One of the things that distinguishes a master artist from a novice, at least in a realist school of art, is attention to detail. God, being a master artist, created a masterpiece so realistic that no matter how carefully we look, the appearance of age is perfect and consistent. This explains all of the evidence for things that appear older than ten thousand years, whether on earth or in the heavens, including light of stars created en route to earth. This is the YEC explanation often cited by opponents, but it has largely been dropped in recent YEC writing.

Currently, many scientists within the YEC community have adopted a different interpretation of the evidence, the universe expanding out of a *white hole. According to this explanation, our galaxy is thought to be near the center of a finite, bounded universe. Being close to the center of gravity, the gravitational time dilation predicted by general relativity causes time to run slower here than it does farther from the center of gravity. Thus during the fourth day of the creation week, "while one ordinary day was elapsing on earth, billions of years worth of physical processes were taking place in distant parts of the universe."[42] As a result the stars appear very old, even though the earth is young. Numerous geological features are listed to show that the earth appears young, which of course differs from evidence cited by other models that the earth appears

---

[42]D. Russell Humphreys (2001), "Seven years of starlight and time," *Acts & Facts* 30 (8), www.icr.org/article/446. More details on white-hole cosmology can be found in three parts at Larry Vardiman and D. Russell Humphreys (2010), "A new creationist cosmology: In no time at all, Part 1," *Acts & Facts* 39 (11): 12-15, www.icr.org/article/5686, "Part 2," www.icr.org/article/5830/, "Part 3," www.icr.org/article/5870.

old, each questioning the methods and assumptions of the other.[43] This explanation also appeals to apparent age, but proposes a mechanism by which the stars and earth could appear to be different ages.

The YEC explanation of the fact that conditions are suitable for life is that these represent the direct plan and work of the Creator, a demonstration of his knowledge and power. No other explanation is considered necessary for why certain conditions exist or why values occur at certain levels. Those are the levels necessary for life to exist, so that is how God created them.

3.3 WHAT DIFFERENCE DOES IT MAKE?

For each of the areas of origins, after examining the evidence and various interpretations of the evidence, it is reasonable to ask what difference it makes. What difference does it make in the way we view ourselves as humans or in the type of research we choose to pursue? For all of the various areas of origins, we will find that the greatest difference, regardless of how the models wind up falling in groups as to their interpretation of the evidence, is a division between naturalistic and supernaturalistic models, or atheistic and theistic, with effectively deistic models sitting on the fence.

One of the major unresolved questions in astronomy is whether we are alone in the universe. Are there other living things, particularly any other sentient beings, in the universe? Naturalistic models predict that life is probable. This is not just something said for the sake of winning the debate, it is something they firmly believe. As a result, NE fully supports research projects such as the Search for Extraterrestrial Intelligence (SETI), the search for electromagnetic signals that might indicate intelligent life elsewhere in the universe, and astrobiology, the search for other planets with conditions suitable for life. Most theistic models, on the other hand, feel such research is a waste of time, believing their calculations that show the likelihood of life arising by chance even once to be impossibly low. Deistic models tend to be neutral on this issue, not

---

[43]For evidence showing the earth to be old, see Gonzalez & Richards (2004). Other authors have criticized the white-hole model on the basis that the math does not work. See Poythress (2006: 103) and Ross (2004: 166-70).

actively pushing for research that would tend to bolster the claim that life could arise spontaneously, but not avoiding it either.

What difference would it make whether we are alone? If it could be shown beyond a doubt that life exists nowhere else in the universe, it would call into question the feasibility of life developing spontaneously from inanimate matter, compelling but not incontrovertible evidence for the involvement of a Creator. On the other hand, if life were to prove common in the universe, it would tend to support naturalistic models of abiogenesis and evolution. If any sentient life were found, it would necessitate development of a whole new branch of theology, to explicate their relation to the Creator.[44]

For now, these must remain as unresolved questions, but we are ready to move on to the first step that would be necessary for life to develop, here or elsewhere, the question of abiogenesis.

---

[44]Some authors have already addressed in a theoretical way the question of how nonhuman sentient life would relate to a Creator, including C. S. Lewis in what is commonly known as the space trilogy (*Out of the Silent Planet*, *Perelandra* and *That Hideous Strength*).

Origin of Life

• • •

A*biogenesis*, the scientific name for the origin of life, is a topic many biologists seem to want to dodge, in spite of the fact that their profession would not exist had it not occurred, to say nothing of the professors. It is glossed over in the evolution unit of biology textbooks with a quick obligatory reference to the Miller-Urey experiment. When students ask about it, teachers often repeat the line found in many textbooks and other places that evolution is the study of how life changed, not how it started in the first place. While this may be true, it is also more than a little disingenuous, since it is a valid scientific question, one that obviously is closely related to evolution as shown by the fact that evolutionary scientists now routinely talk about *prebiotic evolution.

So why is there so much reluctance to talk about the topic? Mostly because there is so little evidence and no good proposed mechanism for how life could have arisen. That may sound like an extreme statement, but it is true.[1] There are several proposals on the table describing how different parts of the process might have occurred, but nothing even vaguely resembling an overall explanation. Ultimately, whether we accept a natural or supernatural explanation is largely based on our philosophical presuppositions, because real evidence is nearly nonexistent.

---

[1]A good summary of problems with current theories of how life could have arisen can be found in Conway Morris (2003: chap. 4).

4.1 WHAT IS THE EVIDENCE?

One of the biggest problems in discussing the origin of life is there is no record of what happened, and in all likelihood, no direct evidence will ever be found. Molecules do not fossilize, although sometimes we may be able to infer the existence of certain elements or compounds from the presence of certain minerals. Single cells fossilize rarely, and even when they do, they leave few clues that would help us to determine the details of their structure.

If cells arose gradually, as predicted by all of the evolutionary models, certain things must have preceded the first true cell, including the presence of organic molecules necessary for life. But existence of the molecules by themselves is not sufficient, since only specific arrangements would be useful in building a cell, a problem referred to as information. And even if all of the molecular components could be formed, a cell is far more complex than the sum of its component parts.

Two distinct lines of argument have arisen regarding the origin of life. From one side, evolutionary scientists have sought to demonstrate methods whereby the various components of life could have been generated from inorganic matter. From the other side, opponents of evolution have sought to show that the probability of life arising by chance is so low that it is effectively impossible. We will examine each of these arguments in turn. A summary of the evidence and the general lines of interpretation can be found in table A1.3.

Life from nonlife. There is really no direct evidence of what conditions might have been like on the earth when life first arose, but there is a fair amount of indirect evidence based on the minerals found in rocks formed during that period. As with other fields, our understanding of the conditions under which certain minerals form has improved over time, based both on observation and chemical bonding theory.

Certain facts are clear, including the limited amount of time involved. The oldest minerals found on the surface of the earth have been dated at 4.2 billion years old, from which the inference is made that the crust cooled sufficiently to allow rock formation at that point. The first definite fossils have been found in rocks dated at 3.6 billion years old.[2]

---

[2]We will briefly discuss the question of radiometric dating in chapter five. The exact dates given by different authors vary and change slightly as techniques improve, but the net effect over the last

Thus the maximum time allowed for the origin of life is about 600,000 years. But there is some evidence based on carbon found in graphite dated at 3.8 billion years old that there may have already been photosynthetic organisms at that time,[3] and there are suggestions life might have appeared almost as soon as conditions became suitable, shortly after earth's surface cooled below the boiling point of water. What is in question is whether that time is sufficient for generating living, reproducing cells.

In the absence of any direct evidence, scientists in this field attack the problem using a number of indirect approaches. Either they specify the conditions that would have been necessary for life to arise, look for evidence of locations where those conditions might have been met, or try to construct viable scenarios of how the necessary steps could have occurred. Over the years many different locations have been proposed, from Darwin's "warm pond" to the edge of the ocean, the atmosphere, the surface of clays, deep sea vents, and space. Yet many problems remain, including the variety of conditions necessary for forming the various compounds, the randomness of reactions and the complexity of cells.

Organic precursors. Almost any biology textbook you pick up will contain a description of the Miller-Urey experiment. Briefly, Stanley Miller, a graduate student working in the laboratory of Harold Urey at the University of Chicago in 1952, sealed water, methane, ammonia and hydrogen in a glass apparatus, heated the mixture and passed a spark through the vapors. The gases were then condensed and any larger products trapped. The "experiment" was allowed to run for a week.[4] When the products were analyzed, Miller found several different amino acids had been formed. Since that time, similar work has led to the creation of most of the basic subunits of the macromolecules of life from inorganic molecules, including all of the essential amino acids, sugars, fatty acids and the nitrogenous bases necessary to form

---

few decades has been to reduce the time available for the origin of life.

[3]Conway Morris (2003: 108).

[4]Although usually called an experiment, this does not fit the formal definition of an experiment in which the scientist is isolating one variable to test its effects in a replicated and randomized study. This lax use of terminology by scientists and science textbooks causes problems, but that is an issue for another venue.

RNA and DNA.[5] Astrobiologists have recently discovered that some organic molecules are also present in comets, apparently having been formed in space.

While this is often touted as evidence that organic molecules can be formed easily from inorganics, it is not the full picture. All of the work was done in varying forms of a reducing atmosphere, one without free oxygen present. In the presence of oxygen all these organic molecules quickly degrade into inorganic compounds. There is evidence, based on the type of minerals found in different rock layers, that the amount of free oxygen in the atmosphere has increased over time, including a rapid increase starting about 1.9 to 2.45 billion years ago.[6] What is less obvious is whether there was a time at which there was no oxygen present, and if so how long it lasted. The standard scientific view is that earth's early atmosphere contained at most 0.1 percent oxygen, but others cite sources of oxygen that would have been present in the early earth, and claim very low levels of oxygen would have been sufficient to cause the breakdown of any macromolecules generated (Thaxton, Bradley & Olsen, 1984: 76-77). Since the evidence is somewhat ambiguous, proponents of different models make statements that favor their arguments, without admitting that the evidence is unclear.[7]

A second problem is that although all of the organic molecules can be formed, they form under different conditions, and conditions that favor the formation of one often favor the breakdown of another. Thus the problem of getting all of the compounds together in a living cell is much like the problem of making a cream puff. The filling needs to be made in a pan on a stove, then put in a refrigerator, while the shell is combined in a bowl, baked in an oven, then cooled, before the two parts are put together. All of the steps need to happen to the right amounts of the right components in the right sequence using the right tools in order to form a successful final product. Simon Conway Morris, in *Life's*

---

[5]These subunits are called monomers, from which polymers (long chains) of protein, carbohydrate, lipids and nucleic acids are built. These four types of macromolecules are considered to be the basic building blocks of life.

[6]For the later date see Conway Morris (2003). For the earlier date see Biello (2009).

[7]YEC supporters claim there was no time that earth lacked oxygen, but they also say the earth is less than 10,000 years old.

Solution, provides an excellent summary of the difficulties involved (Conway Morris, 2003: chap. 4).

Random reactions. Even if we could create and collect all of the molecular components in one place at the same time, that would just be the first step. In living things those subunits are quickly combined in a very specific way by *enzymes, but how could that have happened before enzymes existed? Each enzyme has a specific shape that facilitates a particular reaction. There are several distinct problems with organic reactions in the absence of the enzymes that are normally present only in living cells: *racemic mixtures, undesirable reaction products, decomposition and reaction speed. There is also the problem of replication.

Because each carbon atom can bond to four other atoms, sometimes the molecules formed are mirror images of one another, or in the language of chemistry they have right- and left-handed forms. Thus both sugars and amino acids are said to have *d* and *l* forms, from the initial letters of the Latin words for right and left, respectively. In living things, all sugars are in the *d* form, while only *l* amino acids are used. As with the physical constants discussed in chapter three, no one knows why. It seems that the choice is random. But when they are produced in nonliving systems, the result is a racemic mixture of the two forms, in which half are *d* and half are *l*. Chemically, in terms of their bonding properties the *d* and *l* subunits are nearly identical, but biologically the properties of larger molecules made from a racemic mixture would be very different.[8] An analogy may be helpful: you have undoubtedly seen folding chairs stacked up against a wall—they fit together well either direction, but if put together in random order the stack loses its integrity and strength.

A second problem once you have the proper components is that in nonliving systems, reactions happen randomly, wherever they can. If we have amino acids, sugars and nitrogenous bases together in solution, there is no guarantee the amino acids will all join to form a protein, while the sugar and base join in just the right configuration to form

---

[8]The *d* and *l* forms (enantiomers) usually have the same physical properties, except they rotate polarized light in opposite directions, but may have different ability to bond to other enantiomers. Reactions between *d* and *l* forms of amino acids or simple sugars seem to be equally likely.

nucleotides. Extending the analogy of the folding chairs, if we also have folding tables, it would make sense to put them in their own stack, all oriented the same direction. But what happens naturally in the absence of enzymes is that tables and chairs all get stacked together, in random order and orientation. Predictably, the result is a mess, not the ordered useful arrangements we find in living things.

The third problem is that of decomposition. Most chemical reactions are reversible, and in most cases the reaction that breaks something down proceeds more easily than the one to build it. This is related to the problem of speed. Enzymes lower the energy needed to build molecules by holding the reactants together in a favorable configuration. Without this, the rate is very slow. The problem is that the enzymes themselves are proteins, very specific arrangements of amino acids. How did the first enzymes form, without other enzymes to assist in the process?

A related but slightly different issue is that of self-replication. Even if an enzyme were to arise by chance that could catalyze a specific reaction, it would only be one enzyme and would itself be subject to degradation. In cells, enzymes are coded for by RNA, which in turn is coded for by DNA. The process involves numerous enzymes and cofactors at each stage. How did this complex process develop? The bottom line is that no one has proposed a reasonable stepwise process.[9] That does not mean that none exists, but it does explain why textbooks do not talk about it.

Protocells. The next step that would have to take place for life to arise in a stepwise manner is the sequestration of the organic molecules. Placing the molecules in a protective enclosure would make them more concentrated, facilitating reactions, and protect them from degradation by oxygen. The most likely candidate for this is thought to be coacervates.[10]

*Coacervates are collections of lipids, hydrophobic molecules that

---

[9]Currently the best guess is the idea of an "RNA world," in which RNA was the first self-replicating molecule, and gradually other sections of RNA became attached which could code for proteins. But this leads to the question of information, discussed later. Current theories and problems with them are summarized by Bradley (2004).

[10]Recently, some scientists have suggested that porous limestone could have trapped organics, making them more concentrated. This solves the problem of concentration, but not the question of the origin of the cell membrane, which is then considered as a separate issue.

cluster together to form a bubble in water. Small amounts of other substances can sometimes be caught within this bubble. Because cell membranes are made mostly of phospholipids, there is some similarity in structure.

Nevertheless, the difference between coacervates and cell membranes is huge. Not only are phospholipids more complex than the simple lipids usually found in coacervates, but cell membranes also contain a vast array of proteins embedded in and attached to the wall, along with numerous associated structural fibers. Again, no stepwise process has been proposed for transforming coacervates into functional cell membranes.

Cells. At one time we thought cells were basically blobs of jellylike material, cytoplasm, in which floated a few organelles. We now know that the cell is entirely filled with internal membranes that differ from each other but are continually exchanging material, that molecules and organelles are carried around the cell on a complex trackway of fibers, and even within the nucleus there is a very specific structure that seems to hold the chromosomes in a particular arrangement.[11] The cell is a highly complex integrated system, with molecular machinery as sophisticated as any human factory.

Any cell must be able to carry out a certain number of functions. At a minimum it must be able to get and use energy and reproduce. Getting energy involves having a mechanism to transport an energy-containing molecule through the cell membrane. Using it involves enzymes that can both break down the molecule and convert the energy into a form the cell can use, usually ATP. Reproduction involves taking in substances necessary to make another cell, and being able to make new components identical to those already in the cell, including DNA, RNA, proteins, phospholipids and other components. Clearly this is not a simple process.

The simplest known cell is the bacterium *Carsonella ruddii*, an obligate parasite that must live within another living cell. Yet its DNA contains 159,622 *base pairs, each pair comprising either adenine and thymine or cytosine and guanine, in a very carefully specified order

---

[11]The structure and purpose of the nuclear lamina and matrix are still under debate, but evidence is growing that they differ in different cell types and may influence gene expression. For a very technical description see Vlcek, Dechat & Foisner (2001).

comprising 182 genes.[12] Scientists trying to figure out what the theoretical lower limit is have proposed a minimal cell that would contain 113,000 base pairs and 151 genes (Forster & Church, 2006).[13]

The question for origin of life scientists is how this complexity could have arisen in a stepwise manner. Despite occasional exaggerated claims to the contrary, scientists are far from being able to create life in the laboratory.[14] Life is too complex for such a reconstruction effort, at least given the knowledge and techniques we now have available. Even making the DNA to control the cell is not merely a matter of being able to link thousands of base pairs end to end; they have to be linked in a very specific order that conveys information.

Information. Much of the evidence relating to the difficulty of generating the information contained in the cell, particularly in the DNA, has come from supporters of intelligent design, who have used it to challenge Darwinian evolution. Most of the response to this argument has come from biologists (not the biochemists actually working on origin of life), who say that many of the arguments are not scientific. Both sides have a valid point.

As was discussed in chapter two, many of the key figures in the ID movement come from a background in philosophy or math, and approach their arguments based on the accepted practices of their fields. Thus the claim that the arguments are not scientific, meaning empirically based, is valid. On the other hand, this does not mean that the arguments themselves are invalid.

Biology has always had difficulty accepting mathematical ideas. Part

---

[12]For a summary of three articles that appeared in *Science*, see Roxanne Khamsi, "Bacteria boast the 'tiniest genomes' to date," *NewScientist* (12 October 2006), http://www.newscientist.com/article/dn10259-bacteria-boast-the-tiniest-genomes-to-date.html.

[13]The smallest genome and minimal size are constantly changing as a result of new research, and there is not full agreement among researchers about what criteria to use, resulting in different reports. Many consider *Mycoplasma pneumoniae*, at 816,000 base pairs and 189 genes, to be the smallest free-living cell.

[14]In May 2010 Craig Venter announced he had created "artificial life." As many have pointed out, what he did was decipher the genetic sequence of a bacterium, rebuild the DNA artificially with minor modification, and reinsert that artificial DNA into an enucleated cell, which was then able to live and reproduce. But there is a big difference between copying a set of instructions and placing them in a working machine that can read and follow those instructions and creating both the instructions and machine from scratch.

of the reason Mendel's work was neglected for so long is that it was based on mathematics. When population geneticists reintroduced mathematics to biology in the early 1900s, their ideas were also opposed for a long time (Schwartz, 1999). So it is not unexpected that again this recent incursion of mathematics into science has been met with criticism, especially when many scientists also oppose the conclusions from a philosophical perspective.

The arguments regarding information can be classified into the nearly ideal code, the independence of information from the carrier, and the idea of specified complexity. While most scientists generally accept the first two lines of evidence, although with differing interpretations, many reject the validity of the third, for reasons we will discuss. A fourth line of evidence, irreducible complexity, while distinct from the other three, is often mentioned in the same context and will be discussed here as well.

Nearly universal and ideal code. To transmit information it is necessary to encode it in some way, be it in letters, binary code, pictures or non-verbal expressions. To be useful code, the recipient must also be able to interpret the code properly. Information in the cell is encoded in the DNA, copied into RNA and translated into protein. The *genetic code that does this turns out to be nearly ideal, given the constraints imposed on it physically. It is also nearly universal among all living things.[15]

Many places describe in detail the coding system used in the cell.[16] Those who have had biology recently are undoubtedly familiar with it, while those who have not probably do not care about the details. Suffice it to say that four bases (commonly abbreviated ATGC) are arranged in order on the DNA. It is the particular order that carries the information, in the same way that the sequence of letters on this page conveys information. The information is copied onto the RNA (with U replacing T), then each group of three letters (called a triplet) codes for a particular amino acid, which are joined in order to make a protein. The code used is nearly universal, so that DNA from one organism placed into another

---

[15]There are a few organisms with slight modifications in the genetic code.
[16]For a good, simple version, see "Code" (2003), *DNA Interactive*, Cold Spring Harbor Laboratory, www.dnai.org/a/index.html.

organism will make exactly the same protein, the principle behind genetic engineering. It is also nearly ideal, in the sense that most errors in translation tend to result in substitution of a similar amino acid, resulting in a similar protein. This line of evidence is noncontroversial, although the interpretations of it differ.

Independent of carrier. A second line of evidence that most scientists would have no trouble accepting is that the information contained in a carrier is independent of the carrier itself. We discussed earlier the difficulty of forming organic compounds, including DNA or RNA, in a nonliving system. But it is not enough that the nucleotides be connected in random order, because the role of the nucleic acids is to store and transmit information, particularly information about how to make proteins and control the cell. Alignment of the nucleotides in an order that conveys information requires a higher level of organization than producing and linking the nucleotides randomly.

The controversial aspect is not the independence itself, but the source of the information. Again, an analogy will help. You are reading text on a page, but that same information was transmitted to the printer by binary code in the computer, and originated not in the page or the computer but in the mind of the author. Similarly, the information in a cell is transmitted from generation to generation by the DNA, and transferred from DNA to RNA to protein, but where did it originate in the first place?

Something contains information if it conveys a message, independent of the physical form and independent of the source of that information. As we will see in discussing interpretations, the origin of information is explained by different models in accord with their presuppositions. We will also come back to this topic in chapter five, as it turns out that although the origin of information cannot be detected empirically, it may be possible to detect changes in the DNA over time.

Specified complexity. The third proposition related to information is far more controversial, with some presenting it as crucial evidence and others denying it has anything to contribute to the debate. On the one hand are those who hold *specified complexity to be direct evidence of the work of the Creator; on the other, those who say the complexity can be explained by natural causes. The difference, once again, is based on the philosophical position from which one views the evidence, rather than anything inherent in the evidence itself. Since the argument is mostly over whether this should even be admitted as evidence, that will be the focus of this section.

Specified complexity is based on a new area of mathematics, complexity theory, an offshoot of information theory. Just as the field of statistics was developed in conjunction with and contributed greatly to population genetics, but was opposed by those committed to Darwin's paradigm of blending inheritance, opponents claim complexity theory has nothing to contribute to science. Whether that is true remains to be seen, but history seems to have a way of repeating itself when it comes to contributions of mathematics to the natural sciences, so it would be unwise to dismiss it too quickly.

The basic idea of specified complexity is that complexity can be either specified or random. Any system with multiple components is complex, in that those components could be put together in any one of multiple configurations. So any rock showing multiple mineral crystals is complex, but does not convey information because that complexity is not specified. On the other hand, a rock that has been carved into a particular shape by a sculptor is specified, conveying a degree of information that varies with the complexity of the carving and the intent of the sculptor.

The presence of specified complexity is tested based on the probability of a certain occurrence. As with other historical sciences, the origin of life is not amenable to experimental testing because it is not repeatable. Thus estimates must be made of the likelihood of a system arising as the result of an undirected series of events. As we saw in chapter three, when we have only one example as a basis, this process is fraught with error and highly dependent on the assumptions made by the one setting the independent probabilities.

Those who wish to admit specified complexity as evidence often speak of the low probability of life arising by chance, given its obvious complexity. Those opposed to admitting it as evidence say that life did not arise by chance. Rather, although it arose in an undirected manner, selection of forms with increased function means that the process is not random. In the first interpretation, the overall probability of life is impossibly low, a product of the low probability of each necessary event occurring in the right order. In the latter, the probability is contingent: although variation may arise randomly, only those variants that are more successful at replicating themselves (whether cells or prebiotic molecules) survive to go through the next round of variation and selection, thus the probability of a more successful form remains the same in each generation, low but not impossibly so.

In our experience, all systems that demonstrate specified complexity and contain information reflect intelligence. Most animals have some way of communicating information to other members of the same species. More complex systems, able to communicate more details, we associate with higher intelligence. The only unambiguous examples of highly specified complexity we have are human artifacts. In cells we have an extremely complex system. Whether we are willing to attribute that to intelligence, or how we think the intelligence acted to create it, depends entirely on our philosophical presuppositions, since the code is there, but no claim of authorship has been found in it.

Irreducible complexity. Despite the similarity of the name, specified complexity and *irreducible complexity are very different concepts. The former, as we have seen, is rooted in mathematical theory, while the latter is based on observation of the biochemical machinery of the cell. Although not directly connected to the idea of information, it also questions the idea that the complexity of the cell could originate spontaneously. Furthermore, since the argument is closely associated with intelligent design and vigorously opposed by others for the same reasons, I have chosen to include it here.

The basic idea of irreducible complexity is that there are many structures in the cell that look and function like miniature machines, the most commonly used example being the one made famous by Michael Behe (1996) in *Darwin's Black Box*, the bacterial flagellum. As with manmade machines, many of the components of cellular machinery are essential to its operation; removing any one of them would cause the machine to malfunction. The question is how such a machine could be made in a stepwise manner, adding one part at a time, in a way that each stage would make sense and have a *selective advantage. The contention of irreducible complexity is that they cannot.

While no one debates the complexity of cellular machinery, the idea that it is irreducible is strongly contended. Every time the claim of irreducible complexity is made, someone demonstrates how a simpler system, using some of the same components, performs a similar function in some other organism (Miller, 2004). It should be clarified, however, that the claim of irreducible complexity is not that there are no simpler mechanisms that can achieve the same function or that the parts cannot have other uses, but that no Darwinian mechanism can account for the machine, with each step having a selective advantage.[17] As with the origin of life, so far no one has been able to demonstrate this type of sequence.

4.2 HOW DOES EACH MODEL INTERPRET THE EVIDENCE?

I have to wonder, given the depth of sentiment on this issue, if someone were to find a very clear sign in the cell that read, "I am God, God I am," how many would respond, "That God-I-am! That God-I-am! I do not like that God-I-am!" Tongue in cheek references to Dr. Seuss aside,[18] perhaps of the four origins this is the one in which it is most clear that the choice of model springs from a person's worldview, rather than being directly based on the evidence; the evidence is so scanty that it would be nearly impossible to base any decision on it without viewing it from a particular perspective. Most of what is presented as evidence would be called circumstantial at best.

Cells exist, so they must have originated somehow. If nothing exists outside of the observable natural order, or if God chose not to intervene, cells must have originated in a stepwise manner. On the other hand, an almighty God could have created cells as fully functional units. This delineates the two basic interpretations that dominate the argument. A third postulates direction of natural processes. Thus we again have three basic ways of interpreting the evidence, but the pattern of alliances between models is very different than for the origin of the universe.

---

[17]Behe makes this point repeatedly in response to his critics. See Michael Behe, *Uncommon Descent* (blog), http://behe.uncommondescent.com and Behe (2004).

[18]Dr. Seuss, *Green eggs and ham* (New York: Random House, 1960).

Inevitability. Three of the models—naturalistic evolution, nonteleological evolution and planned evolution—have a prior philosophical commitment to the idea that God did not intervene in natural history. Believing that there is no supernatural intervention in natural events, these three models must come up with a totally naturalistic explanation for the origin of life. Thus life must have arisen as a result of a combination of deterministic events that occur of necessity and random events that occur by chance, selected by survival. Ideally they would like to find a situation in which the necessary events would occur regularly, with a high enough probability to make life inevitable.

Lacking any hard evidence of how life originated, the argument most commonly used is a variant on the anthropic principle described in chapter three—we are here, therefore life must have arisen, so conditions must have been such that life could arise. All we have to do is find out what those conditions were. According to this view, "the production of life cannot be too difficult, because it happened on Earth apparently as soon as conditions had become suitable for life, around 3.8 billion years ago" (Mayr, 2001: 43). This is the standard evolutionary position.

Over the years various locations have been postulated for the origin of life. Darwin hinted at a warm pond.[19] For many years the edge of the ocean, with influx of various components from land, sea and sky, was the main contender, perhaps with clays acting as templates to isolate and organize the molecular reactions (Conway Morris, 2003: chap. 4). More recently deep sea vents, with their intense heat and pressure that would allow reactions to happen more quickly, have gained favor (Martin et al., 2008). However, all face the problems described earlier, that the conditions that favor one necessary reaction tend to cause another key component to break down. Some scientists, including Francis

---

[19]"But if (and Oh! what a big if!) we could conceive in some warm little pond, with all sorts of ammonia and phosphoric salts, light, heat, electricity, etc., present, that a protein compound was chemically formed ready to undergo still more complex changes, at the present day such matter would be instantly devoured or absorbed, which would not have been the case before living creatures were formed.... It is mere rubbish thinking at present of the origin of life; one might as well think of the origin of matter" (Charles Darwin, "Letter to Joseph Hooker" [1845], *Darwin Correspondence Project,* www.darwinproject.ac.uk/entry-922).

Crick, codiscoverer of the structure of DNA, have given up on finding ideal conditions on earth and proposed the idea of directed panspermia, that cells were sent here from another planet: our planet was seeded with life (Crick & Orgel, 1973). Of course, that only pushes the problem back in space and time, without resolving the underlying issue.

According to these models, evolution by means of natural selection occurs not only in living cells but also among molecules, the idea of prebiotic evolution. This idea is particularly applied to replicating molecules like RNA in order to explain how the genetic code became nearly ideal and ubiquitous. A molecule that is better able to replicate itself is able to make more copies, some of which might have a slight variation making them better at copying themselves, so that more are formed. Ultimately, some arose that added the ability to code for other molecules, such as enzymes, that conferred further adaptive advantage to the protocell they were contained in. Ultimately, this type of selection led to an organism that was able to outcompete the rest. The universality of the genetic code is seen as evidence of common descent from that single group of organisms.

The idea of irreducible complexity is strongly disputed by proponents of these three models. As stated previously, they point to the use of similar parts in simpler systems as evidence that the systems are not irreducibly complex. Two terms have been introduced to explain how components could be added to a simpler system, *exaptation* and *spandrels* (Gould & Lewontin, 1979). *Exaptation* refers to taking a component already present in some other system and using it, perhaps with modification, in a new setting. The term *spandrel* is used to refer to a component that was originally nonessential taking on importance of its own. As with panspermia, this pushes the problem back, but the question remains whether it has really resolved the issue, since those parts or earlier systems are themselves complex.

The idea of specified complexity is similarly derided. The rationale is that we do not understand how life originated, but it is a scientific question, which by their definition of science means that there must be a naturalistic explanation to the question.[20] Specified complexity, with the obvious implication that God is the intelligence behind the specification, is viewed as a "god-of-the-gaps" argument. Proponents of specified complexity have replied that chance or necessity is a "naturalism-of-the-gaps" argument, since no stepwise method has been proposed.[21] Both statements, of course, are true. The question is whether one considers it possible that God could have intervened in the creation of a cell, which is not a scientific question.

Immediate appearance. Many who believe God could have intervened also think that life is too complex to have arisen in a stepwise fashion and that it is more likely that God chose to create the first cell directly, fully functional. There is some difference between old- and young-earth creation as to what they believe was created in what order. According to OEC the first living things created were single cells, long before other types of living things, in accord with the fossil record. Young-earth creation does not specify when single-celled organisms were created, since the Bible does not talk about them, but all living things were created within a one-week period, fully formed. Other issues related to the difference between these two, including the degree to which forms might have been modified after creation, we will discuss in chapter five.

The rationale for this position is that living things are seen as having specified and irreducible complexity, which is taken as a sign of intelligence and is also thought to preclude stepwise selection. The contention is made that since in our experience order does not arise from disorder without intelligence as an organizing force, it is reasonable to draw the same conclusion with regard to the origin of life. The position is further bolstered by estimates of the probability of life arising by chance, which according to their estimates is less than the probability

---

[20]Definitions are really the root issue, since they cannot be judged right or wrong based on empirical evidence, but on accepted usage. But if two groups differ in their accepted definition, how do we determine who is correct? As with aesthetics, it is not a matter of "correct," only of what is preferred by each group, and what is considered socially acceptable changes over time. We will return to this issue in chapter eight.

[21]The term *naturalism of the gaps* is used by Reasons to Believe and others, but I do not know the original source of the idea.

of picking one atom at random from all the atoms in the universe (Dembski, 2004: chap. 10). It must be noted, however, as we saw in chapter three, that setting of probabilities in such situations may reveal more about the presuppositions of the one setting them than the actual physical situation.

It is often claimed that creation is not a scientific explanation, both because it invokes the supernatural and because the mechanism, which supposedly would involve either the appearance of new matter or instantaneous assembly of elements already present in the environment, is never discussed by creation proponents. On the other hand, the correct interpretation of the empirical evidence sometimes leads to the imputation of human agency, rather than natural causes, as in the case of forensic science. The difference, of course, is that in the case of the origin of life the proposed agent is supernatural, a possibility ruled out a priori by naturalism, and direct intervention of a supernatural agent as the causal mechanism is ruled out a priori by methodological naturalism.

Nevertheless, the comparison to forensic science is appropriate. It could reasonably be said that the attribution of a crime to an individual is not a scientific explanation, because it is not a repeatable event that follows either natural law or chance, but it may nonetheless be the correct explanation of the scientific evidence left behind after the event. If natural causation can be ruled out by a high number of low probability events, agency is implied. Sometimes there may not be enough evidence to convict someone of a crime, even though it is clear that a crime was committed and there is only one reasonable suspect. Proponents of creation suggest a similar, if opposite, situation exists with regard to the origin of life. The impossibility of natural causes reveals agency, and God is the only one capable of having done it.

Purposeful direction. For each of the two explanations mentioned so far, the philosophical commitments of the model wholly determine the interpretation of the evidence. If there is no divine intervention (NE, NTE, PE), there must be a stepwise natural process to account for life. If God created specific living things, as indicated by a creationary (YEC or OEC) interpretation of Genesis, creatures would have appeared with no intermediate steps. The third explanation, espoused by directed evolution, is not philosophically tied to either a gradual or immediate solution, so it is likely that within this position there will emerge a variety of explanations of mechanism, ranging from slow to nearly instantaneous. The thing they will have in common is the idea that God directed low probability events to achieve his purposes in creation.

As far as I know, no attempts have yet been made to explain the origin of life from a DE perspective, but as with the other models it is possible to predict the form an explanation would take based merely on the suppositions of the position, being related to the argument for specified complexity. Intelligent agents can create complex forms in either a stepwise or immediate manner. When making something we typically collect the materials, then assemble them according to some predetermined plan, often modifying the pattern as we go to achieve the desired result. Applied to the origin of life, this would mean that although certain raw materials might be formed by deterministic processes, the low probability of them coming together in the proper arrangement by chance could have been overcome by the action of an agent.

4.3 What Difference Does It Make?

As we saw with the origin of the universe, the model we hold strongly affects the type of research we conduct or value. In this case, it is not primarily theism or atheism that directs the choice, but whether we accept the necessity of science seeking only naturalistic causes, which reflects the question of whether God ever intervenes in scientific processes.

The charge has been made that the ideas of specified complexity, irreducible complexity and creation positions in general are science stoppers. That is, when one reaches a certain point the conclusion is drawn, God did it, and therefore we stop looking for a scientific mechanism. As with most such assertions, there is some truth to this. If God created, by fiat, fully functional cells with all of their components, we will never be able to determine a stepwise mechanism, and it is therefore foolish to spend time and money looking for one. On the other hand, perhaps it would be better viewed as a redirection of science rather than a stoppage. Other types of scientific questions are suggested based on the prediction that we would expect complexity at every level, for example, looking for structures and mechanisms directing processes in the cell that so far are thought to be random, such as the movement of the proper tRNA into the ribosome, or the arrangement of chromosomes in the nucleus, or the position of genes on the chromosomes.

Conversely, for those who hold that there must be a stepwise natural progression, finding the key to the origin of life is the search for the Holy Grail. If it could be demonstrated that life can be formed without divine intervention, it would immeasurably strengthen their position, which until then is vulnerable. Thus, most of the researchers in origin of life will be from this camp, and it is inevitable that they will find fault with mathematical arguments saying that their pursuit is in vain.

Origin of Species

· · ·

The focal point of the debate between creation and evolution, the main battleground, is without a doubt the origin of species, both because of its historical primacy and its prominence in education. In this chapter I will look at a broader range of evidence and spend less time describing it in detail but more time evaluating its relevance, for several reasons. Admittedly, this is the area I know best, having studied and taught it for many years. But more important, people generally are more familiar with the biological and geological evidence, having been exposed to it in high school biology classes, than with the astronomical, biochemical or anthropological evidence of the other three origins.

Unfortunately, much of the information in high school biology textbooks is at least ten years behind the latest research in science when published, and the books are used for five to ten years. Given the current rate of advance of scientific knowledge, this means the arguments in them are far out of date. Moreover, as in popular scientific writing, inferences are commonly stated as if they were facts, without recognizing their dependence on background knowledge and assumptions. Even the selection of evidence and the choice of language used to present it reveal the perspective of the writer. Thus, a major purpose in this chapter, as in the book as a whole, is to distinguish the evidence, which we should all be able to agree on, from the inferences, which will differ based on our philosophical presuppositions.

It may seem odd, but in some cases different models do not even agree on what constitutes evidence. It should be clear by now that there is no such thing as evidence for or against a certain position. The data exist independent of a position but are interpreted from the perspective of the observer. As a result data that may appear inconsequential from one vantage point may appear very important from another. Thus, sometimes one model considers certain data to be evidence, while another considers the same data to be anomalies or errors. Obviously, anything excluded from evidence does not require an explanation and therefore is not considered when evaluating which interpretation, which model, provides the best explanation of all of the evidence.

5.1 WHAT IS THE EVIDENCE?

When Darwin wrote *On the Origin of Species by Means of Natural Selection*, the main evidence that he cited was paleontological and geographical. In the first half of the twentieth century the new field of genetics began to exert a strong influence on evolutionary theory, an influence that has continued to the present day. Advances in molecular genetics over the past twenty years have drastically changed the evidence cited for evolution and rearranged putative evolutionary relationships, but outdated information is still found in many books. While paleontologists of necessity still argue from *morphology, the structure of the organism, biologists have largely abandoned evidence from body structure in favor of genetic similarities. In this section we will examine evidence in three broad categories: fossils, genetics and similarities at both an organismal and genetic level. A summary of the evidence and interpretations can be found in table A1.4.

Fossils. Fossils have provided a great deal of evidence about the diversity of life that existed on this planet at some time in the past that does not exist today, both forms very similar to those currently in existence and some totally unlike anything we know today. Species appear in and disappear from the fossil record, with very little change in between, and there are often sharp boundaries between the layers of fossils. There are also differences between fossils found in different parts of the world. Many explanations have been proposed to account for these patterns, as we will discuss later in the section on interpretations, but first we must look briefly at the evidence for layering in fossils and how those layers are dated.

Sorting. The first thing that is apparent when looking at a series of *sedimentary rock layers is that the fossils found in each layer are different. Generally, lower layers contain traces of marine organisms, some very different from extant forms, while the highest levels contain organisms much more similar to current species. Land-dwelling forms are generally found in different layers than marine forms. Certain fossils, called index or indicator fossils, are common in one layer but totally absent in all others. In various places around the world, layers containing these index fossils are found in the same relative order from bottom to top. Although no single location contains all the layers, the relative order of those present generally remains the same from location to location.

In many places sedimentary layers alternate with *igneous material. Sometimes the igneous material appears to have perforated through or intruded between sedimentary layers, while other times it spread over the existing surface layer. The type of igneous rock formed from lava on the surface differs from that formed from magma underground, allowing a reasonable inference to be made as to where the rock was formed. Rock layers may also be modified by folding, faulting, overthrust and erosion.

Dating. We often talk about dating fossils. In some sense this is a misnomer, as it is impossible to date most fossils directly. Rather, it is the layer that the fossil is found in that is dated, either relatively or absolutely. Relative dating employs the principle of *superposition, the logical idea that new layers are normally placed on top of older layers, thus the lower the layer, the earlier it was deposited. Although there can be exceptions due to intrusions of igneous material, it is hard to imagine how a sedimentary layer could be placed under any existing material.

Absolute dating involves the use of radioactive elements present in igneous rock, which decays at known rates. Since this is based on igneous rock, it can only be used to date fossils if igneous material such as ash is incorporated in the sedimentary layer containing the fossil. Otherwise, igneous material in layers above or below the fossil-bearing layer can be used to delimit the age range. Igneous rock layers in one location show a pattern that the lower layers are older than the higher layers based on *radiometric data, as would be expected based on superposition.[1] Young-earth creation questions both the methods and results of radiometric dating.[2]

It is important to note that this evidence for sorting and dating represents only the major trends. When dealing with the real world, there are always exceptions. Young-earth creation supporters frequently cite these exceptions, such as wood and pollen found in rock identified as Pre-Cambrian, sequences that appear out of order, paraconformities where there does not appear to be any discontinuity between rocks identified as being from very different geological periods, and anomalies in radiometric measurements.[3] More recently questions have been raised about how soft tissue could be preserved in fossils dated at 70 million years old.[4] Scientists must determine whether those exceptions are errors, odd events caused by unusual local disturbances that can be identified, or whether they represent an important pattern that might change the whole analysis, resulting in a simpler, more consistent interpretation. Throughout history there are examples of data that were ignored, explained away and even ridiculed by most scientists that turned out to be vital, for example, retrograde motion of the planets and transposons, resulting in major paradigm shifts. On the other hand, most such data are consigned to the dustbin of history, having made no impact. Only time will tell what will happen to the anomalies in this field. Because of their controversial position, I will not discuss them here in detail, with the caveat that they should not be forgotten or discarded lightly.

Stasis and saltation. As Darwin looked at the fossils, he noted what

---

[1] Exceptions to the expected pattern of older igneous rocks on the bottom can usually be accounted for by folding, intrusion or other well-known processes.

[2] YEC is the only model to question radiometric dating methods. Like many other important questions, I can only mention it here. For a report of the findings of the creation research project "Radioisotopes and the Age of the Earth" (RATE) see Vardiman, Snelling & Chaffin (2005). For a more readable summary see DeYoung (2005). Brief defenses of the validity of the standard model can be found in Miller (1999: chap. 3) and Falk (2004: chap. 3), and more detailed explanation in Young & Stearley (2008: chaps. 14-15).

[3] Examples of geological anomalies are cited in Vardiman, Snelling & Chaffin (2005).

[4] The presence of soft tissue in dinosaur bones was reported by Schweitzer et al. (2005), contrary to conventional views in the field that thought such preservation impossible.

appeared to be a progression, with simpler fossils in lower layers and more complex ones higher up, but there were major gaps rather than the smooth transition of forms he proposed. He explained that those gaps were expected, both because deposition and fossilization do not occur at all times in all places, and because many of the deposited sediments are later eroded, leaving us with a very imperfect fossil record (Darwin, 1859: chap. 9).

For a long time after Darwin, paleontologists expected that as more fossils were found, the gaps would not be filled completely but there would at least be indications of gradual changes in species. What they found instead was that most species change little from the time they appear in the fossil record until the time they disappear, often a period of millions of years, a phenomenon called *stasis. Many fossil forms have been found that have characteristics intermediate between two other known forms, but these do not represent a smooth transition, rather in almost every case there is an abrupt change from one form to another, a phenomenon called *saltation.[5]

In 1972 this regular pattern of stasis and saltation in the fossils was given the name *punctuated equilibrium by paleontologists Steven Jay Gould and Niles Eldredge. Although resisted for a long time by paleontologists and biologists committed to *gradualism, the overwhelming evidence has led to broad acceptance of this idea. As we will discuss in the interpretation section, there is still disagreement about whether these saltations in the fossil record also represent abrupt changes in form or whether there were rapid but still gradual changes that were not fossilized. Certainly there are fewer transitional forms than were expected based on gradualism.

The question of whether a certain fossil is transitional is a tricky one because the wording itself implies an interpretation. The term *transition* implies an evolutionary relationship exists, which not all models accept. Certainly, at lower levels of *taxa (changes from one *genus or *family to another), there are forms that seem to have intermediate characteristics and appear in the fossil record at about the right time to

---

[5]Stasis and saltation come, respectively, from the Greek word *stasis* (standing still) and the Latin word *saltus* (leap).

be a transition. Fossils that could be classified as transitional between higher taxonomic levels, particularly from one *phylum to another, are essentially nonexistent.

Extinctions and explosions. At various times in the fossil record there appear to be massive die-offs of many species of organisms at the same time. In one fossil layer there will be a certain diversity of forms; in the next layer above it most of those forms are missing, replaced by a totally different biota. Where the layers appear to be sequential in time, evolutionary models explain the discontinuities as *mass extinction events, followed by rapid speciation.[6] The best known is the so-called K-T boundary at the end of the age of the dinosaurs. Below that boundary the majority of the large animal fossils found are dinosaurs. Above that boundary the largest animals are mostly mammals.

There are also times where there is no disappearance, only a rapid appearance of new forms. Every major group of organisms from every kingdom appears in the fossil record suddenly in a form that is clearly similar to its modern descendants. The best known of these is the *Cambrian explosion. During a relatively brief period of time geologically, most of the extant animal phyla appear for the first time in the fossil record, along with many other animal phyla that are now extinct.[7] Many scientists have looked for transitional forms between the various phyla or between them and the few soft-bodied invertebrates present in lower strata, but so far no clear transitional forms have been found.[8]

Geographical distribution. Another interesting pattern is found by comparing fossils at different depths. Fossils in the upper layers are

---

[6]Rising and falling of water levels are thought to introduce gaps in the fossil record. Where these occur there is usually uneven erosion of the top layer, an unconformity, indicating the presence of a gap. Where layers are sequential, the boundaries between them are usually flat. Paraconformities, cases in which there are flat boundaries between layers identified as being from very different geological ages, are cited by creation supporters as a challenge to the standard interpretation.

[7]Based on radiometric data, the Cambrian explosion is thought to have occurred about 540 million years ago, within a period of perhaps 5-10 million years ("Claim CC300," *The Talk Origins Archive* [2006], www.talkorigins.org/indexcc/CC/CC300.html). This sounds like a long time, but it is only about 0.1-0.2% of the age of the earth.

[8]"Almost all of these phyla appeared seemingly full-fledged in the late Precambrian and early Cambrian, ca. 565-530 million years ago. No fossils intermediate between them have been found and no living intermediates are in existence"; Mayr (2001: 51) believes the molecular evidence provides evidence of evolution in the absence of fossils. For a nonevolutionary perspective, see Meyer et al. (2003).

often very similar to the existing organisms in an area, and these vary greatly from one continent to the next. Thus, in Australia we find many fossil marsupials, but these are rare in other parts of the world. The large mammals of Africa are very different from the large mammals of South America, and the fossils in each location are more similar to the existing animals than to one another. Yet when we get down to the fossil layers containing dinosaurs, the pattern changes. Fossil layers in Africa and South America contain fossils that appear identical. In fact, in some cases the fossil beds on the Atlantic coasts of the two continents can be matched up layer by layer. This was one of the lines of evidence that led to the widespread acceptance of *plate tectonic theory.[9]

There is also abundant evidence that different layers of fossils in a particular area represent different biomes or climatic conditions. In one layer, large herbivore remains are present, along with fossilized pollen of grasses, indicating a relatively dry terrestrial environment. In another layer in the same location there are marine fossils. In yet another, the presence of large ferns and oversize insects seems to indicate a very warm, moist environment. Advances in palynology (the study of fossil pollen, spores and similar microscopic remains) have allowed inferences to be made about the climate of the area in a given period even in the absence of larger fossils, since the plants in an area identify the biome and determine the types of consumers that can live there.

Genetics. Although much more could be said about recent advances in paleontology, they have filled in details rather than breaking new ground in the origins debate.[10] In the last fifty years the rapidly developing field of genetics has had a far greater impact. It is hard for us to imagine—having been raised in a time where everyone grows up knowing the shape of a DNA molecule, how many chromosomes a human has, what differentiates male and female, and the influence of genes on various disorders and diseases—that only a hundred years ago none of this was known. In Darwin's day, and for fifty years afterward,

---

[9]The second major line of evidence leading to acceptance of plate tectonics is the pattern of sediments and magnetic reversals on both sides of the mid-Atlantic ridge.

[10]Recent advances in paleontology involve, for example, use of CT scans to see the internal structures of fossils, electron microscopy to reveal structures of chromatophores that give evidence of the original color of the organism, and bioengineering to reveal how animals moved.

inheritance was thought to be controlled by a blending of parental traits, making rapid changes of form impossible.

Selection. The line of evidence Darwin used to begin his famous treatise is still evident today, although greatly modified by our understanding of the genetic basis of inheritance. Darwin used illustrations from artificial selection, particularly pigeon breeding, to illustrate the degree of change possible in organisms under selection. He then extended this to an argument that selection under natural conditions, *natural selection, could similarly cause changes in species. Based on the wide range of forms produced by pigeon breeding, he thought there was no limit to what artificial selection could accomplish. We now know this is not the case. As both plant and animal breeders have repeatedly found, it is impossible to continue selection for any particular trait past a certain point. We also know that natural selection of an adapted species in a stable environment tends to select against the extremes, the very ones that would be necessary to effect any change in the species. Some of the statements made in textbooks and elsewhere in the origins debate do not take this into account and are therefore misleading.

For decades one of the obligatory examples in the evolution unit of biology textbooks was the peppered moth. This moth has two color morphs, one mostly white with black speckles, the other mostly dark. Before the Industrial Revolution in England, the former predominated. During the time that coal dust coated the trees, the darker form gained ascendancy, only to fall in numbers as the environment was cleaned up. This is cited as an example of natural selection, and it appears to be an excellent example of that.[11] Unfortunately, it says nothing about the origin of new species. Both forms were present in all three periods, only the relative numbers changed and no speciation occurred. Interestingly, peppered moths were dropped from the seventh and subsequent editions of *Campbell Biology* (Campbell and Reese, 2005), an influential college textbook, and the display on the peppered moth has been removed from the evolution exhibit at the Chicago Field Museum.[12]

---

[11]Some question even this interpretation of the peppered moths, claiming that similar changes have been observed in areas where there was no effect of pollution. See Wells (2003).

[12]Campbell is an encyclopedic text that has long been the unofficial standard text for AP biology,

One step closer to speciation are the frequently cited studies where bacteria in culture develop antibiotic resistance or the ability to survive on a restricted substrate. Although in this case the traits are new and do indicate new and potentially useful changes in the genes, not once in fifty thousand generations has sufficient change occurred to merit the designation of a new species.[13]

Another common textbook example is the Galapagos finches.[14] There is general agreement that here and in other cases a number of species seem to have arisen from the introduction of a small founder population to an isolated island group. A similar situation exists for ring species, in which a series of related species extend over a broad geographical area. In many cases neighboring species can form fertile hybrids, but the ones at the two ends are unable to interbreed. What is in dispute in both these cases, as we will discuss more in the interpretation section, is to what degree this can be *extrapolated to the origin of higher order taxa.

Population genetics. Perhaps no field had a greater influence on the rise of the neo-Darwinian synthesis in the first half of the twentieth century than did population genetics.[15] Properly, the contribution of this field is not empirical evidence but theoretical mathematical models of how speciation could occur. Developing new statistical methods as they went, pioneers in this field demonstrated how the frequency of different forms of a gene, called *alleles, could change in a population. Biology textbooks talk about this mainly in terms of the Hardy-Weinberg equilibrium, which states that the allele frequency will remain constant as long as there is no gene flow, genetic drift, nonrandom mating, selection or mutation.

Gene flow occurs when an individual enters or leaves the population. To the degree that this individual is different from the population average, it will shift that average. Genetic drift is the result of a small

---

the one all other texts are compared to. For a more complete look at the rise and fall of the peppered moth, see Hooper (2002).

[13]R. E. Lenski, "Experimental evolution," *E. coli Long-term Experimental Evolution Project Site,* http://myxo.css.msu.edu/ecoli.

[14]Many criticisms are offered of textbook presentations of the Galapagos finches. See for example Wells (2000). Primarily, these criticisms involve the problem of extrapolation.

[15]For a history of evolutionary thought, including the importance of population genetics, see Schwartz (1999).

population size, because a small sample will often differ from the average based on random chance.[16] Nonrandom mating can include like with like, like with dislike, preference for a certain form, or many other variations. Selection similarly could be based on many different factors. All of these would change the allele frequencies (remember that alleles are different variants of a gene), but would not change the alleles present, which is solely the domain of mutation.

Many current textbooks claim that if there is a change in allele frequencies, evolution has occurred. In the broadest sense of the term *evolution*, meaning change over time, this is certainly true. But population genetics shows that any new allele, even one with a strong selective advantage, would take thousands of generations to become predominant in a population. Even this does not mean that a new species has formed, any more than a field of a selected variety of soybeans represents a new species. To form a new species, we need not new alleles but entirely new genes, and the main mechanism postulated for this is mutation.[17]

Mutation. Natural selection can only select among the various alleles present in a population. This is what places a limit on how far the population mean for a particular trait can be shifted. To go beyond this point would require, at a minimum, new alleles, which arise by mutation. Some mutations have effects that can be beneficial, neutral or harmful, depending on the environment. Most of these cause small changes in the overall organism, not large enough to cause speciation unless thousands of different mutations accumulated. Many mutations are deleterious, independent of the environment.[18] Furthermore, in order to have an effect on the population, the mutation must arise in one of the *germ-line cells, those that produce the gametes, not one of the *somatic cells of the organism. To go beyond changes within the species to the origin of new species would require not new alleles but totally new

---

[16]Random genetic drift can also occur in a larger population if the genes are nearly neutral in fitness.

[17]Speciation often also requires new gene regulatory networks and frequently involves large-scale changes in the chromosomes, but for simplicity we will restrict our consideration to the genes themselves for now.

[18]A Cornell geneticist (Sanford, 2008: chaps. 2-3) documents how deleterious most mutations are. Geneticists favoring other models will disagree with his conclusions in other chapters, but agree that favorable mutations are extremely rare.

genes that would code for the component parts of that new species.[19]

Many genes code for individual proteins. Most of the structural components of cells, the channels that regulate the flow of molecules into a cell, and enzymes that facilitate chemical reactions are proteins. A mutation in a gene will often lead to a change in the protein it codes for.[20] In most cases, since mutation and natural selection have been functioning for a long time, the mutant form is less advantageous or at least no more advantageous than the original. In a stable environment it is likely that the most beneficial allele has already been found.[21] Even if a beneficial mutation arises, it is likely to make that species better able to survive, not create a new species.

On the other hand, some mutations can cause major changes in an organism that appear to be potentially beneficial but on closer examination are not. One example commonly found in textbooks is the mutation that leads to a second set of wings in fruit flies. Unfortunately, this mutation, like most other major changes in form, is detrimental.[22] Most insect larvae have two sets of wing buds. In some orders of insects, like butterflies and dragonflies, the two wings are similar in size and both function in flight. In others, like beetles, the forewing develops into a protective cover. In flies, the rear wing bud normally develops into a haltere, a small structure used for stabilization, much like the rear fins at the tail of a plane. Although a mutation can change this into a second pair of wings, the resulting fruit fly can no more fly than a plane could with a second set of wings in the tail.

Homeotic genes. One special class of genes, *homeotic genes, has a major influence on the overall structure of the organism.[23] Discovered in

---

[19]According to standard genetic theory, speciation would require new genes in germ-line cells. This is changing as more is found out about the role of the epigenome in regulating gene activity. Epigenetic changes can also be inherited. See the following discussion of non-Darwinian evolution.

[20]There may not be a change in the protein if the change in the DNA is in the third position of a codon, which, due to redundancy in the code, often leads to no change in the amino acid coded for.

[21]"Most mutations are bad for the same reason that most typos in computer code are bad: in finely tuned systems, random tweaks are far more likely to disrupt function than to improve it" (Orr, 2009).

[22]Four-winged fruit flies are discussed in Wells (2000).

[23]The major homeotic genes in animals are the Hox genes. Hox genes code for transcription factors

the last twenty-five years, these genes direct the early development in embryos of animals, plants and fungi, giving the body its overall form. Homeotic genes have been found in a wide assortment of organisms, with similar functions in diverse organisms. For example, one gene directs the polarity (head-tail) direction in animals. Another directs the formation of appendages, whether any one of the many varied appendages of insects or the limbs of vertebrates. Yet another initiates the formation of an eye, whether that be the compound eye of a fruit fly or a vertebrate eye.

For the purposes of this book it is not necessary to discuss in detail the function of these genes, which is quite complex. It is enough to point out that, as with other genes, most mutations that occur in the homeotic genes cause major disruptions of the structure and are either lethal or strongly disadvantageous. Nevertheless, nearly identical forms of the genes exist in different species, with similar effects but variation in the DNA base sequence. Genes with sequences similar to those found in vertebrates have been found in numerous animals, including some like the starlet sea anemone (in the same phylum as jellyfish) that have a very different body structure and method of development (Ferrier & Holland, 2001; Hui, Holland & Ferrier, 2008). The similarity of these genes and their arrangement on the chromosome across a wide range of organisms will be discussed shortly.

Genome complexity. Another special class of mutations, largely overlooked even in advanced textbooks on evolution, involves changes in the structure or number of chromosomes. In many cases organisms thought to be closely related evolutionarily have different numbers of chromosomes.[24] On the one hand, this serves to enforce reproductive isolation between similar species. Animals, far more than plants, are very sensitive to differences in chromosome number. On the other hand, it raises the question of how those differences arose in the first place, since the first individual with a change in chromosome structure would have had difficulty mating with any extant organisms, unless a second individual

---

which switch on a cascade of other genes, causing major effects.

[24]In one extreme example the Chinese muntjac has 23 pair of chromosomes, but the Indian muntjac has only 4 (Futuyma, 1998: 292).

with the same change were present at the same time and place.[25] In some animals, it is thought that *parthenogenesis has allowed sterile organisms to reproduce asexually, forming individuals who can then mate, but this process appears to be rare and has not been demonstrated in mammals or birds (Mayr, 2001: 181-82). This is an area that deserves far more attention.

Another area of recent research is that of multiple uses for genes. Genes were originally thought to be continuous sequences leading to a single protein. It is now known that in *eukaryotes (which includes all animals, plants and fungi) within the region known as a gene there are several sections known as *exons, each of which codes for a *domain, a functional component of a protein. For example, one domain may code for a section of a protein that allows it to bind to the DNA, and another may produce a section that binds a hormone that regulates *gene expression. In some cases it appears that a protein may be formed by combining domains produced by genes on different chromosomes. So far, it is not clear how the cell knows what domains to combine in what order. Even more amazing is that some sections of the DNA appear to code for more than one gene product, depending on which strand is read, or changes in the *reading frame. This would be like constructing a sentence that can be read both backward and forward, with two different meanings, or one that could be read forward with two different meanings, depending on where the string of letters is divided to form words.[26]

Similarities. In evolutionary biology the term *homology refers to traits that are similar by descent, whereas *analogy is used for traits that are similar by *convergence; for example, the streamlined shape of aquatic animals from fish to seals to penguins. Since use of these terms prejudges the issue, I will avoid them and stick with the more generic term *similarities*.[27] We will first examine several similarities at the organ-

---

[25]The difficulty of a male and female of a new species arising by chance was mentioned as early as 1692 (Sober, 2008: 117).

[26]For a summary of multiple use of sections of the DNA, including antisense transcription, overlapping same-strand transcription and long-range interconnected transcription, see Kapranov, Willingham & Gingeras (2007).

[27]Avoiding the term *homology* also avoids the circularity argument. It has been correctly pointed out that if a homology (defined as being similar by descent) is used as an evidence of evolution, this is circular. However, if a similarity is used as evidence of evolution, it is no longer circular.

ismal level that are commonly found in textbooks, although not widely used anymore in professional debates, followed by similarities at the molecular level, which are considered to be stronger evidence, being directly related to the hereditary material.

Embryological. It seems no introductory biology text would be complete without an illustration of the similarities of vertebrate embryos. Embryological similarity is a line of evidence that has been used since the time of Darwin, who, not being an embryologist himself, depended on the work of Haeckel. Some have averred that Haeckel's drawings were faked (Wells, 2000: 82).[28] Whether he was purposefully deceitful or was limited by the technology of the day and so saw what he expected to see and chose to present only the evidence that best illustrated his conclusion, I will leave for others to debate. If the latter, he was no worse a scientist than any alive today. Motives aside, we now know there were several problems with his reported observations.

First, the pictures are selected for maximum similarity of appearance. The stages shown are the ones that look most similar, whereas earlier and later stages appear far less similar. Several vertebrate groups that do not have a similar-looking stage are not represented at all. Second, and more important, now that we are able to look at a cellular level we know that many structures that seem similar externally arise from totally different processes, thus defeating the argument that they are developmentally similar (Wells, 2000). A strong case could be made that this line of evidence, no longer used in professional science, should be dropped from textbooks.

It would be a mistake, however, to think that embryology has faded from importance in the debate; in fact, it could be said to be more important than ever. Most of the recent work has been done under the name evolutionary developmental biology, or *evo-devo for short. A mix of embryology, genetics and evolutionary theory, evo-devo is investigating topics like the origin of feathers and the modification of overall body form. It has provided many examples of how minor mod-

---

[28]Mayr admits that Haeckel used a dog embryo instead of a human, since the latter was at that time not readily available, but Mayr claims this did not change the veracity of his drawings (2001: 28). Some say the charge of fakery was made by some of his peers as well.

ifications in timing of gene expression in early development could lead to adult forms that appear quite distinct (Futuyma, 1998: chap. 23). A common example would be vertebrate forelimbs, where the number of bones is nearly identical but the relative size of the bones and therefore the overall structure differs greatly. Evo-devo would hypothesize this is due to identical genes causing bone growth being active for longer or shorter periods of time during development, rather than changes in the genes themselves.

Vestigial structures. A second argument from similarity found in almost all introductory textbooks concerns structures thought to be vestigial, that is, structures that were functional in some close relative that are present in a reduced form with no known function in another organism. The problem with this line of evidence is that the number of vestigial organs is rapidly shrinking. For many years opponents of evolution have predicted that functions would be found for structures labeled vestigial, and this has been the case (Wells, 2000). In most cases serious treatments of evolutionary theory now restrict themselves to one or two paragraphs about vestigial structures.[29] If this line of evidence is retained in textbooks at all, perhaps in the interest of fairness it would be good to indicate the number of structures once thought to be vestigial that have been shown to have an important function.

On the other side of the coin, evo-devo has revealed a number of cases where structures begin to form during development only to be reabsorbed so they are not present in the adult organism. To the extent that functional structures are present in related species, the initial development of these structures could also be considered vestigial in that they appear to contribute nothing but take energy to produce.[30] The number of instances is expected to rise as the development of more organisms is investigated in detail. It remains an open question whether the proto-structures fulfill some role that could not be achieved in their absence.

---

[29]Mayr (2001: 30-31) devotes only one paragraph of the whole book to vestigial structures.

[30]Multiplication of cells followed by apoptosis, specified death of certain cells, is a common feature in embryo development. For example, the hands of humans begin as a single bud, then develop a webbed appearance, later dividing into fingers by apoptosis. Should the webbed areas be considered vestigial?

A related issue that is often raised is the question of how perfect organisms are. Evolution tends to point to organs or systems that appear to be imperfect, to challenge the idea of a perfect Designer. Creation responds with the idea of design constraints: systems, whether human designed or biological, cannot be optimized for any particular aspect without making some other aspect of the system less than optimal (Dembski, 2004: chap. 6). Ironically, this is exactly the same argument used by evolutionary positions to explain why natural selection does not achieve perfection (Gould & Lewontin, 1979). In any case, there is agreement from both sides that organisms are remarkably well adapted to their environment.

Noncoding DNA. For a long time, DNA with no known purpose in the cell was called junk DNA. As with vestigial structures, the problem was the key word *known*. For thirty years after the elucidation of the structure of DNA and its role in inheritance, little attention was paid to noncoding DNA, the 90% that does not code for protein, but since the 1980s studies have revealed that at least the vast majority of DNA has a function. While scientific journals started putting "junk DNA" in scare quotes in the middle of the 1990s to indicate that the name no longer fit, textbooks and popular science writers have been slow to follow suit.[31] The focus on genes as the basis of heredity similarly limited research on factors outside the DNA base sequence that also play a role in inheritance, a field now known as *epigenetics.[32]

Many high school textbooks still talk about *pseudogenes, sections of DNA with a sequence similar to coding genes but that do not produce a protein, as evolutionary baggage. It is now known that many of the "pseudogenes" are transcribed into RNA and serve as regulators of the "real" gene.[33] Other regions of the DNA have been found to code for *micro-RNA, which also has a regulatory role. *Introns, regions in the middle of a gene that are transcribed into RNA but cut out of the final

---

[31] The work submitted by Wells (2011) was new to the general public but accepted by geneticists for over twenty years. For the most recent information see the ENCODE project (www.nature.com/encode/#threads).

[32] " 'I think this will come to be a classic story of orthodoxy derailing objective analysis of the facts, in this case for a quarter of a century,' Mattick says" (Gibbs, 2003).

[33] Pseudogenes may also be involved in repairing a gene that has been damaged by mutation.

product were once thought to be inefficient but have been found to actually increase the efficiency of transcription (Brinster et al., 1988; Le Hir, Nott & Moore, 2003). Similarly, the length of repeated sequences in the *telomeres has been shown to be important. Even *transposable elements, once thought to be selfish DNA that was deleterious to the species, are now being touted as a major player in evolution (Biémont, 2010).

Gene order. As more and more genomes or sections of genomes are sequenced, it is becoming apparent that there is a great deal of similarity not only in the genes present but also in the order of genes on the chromosome from one species to another, and in many cases this order appears to be important. This is particularly evident in the sequence of homeotic genes.

In fruit flies there is a single set of homeotic genes that controls early development of the body plan. Several of the genes are expressed in the same order in the embryo as they are found on the chromosome. In mammals there are four sets of homeotic genes, each of which is very similar in sequence to the set found in fruit flies and likewise are expressed in the same order in the embryo as they are on the chromosome.[34]

Generally, organisms that are thought to be more closely related evolutionarily have much greater similarity both in the genes present and their order on the chromosome than organisms thought to be more distantly related. This applies not only to the coding genes but also the noncoding sequences. We will return to this in chapter six.

Molecular sequences. Although organisms in different kingdoms have a very different external appearance, at a chemical level they must perform many of the same functions, including reproducing and using energy. In many cases the chemical compounds used to perform these functions also show a great deal of similarity. Ribosomes, cytochromes, actin and myosin are a few of the many molecules whose sequence has been compared across a wide range of organisms.

Although there is a great similarity in the structure of these compounds, there are also differences. In most cases the differences in the

---

[34]"Remarkably, and for unknown reasons, the sequence of the genes along the chromosome matches the sequence along the body of the segments whose identity they control" (Futuyma, 1998: 666).

DNA are small, resulting in the substitution of one amino acid for another in the protein. As genetic distance increases, the number of differences between one species and another also increases. On the assumption of an evolutionary relationship, the sequence of amino acids or nucleotides can be used to draw *phylogenetic trees representing the purported branching pattern of the organisms.[35] In many cases any single tree, based on a single molecule, matches fairly well with the division of organisms based on traditional morphological classification schemes. In other cases surprising results have been found that have led to modification of the classification to match the genetic data, since the genetic data is considered by most evolutionists to be a more reliable record of relationships than external characteristics (de Jong, 1998).

As various trees are traced backward, more and more discrepancies arise between the different trees as they approach the root, particularly within bacteria and archaebacteria. Formerly, the expectation of evolutionary models was that all the trees would be identical, leading to identification of a single last common ancestor (LCA). But instead of a single root, at the base the relationships appear to be more similar to a web. At this point similar molecular sequences are found in organisms thought to be totally unrelated based on other molecular sequences. It appears that common parts were swapped from one organism to another in some way. This has led to the development of new explanations that will be discussed in the following interpretations.

Symbiosis. The last line of evidence we will consider is *symbiosis, two organisms living together in an integral relationship. Symbiosis can include parasitism, where one benefits at the expense of the other; commensalism, where one benefits but there is no apparent harm or benefit to the other; and mutualism, where both benefit from the relationship. An example of mutualism is the relationship (often exclusive) between a plant and its pollinator. In other cases of mutualistic relationships the two organisms are not known to exist independently of the other and are so mutually dependent as to act as one organism. In

---

[35] As with fossils, there is often great similarity within closely related groups, but a noticeable jump between one group and other groups (Milton, 1997: 183).

many of these cases one of the partners is a photosynthetic organism, an *autotroph, living inside a *heterotroph, an organism that needs to obtain its nutrition from an outside source. The heterotroph can be a protozoan, fungus or animal that provides protection and carbon dioxide to an alga living inside it, which in turn provides carbohydrate to its host (Ryan, 2002).

As early as 1918 scientists had noticed the similarity between *prokaryotes (organisms including bacteria and archaebacteria that do not have a nucleus) and the mitochondria and chloroplasts found in eukaryotes (organisms including protists, fungi, plants and animals that have a nucleus) (Ryan, 2002). As investigation progressed from visual to biochemical, more and more similarities appeared between prokaryotes and the mitochondria and chloroplasts, including membrane structure and DNA with similar sequences. This led to a major addition to evolutionary theory, as will be discussed in the next section.

5.2 HOW DOES EACH MODEL INTERPRET THE EVIDENCE?

As with the origins of the universe and life, it is useful to categorize the interpretations of the evidence into three basic positions, but it is also important to remember that there are many variations within each. The neo-Darwinian synthesis has grown by accretion of various concepts over the years, and continues to do so, but retains Darwin's basic ideas that evolution is gradual and primarily driven by natural selection, and that organisms are related by *common descent. A second position, while agreeing that organisms are related by common descent, argues that speciation is rapid and saltational. The third posits direct creation of forms, followed by relatively minor modification within that form by natural processes.

In this section you will note that I rarely use the term *evolution*. This is because the term has so many distinct definitions. In various contexts it is used to mean (1) change over time, (2) change in allele frequency in a population, (3) common descent, (4) origin of new species (microevolution), (5) origin of higher order taxa (macroevolution), (6) origin of all organisms by natural, undirected processes (naturalistic evolution), and (7) the current neo-Darwinian synthesis as an explanation of the mechanism of change.[36] Opponents of evolution sometimes charge that proponents use a bait-and-switch technique, asserting that evolution—definition 1 or 2—has been observed (which is true), therefore evolution—all definitions—is a fact (which does not logically follow).[37] As with the charge of fakery, I am not sure it is proper to aver ill intent; for many proponents of evolution the mechanism is thought to be the same at all levels, so the connection between the definitions is so close that they are not even aware of the difference.[38] Nevertheless, since it is entirely possible scientifically that different mechanisms may be involved at different levels (changes within a species, origin of new species, origin of higher taxa), I will avoid confusion by eschewing the term.[39]

Neo-Darwinian synthesis. By far the dominant interpretation of the evidence today is the neo-Darwinian synthesis. It would be a mistake to think of this as a monolithic, static position that is unquestioningly accepted. In fact, it is continually changing as the relative importance of different processes is debated. Change in consensus often comes by attrition, as opponents of newer ideas die and are replaced by the younger generation.[40] Some authors have proposed the term *meta-Darwinian* to differentiate newer arguments from the neo-Darwinian position that arose from the assimilation of genetic theory in the middle of the twentieth century (Fowler & Kuebler, 2007), but at least two of those arguments, discussed in the next paragraph, have become widely accepted, as

---

[36]Six definitions of evolution, very similar to the first six proposed here, are listed in Meyer & Keas (2003).

[37]See, for example, Tas Walker, "Don't fall for the bait and switch," *Creation Ministries,* http://creation.com/don-t-fall-for-the-bait-and-switch.

[38]For example, Mayr (2001), after defining evolution as "change in the properties of populations of organisms over time" (p. 8), claims evolution is a fact (p. 12). At the end of the book he repeats the same idea, saying that evolution is a "plain fact, not a conjecture or assumption" and "a fact so overwhelmingly established that it has become irrational to call it a theory" (p. 264). While no one would dispute this, using the definition of change over time or change within a population, throughout the book he has used the same term, *evolution,* to refer to concepts as diverse as speciation and the "evolution" of human ethics. Creation supporters call such usage "equivocation," but to Mayr all the processes are part of the same continuum of accumulation of small changes.

[39]The one exception will be in the last subsection, where *evolution* and *creation* are used as shorthand for comparing the neo-Darwinian synthesis and a creationary interpretation, respectively.

[40]Max Planck wrote, "a new scientific truth does not triumph by convincing its opponents and making them see the light, but rather because its opponents eventually die, and a new generation grows up that is familiar with it." (Cited in Kuhn, 1996: 151).

shown by their inclusion in high school textbooks. In one form or another, this is the most common interpretation in models committed to naturalism or methodological naturalism: naturalistic evolution, nonteleological evolution and planned evolution.

The basic contentions of this interpretive framework are descent from a common ancestor, gradualism and the importance of natural selection; these are the legacy of Darwin.[41] The first major addition to this, based on advances in genetics in the first half of the twentieth century, was the idea that new variation can arise as a result of mutation, not just mixing of parental types. In the second half of the twentieth century two major ideas gained acceptance: punctuated equilibrium and *endosymbiosis. Punctuated equilibrium, discussed earlier, is based on the observation of saltation in the fossil record. As interpreted by neo-Darwinism, these saltations are gaps in the fossil record caused by periods of relatively rapid mutation and speciation, perhaps due to shifts in environmental conditions, rather than real jumps from one form to another. Endosymbiosis is the proposition that mitochondria and chloroplasts originated as symbiotic organisms living within the cytoplasm of another organism, and these gradually lost their ability to live independently. Both of these interpretations, initially strongly opposed and even mocked, have come to be accepted as part of evolutionary theory, as shown by their treatment in textbooks. Many other ideas are still competing for acceptance, including exaptation, neutral theory and complexity theory (Fowler & Kuebler, 2007: chap. 8).

Within neo-Darwinian explanations, one of the greatest areas of difference is the question of teleology. Both naturalistic and nonteleological evolution hold nonteleological positions, saying in essence that evolution is not directed or goal oriented, so if history were given a

---

[41]"Natural selection can act only by taking advantage of slight successive variations; she can never take a leap, but must advance by the shortest and slowest steps" (Darwin, 1859: chap. 6). Different authors attribute different numbers of basic ideas to Darwin. Common descent and gradual improvement are listed as the two essential requirements of Darwinism by Fowler and Kuebler (2007). To these two, Gould (2002) adds a third, that selection is at the level of the organism, something often assumed by other authors writing on the subject. Sober (2010) claims natural selection and common descent are the two key components. Mayr (2001: 86) attributes five components of neo-Darwinism to Darwin, including the basic idea of evolution, branching common descent, gradualness, the multiplication of species and natural selection.

second chance, things might turn out very differently. Planned evolution, on the other hand, states that God worked through evolutionary
methods to produce the outcome he had in mind from the beginning.
We will return to this important question and its logical implications for
humans in chapter six.

It is also important to mention that a number of scientists who philosophically and theologically would fit within these three models are
dissenters from Darwinism, challenging the foundational principles of
gradualism and natural selection. We will examine their arguments in
the next subsection.

Dissenters aside, the prevailing neo-Darwinian interpretation views
the evidence as supporting common ancestry with gradual change and
speciation over time. The fossils are viewed as presenting an overall
picture of increasing complexity over time; intermediate forms are
viewed as transitional. The similarity of sequences within the DNA, including mutations in noncoding segments that are retained in a given
lineage, is seen as strong evidence for common descent. Differences in
the phylogenetic trees generated by different molecules, especially at the
base of the trees, are accounted for by *horizontal gene transfer (HGT).
HGT is based on the observation that many bacteria are able to pick up
DNA from the environment (usually in the form of plasmids) and express the genes in that DNA. Thus it is thought that genes could be
transferred horizontally from one organism to another (rather than ver-
tically by normal inheritance) by this method (Brown, 2003; Keeling &
Palmer, 2008).

As is common in every field, scientists present the evidence that best
supports their argument. Thus discussions of saltations in the fossil
record, the limits of selection, the deleterious nature of most mutations
and the length of time necessary to increase the frequency of a beneficial mutation in a large population tend to be minimized by neo-
Darwinians. Certain data presented by creation supporters are excluded
from evidence, explained away as anomalies or exceptions for which an
answer will be found in due course.

Non-Darwinian evolution. The second line of interpretation of the
evidence, while accepting that the overall pattern in the fossils and the

similarity of sequences in various genomes is best explained by common descent, questions the other two main neo-Darwinian tenets: gradualism and the primacy of natural selection as the driving force of change. It takes the saltations in the fossil record at face value and looks for mechanisms that could cause a nearly instantaneous change in form. According to this view natural selection allows the survival of favorable forms but is not the main agent driving the change. Rather, the organism itself, acting as a whole, is in some sense directing its own change, or the changes were directed by God. Proponents of this view include the previously mentioned dissenters, as well as proponents of directed evolution.

One of the first dissenters from Darwin to gain notoriety was Michael Denton, with his 1985 book *Evolution: A Theory in Crisis*. Others have followed, including Richard Milton (1997), a science writer who claims to be neither a creationist nor religious, who presents a thorough critique of the arguments of neo-Darwinism.[42] Still others have presented alternate mechanisms, arguing that symbiosis (Ryan, 2002) or major developmental changes (Schwartz, 1999) could lead to immediate speciation within a generation. One of the most comprehensive new non-Darwinian evolutionary models is presented by James A. Shapiro (2011), in *Evolution: A View from the Twenty-first Century*.[43] He argues that various processes can reassemble useful genomic elements in novel ways, leading rapidly to new species, particularly in times of environmental stress. Although each of these views is currently supported by a minority of scientists, that was true of every position at some point. All of these writers claim the mechanisms they present allow evolution to proceed naturally, without intervention from God.

---

[42]Milton also advocates other alternative science, including alternative medicine and paranormal phenomena. His summary of the evidence (particularly unusual data suppressed in mainstream science) is good, but readers should be aware of his views when evaluating his arguments.

[43]For a brief description of this important book and the model it presents, see the review by the present author in *Perspectives on Science and Christian Faith* (forthcoming). Shapiro argues against Darwinism but for evolution: he presents an evolutionary model that is saltational, a teleological model where the cell itself sets the goal, a natural genetic engineering model without an intelligent engineer. He claims horizontal transfer, transposable elements, chromosome rearrangements, genome duplication and cell fusion can occur in a targeted and teleological fashion, citing extensive evidence from molecular genetics to support his claims.

Directed evolution likewise invokes rapid, coordinated changes in the genome or epigenetic control that would produce rapid changes in form in one generation. This could involve direction of quantum or probabilistic events, and invokes the same scientific mechanisms espoused by other dissenters from Darwinism who would disavow direction, and in some cases teleology.[44] In support of this claim of teleology and direction, directed evolution points, as in the origin of life, to the low probability of so many speciation events, which are hard to explain in the absence of agency. In particular it points to the difficulty of undirected change accounting for the rapid origin of new phyla, the problem of the very low likelihood of success of "hopeful monsters."[45]

The question of teleology, it is important to remember, is one that science cannot answer. Science can determine mechanism but not purpose. When an individual scientist, or group of scientists, takes a stand one way or the other on teleology or direction, it must be remembered that this is a position taken based on their philosophical commitments, which imposes a certain perspective on the scientific evidence.

Unlike creationary models, proponents of non-Darwinian evolution view changes at higher taxonomic levels not as new *de novo* creation events but as major modifications of form based on rapid changes in genetic and epigenetic elements. They do, however, agree with the creationary models, to which we will turn next, on some issues, including the danger of extrapolation.

Creation. The third line of interpretation involves direct creation of complete organisms, either in the recent past (YEC) or over geological time (OEC). Currently very few proponents of creation believe every biological species was created individually. Most accept that some change is possible, both at the level of allele frequency in the population and even up to the taxonomic level of the family, but they assert that

---

[44]The idea of God controlling probabilistic events in a way that the result is scientifically indistinguishable from natural events is discussed in Ratzsch (1996: 186-88). Shapiro (2011: 137) claims the process is teleological, but that the cells or organisms themselves provide the goal, which is survival. This is a very different sense of teleology from that used in this book, where the goal is set by God.

[45]*Hopeful monsters* is a term introduced by Richard Goldschmidt for organisms undergoing major changes early in development, resulting in offspring produced which are very different from the parents. A good review of his ideas is presented by Schwartz (1999: chap. 10).

larger gaps are evidence of creative acts that science cannot explain.

If the assertion is made that science will never be able to determine how major groups of organisms arose, in what sense are these scientific models of origins? On the one hand, the two creation models state that a Creator made them, without providing a mechanism. On the other hand, they do provide an explanation for the scientific evidence. The question of whether an explanation of scientific evidence without mechanism should be classified as science belongs to the realm of the philosophy of science, not science itself. We will return to this question in chapter eight.[46]

Both creation positions believe God created separate "kinds," according to the text of Genesis.[47] The question is how these kinds relate to the definition of species.[48] Currently most adherents of this interpretation admit that a certain degree of microevolution takes place by Darwinian mechanisms. Where they disagree is the extrapolation of this to higher taxa, from microevolution to macroevolution. Thus, they will admit that the Galapagos finches arose from a single population, but point out that in the millions of years the finches are thought to have inhabited the islands, none have become anything except finches, and none have extended their range of food outside that eaten by other finches. None, for example, have become shore birds or raptors, although food for those would be present in abundance. At higher taxonomic levels (from reptiles to birds or invertebrates to vertebrates) even greater changes of form would be required. To emphasize the difficulty of this, creation models highlight precisely the evidence minimized by evolution models: the limits of selection, the deleterious nature of muta-

---

[46]The problem of demarcation of science is addressed by Meyer (1994).

[47]"Kinds" are generally taken to represent forms from which all organisms within a family or genus are derived (Scherer, 1998). The study of kinds, called baraminology, after the Hebrew word translated "kind," seeks to determine how many original kinds there were, based on their ability to interbreed.

[48]The question of how species should be designated is an open question. In living organisms the standard definition is ability to reproduce, but paleontologists are limited to examining differences in form. It has been remarked that if paleontologists were to find skeletons of modern dogs, all of which are considered one species biologically, they would undoubtedly classify them as dozens if not hundreds of species. There are also philosophical questions underlying the definition of species. For a summary of the debate see "Species" (2010), *Stanford Encyclopedia of Philosophy*, http://plato.stanford.edu/entries/species.

tions and the saltations in the fossil record. They also question how Darwinian gradualism and natural selection could create complex structural and behavioral patterns, sometimes involving multiple species, such as the structural adaptations of a woodpecker or the symbiotic behavior of cleaner fish and their clients (Morris & Parker, 1987: 84-87), an argument similar to irreducible complexity but on a macroscopic or ecological scale.[49]

Thus, the basic argument is that although Darwinian mechanisms and gradualism are sufficient to account for changes within a species, and even within closely related groups of species, a different mechanism is necessary to account for larger changes. Supporters of non-Darwinian evolution agree with this, although they disagree with the creation explanation of the direct creation of forms. Nevertheless, anyone who questions the idea of gradualism runs the risk of being attacked, ridiculed and branded a creationist, even if they deny that label.[50]

In most of the other categories of evidence, where (neo-Darwinian) evolution cites common descent as an explanation, creation cites common design. Where evolution claims similarity in the order of genes reflects common descent, creation claims the order is important to the function, citing the order of the homeotic genes as an example. Where evolution postulates horizontal gene transfer (HGT), creation attributes the patchwork of genes present in different species of prokaryotes to God giving each organism the mosaic of genes it would need. As mentioned previously, creation cites certain data as evidence that evolution generally regards as anomalies and excludes from evidence. As a result, the two positions completely talk past one another on a number of issues.

While the two creationary models agree on most interpretations related to genetics and similarities, they differ when it comes to fossils. Old-earth creation adheres to a standard chronology of the fossils, including explanations of stratigraphy and dating (see chap. 3). Where it differs from the evolutionary positions is in interpretation of the saltations, which it views as evidence of creative acts scattered over geo-

---

[49]A similar argument is found in Ryan (2002: 242-43, 263), but from a naturalistic perspective.
[50]Milton (1997: chap. 24) describes the treatment he and others received.

logical time. In particular, the rapid appearance of most animal phyla during the Cambrian period and the lack of fossil evidence of transitional forms between them is cited as evidence for that model.

Currently, most YEC models explain all fossils as the result of a global flood. Both are based on a similar interpretation of the early chapters of Genesis, and are connected by most YEC organizations today, although the idea of a global flood is a separate issue from the age of the present creation.[51] The flood is used to explain the order of the fossils, as different biomes were buried separately, with marine organisms buried first, followed by increasingly larger and more active organisms in the upper layers. The flood also explains why the radioactive dates obtained for pre-flood organisms are so old. According to the most current YEC explanation, the rate of radioactive decay increased during two time periods, the first and second days of creation and the time of Noah's flood (DeYoung, 2005: chap. 9).

5.3 WHAT DIFFERENCE DOES IT MAKE?

It has often been noted that what we see depends on what we expect to see.[52] This is true no matter whether we are dealing with general observations of our surroundings or scientific evidence. As we know from optical illusions, our senses can easily be tricked when we are conditioned to interpret things in a certain way. Thus, two people can look at the Grand Canyon, one seeing the results of a global flood, the other the results of millions of years of change, neither able to understand how the other could be so obtuse.

Paleontologists working from an evolutionary perspective frequently look for transitional fossils, while geologists working from a creationary perspective look for discrepancies in radiometric dating and cases of recent and rapid fossilization. Not unexpectedly, each finds what they

---

[51]According to the gap model, an earlier creation by Satan, including the monstrous dinosaurs, was destroyed by God when "the earth *became* formless and void," according to their interpretation of Genesis 1. God then repopulated the world with a new creation in the recent past. This model, which did not emphasize a worldwide flood, was common in the early nineteenth century and was popularized in the Scofield Bible but is not widespread today.

[52]As C. S. Lewis put it less prosaically, "Moreover, he knew nothing yet well enough to see it: you cannot see things till you know roughly what they are" (1938: 43).

are looking for and extrapolates from those cases to general principles they claim apply to every situation. Neo-Darwinians search the Cambrian fossils for missing links, while proponents of OEC search the same fossils for evidence that each phylum appears without intermediate forms.

For those who idolize Darwin,[53] the mantra of common descent by gradual change via natural selection is an inviolable rule, and everything is interpreted in its light. Thus accumulating evidence of rapid molecular change within various lineages "must" have occurred over thousands of generations. Those not bound by this are free to look for mechanisms that would allow rapid speciation over the course of one or a few generations, whether by creation or by major genetic and epigenetic change.

Overall, the evidence points to great similarity between living things, both on a morphological and genetic level. There is no disagreement that speciation can occur based on drift and selection, for closely related species. The question that remains is whether Darwinian mechanisms are sufficient to account for the larger levels of change, whether a jellyfish, an insect and a person all have a common ancestor, and if so whether the mechanisms are the same for the smaller and larger changes, for micro- and macroevolution. If the mechanisms are different, to what degree was God involved in the process? Did he frontload the system at the beginning of creation with capacity to change by itself in response to changing conditions, or did he direct the process step-by-step, or did he create each major branch of organisms separately, using similar components modified to the particular needs of each, and if so at what taxonomic level and on what time scale? There are committed Christians who support each of these models, but there are distinct theological implications of each, which become even clearer when we discuss the origin of humans.

---

[53]As Gould and Lewontin (1979) put it, "Darwin has attained sainthood (if not divinity) among evolutionary biologists." How many other scientists of his era have every known word they have written, including every version of every book and all known correspondence, published online? See darwin-online.org.uk.

Origin of Humans

...

The origin of humans is in one sense merely a subset of the origin of species. From a creationary perspective, humans were created, as were other species; from an evolutionary perspective, humans are one species among many that arose by the same mechanisms. In another sense, however, it is a distinct question that is central to the debate, because the underlying issue is whether humans are qualitatively or only quantitatively different from animals, whether we are unique or just smarter. Is there more to a person than meets the eye (and other sense organs): do we have a soul or spirit (and if so, are the two identical), and do we bear the image of God (and if so, what exactly does that mean)?[1] These are questions science cannot answer, and therefore fall outside the scope of this book. Our focus will therefore be on a question science can address, the origin of the human body.

As we consider the origin of humans, I will try to follow the same format as the last three chapters, first discussing the evidence, then the various interpretations. I say "try" because, as with other fields, much of the actual evidence is highly technical, accessible only to specialists who

---

[1] Some theological positions view soul and spirit as identical, others say that at least some animals have a soul (they are soulish creatures, able to express emotion), whereas only humans have a spirit (we are sentient and bear the image of God). Christians agree that humans are created in the image of God (Gen 1:26-27), but what that means is a longstanding theological debate.

provide us with a summary of the evidence as viewed from their perspective. Even more than other areas of origin, these inferences reflect the personal philosophy of the observer. Our personal philosophy, after all, defines our identity; it reveals how we view ourselves in relation to the world around us, and the question of how the first humans got here bears directly on that.

6.1 What Is the Evidence?

Most of the physical evidence for the origin of the human body comes from one of two areas: fossils and similarities between humans and apes. A summary of the evidence and interpretations can be found in table A1.5. Additional evidence for the origin of humans deals with the origin of language and culture, as investigated by cognitive science, psychology, linguistics and sociology. This is where the social sciences enter the debate. Space unfortunately precludes discussion of these areas at this time.

Hominoids, hominids or hominins? The first area of evidence we will consider, as with the origin of species, is the evidence from fossils. Before we look at the fossils themselves, however, we need to talk a little about the terminology used in regard to human fossils because, again, the terminology reflects the viewpoint of the one using it more than anything about the fossils themselves, and prejudges the issue.

When Linnaeus did his classification in the second half of the eighteenth century, humans were placed in one family and apes and monkeys in another, within the order Anthropomorpha (human form).[2] This reflected the idea of the time that humans were qualitatively different from apes and monkeys. Over time, categories changed, representing sometimes advances in knowledge but more often changes in perspective. Gradually, the name of the order changed to Primates, including prosimians (such as lemurs, the prefix *pro*, "early," indicating their evolutionary origin before monkeys), and simians (monkeys and apes); humans came to be included in the latter category, but still somewhat distinct, the four major categories within simians being old

---

[2]One has to think that if monkeys were doing the classifying, humans would have been in placed in the category Simimorpha (monkey form).

world monkeys, new world monkeys, apes and humans.[3]

Throughout most of the twentieth century, the term *hominid was used to mean humans and fossils thought to be in the evolutionary lineage of humans. Apes were viewed as a separate taxonomic branch. As molecular studies were conducted comparing various primates, the proposed lineage and therefore terminology has changed many times within the last few decades, with the category hominid expanding to include first gorillas and chimpanzees, and later orangutans.[4] *Hominin*, a term first used in 1989, for many years had the same meaning as the older use of the term *hominid*, restricted to humans and related fossils.[5] Recently that term as well has been broadened to include chimpanzees. The newest term for humans and related fossils is *hominan. The constant change in terminology has predictably led to confusion, as specialists in the field regularly switch to newer definitions, while many outside the field continue to use an older set. This sets up a situation where the same person will use the same word differently at different times, and also the same word will be used differently by different people at the same time. Thus it is essential to ascertain what definition a person is using in a particular context. Another confusing term is the word *hominoid*, used in evolutionary taxonomy to mean all human-like animals, including humans, apes and their ancestors. However, the same term is used by creation supporters to mean human-like animals, usually excluding humans. A simplified version of the changes in taxonomy is shown in table 6.1.

It is important to understand how these terms are used when reading other literature, but as I have tried to do throughout the book, in the following section I will eschew them to avoid prejudicing the issue.

Fossils. Since Darwin's time, researchers have been scouring the world for fossils of possible human ancestors, that is to say, fossils with inter-

---

[3]Continued use of the term *primates* (from the Latin for principal, or first rank) indicates there is a sense in which humans are still considered the pinnacle of evolution.

[4]"Hominid and hominin: What's the difference?" Australian Museum, November 11, 2009, http://australianmuseum.net.au/Hominid-and-hominin-whats-the-difference. Diagrams of the changes can be seen at "Ape," *Wikipedia*, http://en.wikipedia.org/wiki/Ape, in the section "Changes in Taxonomy."

[5]"Hominin," *Merriam-Webster*, www.merriam-webster.com/dictionary/hominin.

mediate characteristics or a mosaic of some ape-like and some human-like characters. One feature of paleontology is that if you discover a fossil of a new species, you get to name it, and your name will forever be associated with it. If you find the second or third fossil of a type, it barely deserves mention outside a small group of specialists, unless it

Table 6.1. Hominoids

Old Evolutionary Scheme	Newer Evolutionary Scheme	Newest Evolutionary Scheme	Creationary Scheme
Apes	*Non-hominid Apes*	*Hominids*	*Apes*
Orangutan	Orangutan	Orangutan	Orangutan
Gorilla	*Hominids*	Gorilla	Gorilla
Chimpanzee	Gorilla	*Hominins*	Chimpanzee
Hominids	Chimpanzee	Chimpanzee	*(Human)**
Human	*Hominins*	*Hominans*	
	Human	Human	

*In the creation models, humans are not considered to be hominoids, but a separate category. The various terms hominoid, hominid and hominin are generally used in creation literature only in reference to their use in evolutionary literature.

happens to be very complete or highly articulated (the bones lying in the proper relative positions). As a result, there is a strong desire to find and identify new species. This often results in naming of new species based on a very small number of bones, with fairly small anatomical differences from named species. Later, when more fossils are found in the same area or sediment layer, showing an overlapping range of features, many of the finds may be declared to be the same species.[6] Nowhere is this more evident than in the search for human ancestors. Furthermore, the desire to find human ancestors is so strong that there have been hoaxes and incorrect identification of totally unrelated bones as human.[7] Those who question evolution have used this to challenge both the reli-

---

[6]The same is true in botany and zoology—those whose goal is discovering new species tend to be "splitters," while those who reexamine the results are much more likely to be "lumpers." The former split similar organisms into many species, based on minimal differences, while the latter lump organisms of quite different color or appearance together as one species, as long as there is any evidence of interbreeding. The opposite situation also occurs, especially where small fragments, insufficient to describe a new species, are first designated as belonging to a known species but later reassigned based on greater similarity to a newly described species.

[7]Descriptions of Piltdown Man, Nebraska Man and others are easy to find, but not relevant to the evidence.

ability of the evidence and the explanation, but this is the way things are done in historical sciences, just as in forensics there may be many false leads and many suspects considered based on early evidence, with the number whittled down as the process of gathering evidence continues.

So what is the actual evidence? The number of remains identified as primate is quite limited, and their state of preservation poor, making identification and interpretation difficult. All together there are perhaps a few thousand fossils identified as human or human-like, most represented by only a few fragments of bone. There are less than a hundred significant fossils identified as human-like that are dated at more than 200,000 years old, mostly partial skulls. Only four, nicknamed Ardi, Lucy, MH1 and Turkana boy, are anywhere near complete skeletons.[8] Another fifty fossils are more recent than that, all identified as modern human or *Neanderthal.[9]

The vast majority of the fossils have been assigned to the genera *Australopithecus* and *Homo*, with a half-dozen widely recognized species within each. Other genera and species have been proposed, but it remains to be seen how many will eventually be lumped back in with the accepted categories. In general, the Australopithecines have more ape-like and the Homo more human-like characteristics. The vast majority of the former are dated at more than 2 million years old, and the latter less, although there is a period of overlap, as shown in figure 6.1.

Do these fossils show traits that are intermediate between apes and humans, or show some traits similar to each? Most authors, except those writing from a YEC perspective, think that they do.[10] There are a number of physical characteristics that distinguish modern humans from all

---

[8]"Prominent hominid fossils," *Talk Origins Archive*, www.talkorigins.org/faqs/homs/specimen .html. Ardi is classified as *Ardipithecus*, Lucy and MH1 as *Australopithecus* and Turkana boy as *Homo erectus*.

[9]There is ongoing debate about whether Neanderthals should be classified as a separate species (*Homo neanderthalensis*) or a subspecies of humans (*Homo sapiens neanderthalensis*). Recent molecular studies have been inconclusive, with some claiming there was interbreeding between the two populations, others disputing that.

[10]Hartwig-Scherer (1998: table 9.1) shows which features of Australopithecans are more chimp-like, which more human-like, which are intermediate, and which are unique, with similar numbers of traits in each category. YEC proponents think all the fossils can be clearly distinguished as either human or ape. Some evolution proponents say different YEC authors place the same fossil in different categories, showing how hard it is to distinguish them.

modern apes, including characters related to the skull (such as the size and shape of the brain case, teeth and jaws), those related to upright posture (such as the position of the hole where the spine enters the skull and pelvis shape), and the size and position of the thumb and big toe. In all of these traits modern humans are distinct from modern apes, and there are fossil forms that are intermediate between the two.[11]

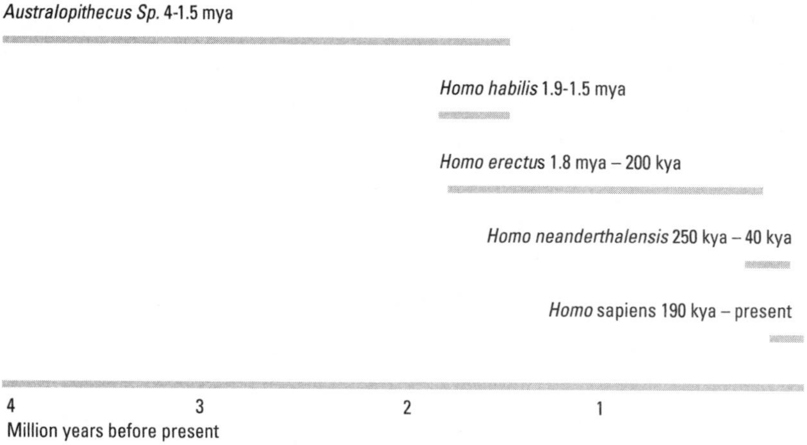

Australopithecus Sp. 4-1.5 mya

Homo habilis 1.9-1.5 mya

Homo erectus 1.8 mya – 200 kya

Homo neanderthalensis 250 kya – 40 kya

Homo sapiens 190 kya – present

4   3   2   1
Million years before present

Figure 6.1. Names and radiometric dates assigned to major hominid fossils

Is there a distinct pattern of transformation in the fossils, so that a distinct path can be drawn of sequential change from a more ape-like to a more human-like form, in conjunction with decreasing age of the fossils? Most paleontologists would agree that there is not.[12] Rather, we see a mosaic of forms. Some earlier forms are more human-like in one aspect, less in another, while later forms are the opposite. This is what has led to the still unresolved debate among evolutionary paleoanthro-pologists whether bipedalism or brain development arose first, and the many different possible lineages that have been suggested over the years.

Fossils identified as *Homo habilis*, often cited in textbooks as the link

[11]For a more complete picture of what distinguishes humans from apes, see Schwartz (1999: chap. 2).
[12]Mayr says there is no fossil record of the branching event between human and ape lineages, that there is a strong discontinuity between various fossil types, and "this is particularly true for the break between Australopithecus and Homo" (2001: 238).

between *Australopithecus* and *Homo erectus*, are a particular enigma. They show a vast range of traits, with brain sizes ranging from 500 to 800 cubic centimeters. Similarly, the evidence of traits related to bipedalism is mixed. Some have interpreted this as misclassification of these fossils, and they would reassign at least some to other species. Some would prefer to eliminate the species altogether (Mayr, 2001: 246), while others claim that after debate, the species is now fully accepted.[13]

Artifacts. Beyond the physical features, is there anything else that distinguishes apes from humans? The traits most often noted are the ability to reason, use of language and tool making (Schwartz, 1999: 70). Of these, tools are the only artifacts directly evident in the fossil record, but artistic or cultural artifacts are taken as evidence of ability to reason, and there are clues about ability to reason and use of language in the size and shape of the braincase.[14]

It has been noted that humans are not totally unique in any of these three areas. All animals can reason, and tests of intelligence have shown that various animals from cephalopods to birds to mammals can solve multistep problems to get a food reward, and some seem to do so out of mere curiosity. Similarly, most, if not all, animals have some form of communication with other members of their own species, including many with quite varied vocalizations. Some use tools, even fashioning them to a particular shape suited to the purpose, although none are known to fashion permanent, reusable tools. Based on this, many researchers (mostly from a nonreligious position) say humans are only quantitatively different from animals, based on our larger brain, social structure, prolonged adolescence and other factors. Others (mostly from a religious perspective) point to abstract thought and spiritual awareness as uniquely human traits.

In the fossil record we find tools associated with fossils identified as early representatives of the genus *Homo*, dated as old as 2.5 million

---

[13]Jim Foley, "Hominid species," *Talk Origins Archive*, April 30, 2010, www.talkorigins.org/faqs/homs/species.html. It should be pointed out that these disagreements are among evolutionary paleoanthropologists, not between supporters of evolution and creation.

[14]Reasoning is localized in the frontal cortex, the area of the human brain most enlarged relative to apes, and speech is localized in Broca's area. The size of both of these areas can be estimated based on molds of the interior of the skull.

years ago. As with the fossils themselves, there seem to be distinct periods of stasis and saltation in tools, so that it is possible to categorize
the tools into specific groups. Those associated with *Homo erectus* are
simple stone tools, which like the species itself changed relatively little
over the million years it exists in the fossil record. More advanced tools,
called core flake technology, are not found until fossils identified as
Neanderthal or early modern human appear, between 300,000 to
200,000 years ago. The most advanced, blade technology, does not
appear until the Late Paleolithic, within the last 30,000 years. A similar
pattern is found with other evidences of culture, including art objects
and signs of ritual burial, both of which became common about the
same time as blade technology and are found only in association with
human or Neanderthal fossils. Numerous advances, including pottery
and signs of domesticated agriculture, mark the change to the Neo-
lithic period, about 10,000 years ago (8000 B.C.), followed in about 3500
B.C. by metal tools.[15]

Brain size likewise is not continuous. *Australopithecus* skulls reveal a
brain similar in size to that of apes, but the brain size of *Homo erectus* is
almost twice as large as *Australopithecus* (and about two-thirds the size
of humans), although the body is only marginally larger.[16] The brains of
Neanderthals, as well as their bodies, were slightly larger than those of
modern humans, although the shape of the brain case was slightly different.[17] In the time period between *erectus* and modern man several
other skulls have been discovered that are intermediate in size between
the two. These are identified by some as *H. heidelbergensis*, but the few
fossils that exist have been discovered in various places and there is no
consensus on their relation to other fossil forms.

It is important to remember that the only real evidence is that a number
of fossils and artifacts have been found, with a number of different fea-

---

[15]This summary is obviously a gross generalization, as the implements found at different dates vary
in different sites around the world.

[16]YEC points out that there is no direct correlation between brain size and intelligence, as seen by
comparing mice and rats.

[17]Relating to brain structure, Mayr contends that the human brain may contain as many as forty
different kinds of neurons, some perhaps unique to humans, and "What is perhaps most astonish-
ing is the fact that the human brain seems not to have changed one single bit since the first appearance of *Homo sapiens*, some 150,000 years ago" (2001: 252).

tures. Anything beyond that, including classifying them into groups, naming the groups, deciding which represent differences at the level of genus and which at the level of species, dating and relationships between them all involve varying degrees of inference. Yet, it is impossible to talk about the fossils in any meaningful way without classifying them into groups, so inference is unavoidable, and with it the underlying background knowledge and assumptions of the one doing the classifying.

Chimps versus humans. The second main line of evidence comes from comparing humans with apes. Originally done at an anatomical level, in recent years the majority of the comparisons have involved molecular similarity. In this section we will look first at similarities in the number and structure of human and chimpanzee chromosomes. We will then examine specific similarities and differences in the DNA sequence. Finally, I will briefly describe some of the techniques used to determine how long ago and in how large a population these changes might have occurred, from an evolutionary perspective.

Chromosome 2. For a long time it has been known that there are many similarities between ape and human chromosomes. Early DNA staining techniques revealed nearly identical banding patterns for many of the chromosomes. As techniques have improved, the true extent of the similarity has become apparent.

All apes have 24 pairs of chromosomes, or a total of 48 chromosomes, compared with the 23 pairs found in humans. But the second longest of our chromosomes, chromosome 2, has a number of traits that give it the appearance of being two chromosomes joined end to end. All chromosomes have a *centromere, a region of the chromosome where the spindle fibers bind during cell division.[18] In diagrams of cell division, this is the middle of the X, the point of attachment between the two replicated sister chromatids. The DNA in this region is composed of many highly repetitive sequences and, unlike regions that code for proteins, remains highly condensed throughout the life of the cell, a state known as *heterochromatin.[19] In the long arm of chromosome 2, there

---

[18]Properly, the spindle fibers bind to the kinetochore, a protein complex, which binds to the DNA of the centromere.

[19]The DNA in the centromere is wrapped around a protein known as CENP-C. In other parts of

is a second region with a very similar collection of heterochromatic sequences. Between this and the active centromere, there is a section that has a sequence very similar to that found at the end of every chromosome, the *telomere. The telomere consists of a short sequence repeated many times; this sequence is usually found only in the telomere. Furthermore, the order of genes found on chromosome 2 matches the order of the genes of two different chimp chromosomes, joined end to end by their short arms.[20]

DNA sequence. For years textbooks have cited the figure that humans and chimps are about 98.5% identical genetically, based on preliminary comparisons of selected sections of the DNA. Within the first five years of the new millennium, scientists determined the complete sequences of both the human and chimp genomes, allowing a base-by-base comparison. Although this brought greater clarity, it also added to the confusion, as different numbers have been published at different times, some based on the older studies, others on the initial analysis of a single chromosome (Weissenbach, 2004), some on the first draft of the entire chimp genome (Chimpanzee Sequencing and Analysis Consortium, 2005), and yet others on later revisions or other work, for example the sequence of the Y chromosome (Hughes et al., 2010). Furthermore, differences are sometimes cited as numbers, sometimes as percentages, making it hard for the average person to figure out why there is such a disparity in the reports. The saying, "Figures don't lie, but liars figure," attributed to Mark Twain, may be appropriate here, as different writers choose which figures to cite in order to make their argument seem stronger.[21]

Starting from the most basic level, the human genome contains approximately 3 billion base pairs, the chimp genome about 2.7 billion (a difference of 10%). Most of this difference is due to *insertions or *dele-

---

the chromosome the DNA is wrapped around proteins known as histones. The variant form CENP-C seems to be involved in binding to the kinetochore.

[20]There is, at the point of junction, a section of DNA of about 150,000 base pairs not found in the two chimp chromosomes, which contains what appear to be copies of sections of genes found elsewhere in the genome. The function of this DNA, if any, is not yet known.

[21]My choice to cite many different, seemingly conflicting, ways of looking at the data is obviously included.

tions, of which there seem to be about 5 million. These insertions and deletions range from 30 base pairs to tens of thousands of base pairs long; about 7,000 are *Alu elements, common in both apes and humans.[22] Some of the difference in size is due to *copy number variation, where certain sections of the chromosome are duplicated in one species. There are also 9 *inversions, where part of a chromosome is flipped in one species relative to the other, along with the chromosome fusion already mentioned.

Apart from such large-scale changes to the genome, in sections that do match up there are about 35 million *single nucleotide substitutions, a mutation involving the substitution of one base pair for another (making them 1.23% different, or 98.77% similar), confirming the earlier estimates. In genes that code for a protein product, the estimate is even higher, up to 99.4% similarity. Even if we consider insertions and deletions within the gene, the number is still fairly high, with about 95% similarity (cited, with references to the original research, in Venema, 2010). There is, however, a difference of about 20% in the *expression* of the genes, how much protein is made from them and when, so similarity of the genes themselves is not the only factor separating humans and chimps (Weissenbach, 2004).

On the other hand, a different picture emerges from a comparison of the coding genes on the shortest chromosome.[23] Of 231 functional genes on that chromosome, only 39 (17%) produce identical proteins in the two species.[24] Another 140 (61%) are the same length but would lead to changes in at least one amino acid, with probably minor impact on the

---

[22]Altogether there are about a million Alu elements in humans, about 7,000 more than in apes. Each is about 300 base pairs long, altogether constituting about 10% of the genome.

[23]In humans, the shortest chromosome is number 21. In general, human chromosomes are numbered from longest to shortest, but the last three (20, 21, 22, excluding the sex chromosomes 23) are all about the same based on visual inspection. When sequencing showed that 21 was actually the shortest, scientists wisely chose not to change the established numbering system. Ape chromosomes used to be numbered from longest to shortest, but after sequencing was complete the numbering was changed to make it easier to compare them with the homologous human chromosome, with two numbered 2A and 2B. See "Mapping chimp chromosome numbers to human chromosomes numbers" (January 2012), *UCSC Genome Bioinformatics*, http://genome.ucsc.edu/FAQ/FAQdownloads#download25.

[24]Note that this is not the same as saying there are no changes in the DNA itself, since many changes at the third base in the codon do not change the amino acid coded for.

function of the protein. But 52 (22%) of the protein products differ in length, and of these 47 (20%) seem to involve major changes (Weissenbach, 2004).

So which is correct? If chimp *genes* that code for protein are 99.4% the *same* as humans, how can 83% of the *proteins* be *different*, with 20% showing major changes? Let me give a simple illustration to show how this works. If we have one gene, coding for a protein 100 amino acids long, the gene itself will contain 300 nucleotides, since 3 nucleotides code for one amino acid. If one of those nucleotides changes, causing a change in one amino acid, we could say that 1/300 of the DNA changed (only 0.3%), or 1/100 of the amino acids changed (1%), or that 1/1 (100%) of the proteins changed. Take your pick—all are true. And although the actual numbers may change or be disputed, the principle still holds: which figures a person quotes will reflect what they want their readers to conclude.[25]

Before we leave the topic of similarities and differences in the genome, we need to briefly mention the Y chromosome. The Y chromosome is special not only because it is the male sex chromosome but also because its structure does not allow it to be sequenced the same way as the other chromosomes, and therefore it was sequenced separately later. The expectation was that a similar pattern would be found there, but instead, as the journal *Nature* (2010) put it, the Y chromosome "reveals a rate of change that puts the rest of the genome to shame." The analysis showed that the chimp Y has only 11 genes whereas the human Y has 16, and that there has been massive rearrangement of the order of the genes.

Molecular clock studies. We frequently read about how long it has been since human and ape lineages separated, or about tracing humanity back to a "mitochondrial Eve" or "Y-chromosomal Adam," or determining the minimum size of populations millions of years in the past. Such statements are clearly inferences, but what is the original evidence? While it is impossible in a limited space to do justice to the arguments, since they involve fairly complex mathematics, I will attempt to explain

---

[25]Jeffrey Tompkins (2011) writing from a YEC perspective, recently conducted a new comparison of chimp and human genomes and concluded they are no more than 89% similar. He claims the algorithm used for computation of similarity compares samples of the genome, not the entire sequence, and that earlier analyses eliminated large regions of noncorrespondence in order to save computing time.

the reasoning behind them sufficiently for the reader to understand the basic principles, potential and limitations of the methods.

Although the specifics vary, most modern versions of a *molecular clock involve studies of *polymorphisms. Polymorphisms (literally "many forms") arise when a mutation occurs, producing two different forms of the DNA. In many cases the mutation causes no change or only a very small change at the level of the individual and therefore is not acted on by selection.[26] Probability theory suggests that most of these *neutral mutations should be eliminated by random chance within a relatively short time, but a few will persist and eventually become "fixed" in the population; that is, all individuals in the population will have that mutation. When the population splits, either due to geographical isolation or speciation, all of the fixed forms will initially be the same in both groups, but other mutations will subsequently arise and be fixed independently in the two populations. Patterns of branching are determined based on the various polymorphisms in different groups. This gives an estimate, in relative terms, of how long the two populations have been distinct. Studies estimating effective population size are similarly based on polymorphisms, but they compare polymorphisms between different individuals within the species.

These calculations rest on certain assumptions, including that the changes are random, occur at a fairly constant rate and generally do not revert to the original form. In order to assign actual dates rather than relative dates, it is necessary to calibrate the molecular clock. This is done by comparing changes in the DNA with changes in the fossils. Choosing a major branching point that is fairly well attested in the fossil record, for example the origin of primates, comparison is made between primates and other mammals to determine how many have occurred since that point. That number is then divided by the time,

---

[26]A mutation may not lead to a change in any gene product if the mutation occurs in a noncoding region of the genome or if the substitution occurs in the third position of a codon. Other changes at a molecular level may be small enough not to affect the fitness of the individual; for example, a change in the intensity of eye color. The idea that many mutations are neutral with regard to selection pressure is called the neutral theory of molecular evolution. While some contentions of the theory are controversial, such as the relative importance of neutral and nonneutral mutations in evolution, use of neutral mutations to construct a molecular clock is widely accepted in evolutionary circles.

giving an average rate of change for the lineage.[27] All of these assumptions are reasonable within an evolutionary model, but of course do not make sense in a nonevolutionary model.

So the actual evidence underlying molecular clock studies is in most cases the number and positions of polymorphisms in the DNA. Since this underlying evidence makes no more sense to the nonspecialist than the astronomical data that comprise the evidence for the origin of the universe, the only thing reported to the public are inferences. In this case, those inferences are that ape and human lineages separated about 4.5 to 6 million years ago, that all humans can trace their mitochondrial DNA to a single woman who lived about 150,000 to 200,000 years ago, and that all men can trace their Y chromosome to a single man who lived about 60,000 to 90,000 years ago.[28] This does not mean these individuals were the only male or female living at the time. Different studies of the size of the ancestral human population within the last 200,000 years have come up with quite varied answers, from more than 10,000 to as few as 1,000, with several authors concluding that there were one or more bottlenecks in the population, periods of low population numbers, sometime prior to 20,000 years ago (Tenesa et al., 2007). As we look at various interpretations of the evidence we will see how different positions reconcile these numbers.

6.2 HOW DOES EACH MODEL INTERPRET THE EVIDENCE?

When we look at the primate fossil record, or the molecular evidence, we do so from a certain perspective, basically either that of evolution or of creation. While it is possible to choose to look from the other side, or even choose to switch sides, it is impossible to look at the evidence from both perspectives at once, just as it is impossible to focus on both sets of images at the same time in Escher's tessellations.[29]

---

[27] Initially it was thought that the rate of mutation should be the same for all species, all of the time, but this has not shown to be the case, so now such comparisons are done only within a given evolutionary lineage.

[28] More properly, Y chromosome Adam represents a relatively small population in which a single version of the Y chromosome is fixed. The original man from whom all these males are descended patrilineally would have lived at some time earlier. The same would be true of mitochondrial Eve (Venema, 2010).

[29] For example, *Day and Night*, http://tessellations.org/eschergallery8.htm.

Looking a little deeper, there are three separate questions, all more in the realm of religion than science, that people already have considered to some degree before they examine the scientific evidence: Is there such a thing as a human soul or spirit, how does God interact with his creation, and how is Genesis to be interpreted? The intersection of belief about those three questions leads to four distinct interpretations of the evidence about human origins. Of the six models, only one, naturalistic evolution, believes that there is no human soul, that the natural world is the only reality. Two models, nonteleological evolution and planned evolution, comprise the second interpretation, based on the belief that the soul exists and that although God may intervene in the world in response to prayer, he does not do so in areas that can be studied by science, including origins. The third interpretation is that held by directed evolution, based on a belief that God regularly interacts with his creation, but that the first few chapters of Genesis tell us nothing about the timing or mechanism of creation. Old-earth creation and young-earth creation comprise the final interpretation, based on the belief that God regularly interacts with his creation and that the first few chapters of the Genesis creation tell us something about how God created. In each case the religious beliefs have a clear and direct impact on both the interpretation of the scientific evidence and on one's view of humanity, so in the following analysis there will of necessity be far more discussion of religious issues than in earlier chapters.

The first two interpretations, comprising the models NE, NTE and PE, take a nearly identical view of the science, although they differ on the question of whether there is a soul. This is possible because all three models accept the principle of nonoverlapping magisteria (see chap. 2) that science and religion answer different questions. The third interpretation, directed evolution, although an evolutionary interpretation of the scientific evidence, is in many ways more similar to the creationary interpretation than to the two other evolutionary positions because of its basic philosophical presupposition that science and religion are interacting and inseparable ways of knowing the truth.

Sentient animal. If, as claimed by the nontheistic model of naturalistic evolution, there is nothing in the universe apart from the empirically observable matter and energy, then logically there is no such thing as a soul and our minds are merely projections of our brain. When we die, when our brains cease to function, we simply cease to exist. Similarly, there must be some natural, totally undirected process that allowed our species to come into being. The only thing that separates us from other animals is our large brain; we are sentient animals.

According to this interpretation, humans evolved slowly, gradually separating from apes and at the same time gradually developing the ability to use tools, domesticate plants and animals, and transmit culture. At least some of the hominids are our direct ancestors, it is simply a matter of figuring out which. The evidence of fusion in chromosome 2 and the similarity of sequence in both functional genes and noncoding regions, particularly the similarity of apparently neutral mutations in both, are viewed as strong evidence of our evolutionary connection with other primates.

The whole concept of molecular trees and molecular clocks is built on an evolutionary model, so the resulting estimate that human and ape lineages diverged 4.5 to 6 million years ago is considered accurate. The difference between this time frame and the far shorter time calculated from mitochondrial DNA or the Y chromosome is explained by the fact that if a mother has only male offspring, her mitochondrial DNA will disappear from the population, although her chromosomal DNA will still be passed on. Over many generations, this has led to the survival of only one lineage of mitochondrial DNA. A similar situation holds for the Y chromosome of a male who has only female offspring. Thus they claim that there was never a time when there was a single human male or female from whom the whole human race descended, rather that there was always a population of individuals, slowly diverging from some common ancestor with apes.

Special animal. Nonteleological evolution and planned evolution are virtually indistinguishable from naturalistic evolution with regard to their view of the scientific evidence. Exactly the same arguments are used to show the connection of humans with other animals. Unlike NE, these two models view religion as a distinct, valid domain of knowledge; from that domain the claim is made that humans have an eternal soul.

Theologically, there is quite a range represented within this position, from positions that view Christianity as only one of many paths leading to knowledge of God (mostly NTE) to positions that view Christ as the only way. The common factor is that God is viewed as external to the created universe, intervening only rarely in miraculous events, if at all. According to this position, it may not even have been necessary for him to specifically intervene to choose one hominid to bear his image (often viewed, at least in part, as the ability to make moral judgments).

On the basis of an evolutionary model, this interpretation also accepts the findings of molecular clock studies. As with the first line of interpretation, one of the inferences drawn is that there was never a severe bottleneck in the human population, down to a single male and female at the same time, thus proponents deny that Adam and Eve were single individuals who were progenitors of the human race. If humans did not arise from a single man and woman at a particular point in time, various explanations are possible of how humans might have arisen. First, awareness of God and sinfulness could have arisen slowly in a group of primates over many generations, so there was no single point in time at which pre-humans became human.[30] This interpretation, in accord with Darwinian gradualism and the idea of non-intervention, is the one espoused by most proponents of evolutionary creation at the present time. Two evolutionary explanations that involve humanness arising at one particular point in time belong to the next interpretation.

Special purpose. The interpretation proposed by directed evolution springs from a very different theological perspective, one that considers God to be continually and intimately involved in creation at all times. According to this view God does not intervene in the world only at particular times; it would be better stated that he is constantly involved in sustaining and directing it.[31] Thus he is always working in the world to accomplish his purposes, whether that be gradually

---

[30]This view of the spiritual origin of humanness is called gradual polygenism (Lamoureux, 2008: chap. 8; BioLogos Foundation, 2011).

[31]Departures from natural law still appear from our perspective to be interventions and are often referred to as such, just as a child may think only of a gift as being given by his parents, when in fact everything the child has is provided from the parents' income.

shaping a human form from an ape lineage or instantaneously imbuing that form with a spirit.[32]

As with the two positions described previously, most of the scientific
evidence is seen from an evolutionary perspective. Thus it is considered
likely that at least some of the fossils discovered are in the human
lineage. However, as with origin of species, DE is far more willing to
consider saltation in the fossil record as a representation of what actually happened, rather than merely the imperfection of the record. As
mentioned before, I do not know of any complete account bridging the
theological and scientific arguments for this position, although there are
definitely scientists who hold it.[33] The main distinction between this
interpretation and the former one is the belief that there was a specific
point at which our progenitors became human, whether God chose one
pair of individuals from an evolving population of pre-humans and imparted to them his image, or imparted his image at a point in time to a
whole population of pre-humans.[34] It is likely that different submodels
would place Adam at different times, from the first representatives of
the genus *Homo* to the first *Homo sapiens* or even some time after that.

There are two areas where DE disagrees with NTE and PE, both in
regard to the molecular evidence. First, DE, along with the two creation models, is more likely to highlight the number of changes between humans and apes, rather than the percent of similarity. According to the evidence, about 40 million changes happened within 6
million years, including substantial changes in both the structure and
expression of about 20% of the proteins. Evolutionary scientists admit
that there was rapid change (they of course say rapid evolution, meaning
gradual change as a result of natural selection) within the human
lineage, far faster than expected. In particular, there seems to have been

---

[32]The term *spirit* is purposefully used here instead of soul, used in describing the previous two positions. The question of whether there is a difference between soul and spirit is an ongoing theological debate, but often the soul is thought of as a general life force, shared by animals, whereas
the spirit is considered that special image of God unique to humans.

[33]Venema notes that some within ID, such as Behe, accept human-chimp common ancestry, and
talks about a position he calls "Evolutionary Creationism that retains a literal Adam and Eve as
biological progenitors of humanity (evolutionary monogenism)" (Venema, 2010: fn. 52).

[34]These two views are called evolutionary monogenism and punctiliar polygenism, respectively
(Lamoureux, 2008: chap. 8).

rapid change in genes related to the nervous system (Dorus et al., 2004). As with the origin of other species, DE claims this would be far more likely if the changes were purposefully directed rather than random. Second, if there was direction, and the timing of change was not random and gradual but saltational, this contradicts the basic assumptions of the molecular clock procedures used to generate time of branching and population sizes.

Special creation. The final interpretation is that held by the two creationary models, old-earth creation and young-earth creation. Although differing in the timing, both of these believe God created two humans, Adam and Eve, creating the body and imbuing them with spirit, without progenitor.[35] This, of course, is a radically different perspective from the evolutionary models. Although Mayr claims, "No well-informed person any longer questions the descent of man from primates and more specifically from apes" (2001: 235), surveys continue to show that nearly half of the US population does question it.[36]

According to this interpretation, all the fossils can be classified as either ape or human, not as transitional. Generally OEC considers all *Homo* fossils to be human, whereas YEC is more likely to consider only *Homo sapiens* to be human. This sort of disagreement among creation supporters is to be expected, in the same way that there are disagreements among evolutionists about classification of fossils, number of species or how they are related. Young-earth creation further questions the dating methods, as with other fossils.

With regard to the molecular data, both models, as with the origin of other species, claim that the similarities to chimps are due to common

---

[35]This view is called punctiliar monogenism, the image of God being given at a single point in time (*punct*, point) to a single human couple (*mono*, single; *gen*, beginning) (Lamoureux, 2008: chap. 8).
[36]In a poll conducted by a pro-evolution journal, 48% of the general population and 16% of high school biology teachers thought "God created human beings pretty much in their present form at one time within the last 10,000 years or so." A further 30% of the general population and 47% of high school biology teachers responded, "Human beings have developed over millions of years . . . but God directed this process." There was no option for what is herein called OEC, but one would assume they would have split their answer between these two categories. The other option was, "Human beings have developed over millions of years . . . but God had no part in this process," chosen by 13% of the general population and 28% of high school biology teachers. For both groups, 9% did not answer or had no opinion (Berkman, Pacheco & Plutzer, 2008).

design rather than common descent.[37] With DE, the sheer number of mutations is seen as evidence against undirected evolution. The idea that organisms are similar by design, not descent, along with the assumption that all changes in genomes have a function, questions the basic assumptions of molecular clocks; thus the results, which are inferences, are rendered invalid.

6.3 WHAT DIFFERENCE DOES IT MAKE?

What difference does it make whether humans have a soul, whether there was a historical Adam or how we interpret the first chapters of the book of Genesis? Not unexpectedly, how important each is considered to be depends on the model one holds, with the models at the extremes being the most adamant about the importance of one thing or another. We will look briefly at three different areas: what difference it makes theologically, personally and socially.

Theological issues. As noted earlier, we cannot talk about the origin of humans apart from our philosophical or religious perspective, and without implicitly or explicitly judging the perspective of others. Advocates of NE, who believe nothing exists that cannot be investigated by empirical science, think and often express that those who believe in the existence of a soul are deluded. On the other hand, Christians and other theists often refer to advocates of NE as lost, deceiving themselves and others.

We could hope for better within the Christian community, but animosity is not infrequent between believers holding different theological, and therefore scientific, positions. Many advocates of YEC are totally convinced that their interpretation of Scripture is correct, and they therefore call all others compromisers, deceived by the lies of Satan, who substitute the changing ideas of science for the eternal, unchanging truth of the Bible. At the same time theistic evolution proponents representing various models claim it is YEC that is violating hermeneutical

---

[37]One prominent OEC organization recently admitted that chromosome 2 appears to be a fusion product, going on to say that God could have "used a preexisting 'template' that he then reshaped to create the physical makeup of human beings, to which he then imparted his image" (Rana, 2010). This is moving away from the traditional OEC position toward a DE position.

principles by forcing on Scripture a scientific interpretation that was never intended, and they criticize creation advocates for ignoring what they consider to be the plain facts of science, thus placing a stumbling block in the way of scientists who might otherwise be more open to Christianity (Carlson & Longman, 2010: 138).

At heart is the question of how to interpret Genesis, including the six days of creation, Adam and the global flood of Noah. Some say taking the words literally is not an interpretation, but that is not the case. Everything we see, hear or experience, we interpret. Anything that we put into words is automatically an interpretation. When I look at the middle light of a traffic light and call it yellow, the cones in my eye are responding to light of a particular wavelength, sending a message to the brain reporting the presence of that wavelength, and the brain matches that with its internal database and returns the result "yellow." But the "yellow" color of many traffic lights is actually amber and might be called "orange" in a different context. Furthermore, if I write, "He went through a yellow light," my meaning would be perfectly clear to present-day readers,[38] but perhaps less so to readers forty centuries from now, trying to figure out what kind of light I was talking about and how someone went through it.

Advocates of literalism admit there are places in the Bible that are not to be taken literally, but they say that literal is the default and there must be overwhelming evidence for something to be interpreted differently. They particularly point out that Jesus and the New Testament writers seem to have spoken of Adam as a single, real individual.[39] Many supporters of evolutionary models say there is overwhelming scientific evidence that the literal interpretation cannot be the correct one in this case.[40] One conservative scholar presents a minority position, that the

---

[38]We automatically translate this into, "He drove his car through the intersection when the yellow light of the traffic light facing his direction was lit, indicating that he should stop if he could do so safely." Notice how much information not in the original is automatically supplied by our knowledge of the context.

[39]Others respond that speaking of what someone did and considering them to be a real individual are not necessarily the same thing. It is common for us when talking about a familiar story, for instance Cinderella, to talk of what she did without clarifying that both we and the audience know she was not a real person.

[40]It should be noted that the question of how to interpret the story of Adam and Eve is not recent

most "literal" way to read Genesis 1, the way that would have come most naturally to the original readers, is not six twenty-four-hour periods or even sequential periods, but as an account of God establishing his temple and taking up residence there (Walton, 2009).

Our choice of interpretation of human origins not only reflects our theology but also influences our theology. If Adam was not a single individual, this would affect our doctrine of sin and therefore redemption from sin. Related to this is the question of death, particularly death before the Fall, which YEC considers to be a major issue.[41] While such doctrines are human creations, not divine revelation, they are deeply rooted in church traditions and in many cases treated with almost as much reverence as the Bible itself.

Clearly this is not an issue that will be resolved easily, and it would be pointless to say that everyone should respect the rights of others to their own opinions, that since we really don't know the mind of the original author we should reserve judgment. We cannot reserve judgment— these beliefs elicit deep emotions; we feel a need for certainty—this issue affects our identity.

Personal identity. A second area affected by our view of human origin is our personal identity. Here the main dividing line falls between theistic and nontheistic positions.

If naturalism is correct and there is no such thing as a soul, at death we utterly cease to exist. The only logical implications of this assumption are nihilism or existentialism—either we say that life is meaningless and do whatever we please, or we create a meaning for ourselves and no one else can tell us whether our chosen purpose is good or bad, a relativistic perspective.

If theism is correct, there is a basis for morality that transcends the individual, and a purpose for living beyond this current life. This gives hope to many, especially in times of suffering, but it raises the theological question of why, if God is indeed good, suffering exists, a question many

---

or exclusively related to the question of evolution. Church fathers expressed various opinions on the issue.

[41]YEC says that since the Bible says there was no death before the Fall, including animal death, so there must have been a very brief time between creation and the Fall. Other Christian models distinguish physical death from spiritual (evolutionary positions) or animal from human (OEC).

great minds have grappled with throughout history, without consensus.

As discussed in chapter one, each of us has a personal philosophy, but that philosophy is strongly shaped by the worldview of our community, so changes in our personal philosophy often necessitate a change in our community. Although some Christian churches and denominations are open to various interpretations of both Scripture and science, many are not. Personal connection with the community makes it difficult, if not impossible, for many to change their position. Individual thought is stifled by commitment to the unity of the whole. As with changes in scientific theory, change often comes only with a new influential leader or by attrition.

Social issues. Our view of what it means to be human has social implications as well, and yet again the basic question of whether there is anything beyond the material comes to the fore. If we are created in the image of God, whether by direct action or a gradual process, we have inherent worth beyond that of animals. Humanitarian efforts do not merely help others and make us feel good, but are reflections of God's love for the needy.

On the other hand, if we are just another animal, distinct only in our degree of intelligence, involved in a struggle for existence, that has implications as well. The logical outcome of naturalistic Darwinism, although many proponents refuse to accept it, is social Darwinism. When there is a struggle for resources, it would be in our best interest to allow the infirm to be eliminated from the population. Others who suffer from various infirmities, mental or physical, should also be removed from the gene pool, whether passively by withholding assistance, or actively by euthanasia. The underlying issues and results of this are adequately documented elsewhere.

So it is clear that the origins debate is not restricted to questions of science. Because it strikes at the heart of what it means to be human, it has ramifications in many areas of society. But the greatest distinction is not between evolution and creation, as often simplistically portrayed. Within theistic positions there are many different interpretations of the scientific evidence, including several variants of both evolutionary and creationary models, as we have seen. All agree that there is a God and that people, made in God's image, have innate worth. A nontheistic position cannot affirm this but must conclude that we are no more than sentient animals, important to ourselves but of no inherent value in the broader picture. This is the message conveyed by textbooks when they state that we, as all other organisms (not *creatures*), are the result of blind natural processes that never intended our existence, and it is this message that proponents of creation and intelligent design oppose, more than evolution itself.[42]

---

[42]See the description of the ID movement in chapter two, particularly note 37.

What We Can Learn from Each

•••

In the previous four chapters I have tried to present the evidence and various interpretations of it as objectively as possible, showing the logic of each position and how the arguments ultimately rest on the philosophical presuppositions undergirding each model. It is now time to evaluate the strengths and weaknesses of each. Here too I will avoid evaluation of the underlying philosophies or associated assumptions, concentrating instead on where each model has made contributions to science that others need to take seriously and where each has weaknesses that need to be addressed.

The question of origins is a puzzle, and it is clear that no model has put the whole puzzle together yet. Moreover, no model even has all the pieces of the puzzle in hand. People working on a large physical puzzle will often collect many puzzle pieces of one color or pattern and try to fit those together, and only later figure out how the sections different people have assembled fit together. The same is true in origins, with regard to both different fields of science and different models of origins. Each group is working on its own section, but sometimes someone looks over at what another person is doing and realizes a piece they have might fill a hole in someone else's section. When the piece is offered, the person with the hole may not believe the piece will fit; indeed often it does not, but sometimes it does.

We are all working on the same puzzle and must eventually work together if it is to be completed. Even if we succeed, because we will be looking at the same picture from two different sides, those from theistic and nontheistic viewpoints will still not see the results the same way.

7.1 WHAT EVIDENCE NEEDS AN EXPLANATION?

Typically in a debate, or in court, each side tries to limit what is admitted as evidence, presenting evidence and associated arguments favorable to its position, while discounting evidence that challenges it. While this is good technique for winning an argument, it is not good science. As a starting point, we need to agree that the evidence exists and deserves an explanation; otherwise we are no better than the six blind men examining an elephant.

Six blind men. I assume most of you have heard the old story of how six blind men each examined an elephant to find out what it was like. One, touching the tusk, thought the elephant to be hard and smooth, and pointed like a spear. Another, next to him but grasping the writhing trunk, said, no, it is more like a snake. The third, who happened to examine the ear, was convinced it was more like a large fan. The fourth, reaching the flat side, said it obviously was like a wall. The next felt the leg and proclaimed the elephant to be like a tree. The last, one hand on the tail, was sure it was more like a rope. Each, utterly convinced that his observation was correct, mocked the others as fools. So it is often with the six models of origins.

Not only is each convinced of their own conclusions, but the six speak different languages as well, making it hard for them to communicate. Within any academic discipline there are structuralists and functionalists, universalists and variationists, presenting prescriptive and descriptive views of reality, respectively, using different technical language. When this is combined with the multiple disciplines that contribute to understanding of origins, both empirical and nonempirical, and with varying underlying philosophical and theological positions, each with its own distinctive vocabulary, it is nearly impossible for all of the different groups to communicate in a meaningful way, nor do they necessarily want to.[1] Those who really wish to do so need to spend the time learning the language of other fields and positions, learning to see the world from their perspective. Furthermore, the actual data in most fields today is highly technical, only accessible to experts in those fields. The summaries presented in nontechnical language are colored by the expectations and philosophies of the presenters and therefore often summarily rejected by other groups, based on disagreement with the underlying philosophy and therefore distrust of everything the other says. Is there any way around this impasse?

Agreeing to disagree. The essential starting point for any meaningful communication is a desire to communicate, not just one way, conveying your views to another, but both ways, actually listening to find where you have common ground, where there are differences and why. Implicit in this is respect for the other person and his or her position. Unfortunately, it is often at this basic starting point that communication breaks down.

There *will* be things in this chapter you will disagree with.[2] Unless you have no position at all, this is guaranteed, because I will point out what I consider the strengths and weaknesses of each model, and no one likes to admit that their model has problems. But my intention is to do this fairly, not to say which model is right or wrong, but to show where each has presented important evidence that others need to consider.[3]

7.2 WHAT CONTRIBUTION HAS EACH MADE?

There would not be a debate unless there were reasonable arguments on each side, arguments that are convincing to the nonscientists who make up the bulk of the population. But in this section I am not talking about arguments or inferences as much as lines of evidence. To reiterate, it is important for each model to deal effectively with *all* the evidence, not

---

[1] Put another way, "Each side develops its own organizations, journals, networks, buzzwords, mythologies, heroes, conspiracy theories, horror stories, dire predictions, standards of orthodoxy, loyalty tests, and so forth" (Ratzsch, 1996: 9).

[2] One of the reviewers strongly disagreed with my analysis in the section "Overcoming the Odds." While I respect his opinion, he represents one of the models criticized in this section. Some of his comments showed that he did not fully understand my argument, which I have attempted to clarify.

[3] Obviously this involves judgment of what evidence is important and will therefore reveal what I think is important, and thus implicitly reveal my position.

just that which can easily be explained based on its model.

It is unfortunate but true that the nonspecialist never sees any of the real data. What is presented as evidence has always already been selected and interpreted to some degree by specialists in the field before it can be presented to the public. This is inevitable given the current state of science and technology, where it is impossible to be an expert in every field, and where so much science is based on indirect evidence.[4] Twenty years ago many of the fields that are now making contributions to the question of origins did not even exist, and most modern methods of data collection and analysis had not been developed either. Unfortunately, the lag time of getting from research to textbook means that few people are aware of the latest evidence, or only get the very abridged version found in the latest news report, which is limited to whatever makes a good headline (which the later correction or response never does). Therefore a major contribution of some groups has been to call public attention to evidence that scientists are aware of, but that is not communicated in the popular press or textbooks.

In the following sections I will not talk about each model individually, but rather four broad interpretations of the scientific data. There are two main evolutionary interpretations: neo-Darwinian and non-Darwinian. As we have seen, there are both atheistic and theistic versions of each, but they approach the scientific evidence in a very similar way, back to the point of the origin of the universe. Among creationary models we have young- and old-earth explanations. I will also show why opposing models may ignore particular lines of evidence based on the assumptions of each model. In other words, we see what we are looking for.

Contributions of neo-Darwinism. We will first consider the "standard" evolutionary position, held by the majority of those in naturalistic evolution, nonteleological evolution and planned evolution. Broadly, contributions in this area are related to two major tenets of neo-Darwinism, gradual change and common descent.

In astronomy, the model of a gradually changing universe has been bolstered in recent years by a number of different lines of evidence.

---

[4]For a description of indirect evidence, see chap. 3, note 7.

Based on predictions made by the big bang theory, detailed observations were made of patterns in the cosmic microwave background radiation. Close conformity of the results with values predicted by blackbody cooling provided strong corroboration of theory. Predictions were made that when the Hubble observatory allowed us to see fainter objects, interpreted as farther away and farther back in time (because of the amount of time it took for the light to reach us), they would have a very different appearance than the current universe; this also has proven true. These and other lines of evidence have converged on a very similar date for the beginning of the universe (see chap. 3).[5]

In genetics, it was predicted that polymorphisms would confirm putative evolutionary relationships, through a gradual accumulation of identical mutations in different lineages (see chap. 5). This has proven to be true in many cases among multicellular organisms, although not among unicellular. The technique used is essentially identical to that used to determine which of the various manuscripts of the Bible are closest to the original. Since the documents were copied word-for-word, any scribal errors that were not caught and corrected would be transmitted to subsequent copies, allowing us to trace the lineage of texts back and reconstruct the original. Thus the general method has broad acceptance and applicability. Examples of identical genetic markers have been found in organisms that exceed the boundaries of "kind" set by YEC, and identical markers are found in apes and humans.

In paleontology, there have been a number of cases where intermediate or transitional fossils were expected in rock of a certain age, and such fossils have been found (see chap. 5). One of the best documented at this point is the whale series. In this particular case there is also molecular evidence linking whales to even-toed ungulates that matches the fossil evidence (Falk, 2004: 105-11). It is true that it is very difficult to predict exactly what these intermediate forms would look like or the

---

[5]As discussed in chap. 3, even many supporters of YEC are coming to accept that the evidence points to an old universe, claiming according to white-hole cosmology that it is possible for distant parts of the universe to be billions of years old, while the earth is only 6,000 years old, due to gravitational time dilation and the effect of a "timeless zone" on the fourth day of creation. See L. Vardiman and D. R. Humphreys (2011), "A new creationist cosmology: In no time at all, part 3," *Acts & Facts* 40 (2): 12-14, www.icr.org/article/5870.

exact rock layers in which they would be found. This is to be expected based on the spotty nature of fossilization and the inherent difficulty of deterministic prediction in biology and geology, which by nature are more probabilistic than the physical sciences.

Supporters of creationary models (OEC, YEC) are least likely to recognize the contributions in this area because of their a priori commitment to separate creation of each kind. Modern creationary models allow for speciation within a kind (i.e., differentiation within taxonomic families) but claim that it represents diversification of forms from a single perfect, highly heterozygous prototypical pair of individuals. They claim each prototype was individually created, and the vast majority of mutations are deleterious and result from the fall of humankind, prior to which the whole creation was perfect. Yet as more genomes are analyzed, we find the same apparently neutral differences in the same spot in forms that are increasingly diverse.[6] Did whales and hippos descend from the same perfect organism within the last six thousand years? If not, why are there so many intermediate forms and genetic similarities?

Contributions of non-Darwinian evolution. In chapter five I mentioned that a minority of evolutionary scientists, including supporters of directed evolution and a few from naturalistic, nonteleological and planned evolution, envision a more saltational evolution. This group has also brought important evidence to the table, primarily in the area of challenges to two key tenets of neo-Darwinism: gradualism and the creative potential of natural selection.

Supporters of non-Darwinian evolutionary models generally agree that polymorphisms and fossils give evidence of common descent, but they question the idea that gradual change can account for major changes in body structure and that mutation plus natural selection is a sufficient mechanism for production of new species. Based on this they have looked for mechanisms that could cause rapid change and have reported at least three—epigenetic changes, symbiotic relationships and developmental genes—any of which could potentially cause speciation in one generation.

---

[6]Evolution models would say "mutations" or "changes," but since that is an interpretation, not actually observed, I have chosen to use the neutral term *differences*, which reflects the evidence itself.

These areas of study have slowly been making inroads into scientific acceptability. As mentioned in chapter five, the idea of endosymbiosis as the source of mitochondria and chloroplasts has now become part of the standard evolutionary theory. Similarly, the concept of horizontal gene transfer, once anathema, has become standard doctrine. Suggestions that other symbiotic relationships could lead to very rapid speciation have been slower to gain acceptance, but it seems likely that as the reductionism of molecular biology is balanced by an increasing emphasis on complex systems and ecological relationships, this area will continue to grow in influence.

Similarly, the first genes identified were ones that had small effects, where different alleles were viable. Mutations in genes exerting larger effects on the organism, especially early in development, usually led to death of the organism, an obvious dead end for evolution. Yet now those same genes are being viewed as potential sources of rapid change from one species to another, or even of larger changes in form. The question remains how such a process could have occurred in the absence of teleological control. Since this challenges not only gradualism but also the more important question of purpose, it faces an even greater battle for acceptance. Yet the evidence points to the existence of mechanisms in the cell that could permit major changes of form in a single generation.

This evidence is opposed by most advocates of evolution because there is no known natural mechanism for bringing about the coordinated change in several genes that would be necessary to produce viable offspring that differ significantly from the parents, and it is opposed by advocates of creation because of their prior commitment to *de novo* formation of kinds. Nevertheless, the evidence is there and suggests a fruitful line of research to determine whether there are currently unknown control mechanisms that could coordinate such a change.[7]

Contributions of old-earth creation and intelligent design. Since intelligent design focuses on much of the same evidence as old-earth creation, we will consider the two together. This group has also contributed

<hr>

[7]Related to this is new information that shows things the experience of parents can influence traits in the offspring. For example see Sharon Begley, "The sins of the fathers, Take 2," *Newsweek*, January 16, 2009, www.newsweek.com/id/180103.

in several areas, primarily by identifying difficulties with a nonteleological model.

Perhaps the earliest contribution of this group to the evidence was
work on the fine-tuning of the various properties of the universe and
solar system at levels suitable for life (see chap. 3). Since these numbers
are closely constrained and since there are so many noncontingent
values, all set at the level needed for life to exist, this was presented as
clear evidence of the handiwork of God. The importance of this evidence is obvious from the formulation of various versions of the anthropic principle, an alternate interpretation that has been widely pub-
licized by the naturalistic community. This alternative explanation
acknowledges the evidence, while at the same time denying its teleological significance.

A second area is the Cambrian explosion (see chap. 5), which until
about ten years ago was not even mentioned in textbooks, even though
the phenomenon of many different phyla appearing in the fossil record
within a very short period had been known for a long time. I believe
much of the reason for this was the publicity given to the phenomenon
by supporters of ID and OEC, who see it as an example of a specific
creative period.[8] Certainly the interpretation given in textbooks is different, where the Cambrian is explained as a period of rapid diversification, with the changes described as occurring rapidly, but still gradually, according to Darwinian principles, the same explanation used
for punctuated equilibria. Differing interpretations aside, public
awareness of the evidence was promoted primarily by opponents of
neo-Darwinism.

More recently, ID has published evidence from mathematics that information is separate from the carrier and requires a separate explanation.
Ultimately, the question of the origin of information is at the root of the
evidence for specified complexity and irreducible complexity (see chap.
4). Although researchers associated with evolutionary models are also

---

[8]It is hard to prove causation, since many factors contribute to such decisions, but the timing is
certainly suggestive. The decision to include the Cambrian explosion in textbooks, when it had
never been included before, and at the same time drop peppered moths and minimize the presentation of vestigial organs and vertebrate homology, came a few years after challenges to the textbook presentations of these topics had been published in popular ID publications.

studying the origin of information, the importance of this line of evidence is often downplayed by the dominant scientific community in the popular press due to its association with ID, with its challenge to the current philosophy of science and its apparent teleological implications.

Contributions of young-earth creation. It is very difficult to evaluate the contribution of young-earth creation objectively, because both the evidence and the interpretations presented by this model are so different from the majority of the scientific community. Thus others feel YEC has contributed nothing to the scientific evidence, while YEC supporters feel that they have made the greatest contributions of all, by pointing out major flaws in our understanding of the age of the earth. Indeed, if they are correct, it would require the rewriting of just about every science textbook, including astronomy, physics, chemistry, biology, geology and anthropology, since major tenets in every branch of science are challenged by the idea of a young earth. At the very least YEC has made a contribution to the public debate by highlighting evidence that is well known in the scientific community but is slow to find its way into the popular press and textbooks.

One of the reasons YEC has contributed relatively little to the evidence is that until recently there were only a small number of scientists in YEC who held advanced degrees in science (Numbers, 1992). In recent years YEC has established its own peer-reviewed scientific journals, publishing original research on radiometric dating, fossils, molecular similarities and other topics.[9] Extensive work has also been done to propose mechanistic young earth explanations for the ice ages (Oard, 1990)[10] and plate tectonics.[11] So far, this work has been largely ignored by the mainstream scientific community.

Although YEC has had little influence on the broader scientific community, it has made the public aware of things widely accepted by the scientific community but not emphasized in textbooks. Long

[9] *Answers Research Journal*, www.answersingenesis.org/arj.
[10] For a shorter summary, see Ham (2006: 207-19).
[11] Many YEC scientists believe in some form of catastrophic plate tectonics, in which the plates became unstable and moved very quickly, triggering the flood. Variations of this can be found in Snelling (2009) and Brown (2001). For a brief explanation, see Snelling, "Can catastrophic plate tectonics explain flood geology," in Ham (2006: 186-97).

before the modern young-earth movement gained strength, geologists were aware that both gradual and catastrophic events played a role in the history of the earth. Nevertheless, textbook presentations of processes such as sedimentation, fossilization and erosion tended to focus on the regular deposition of sediment, the slow mineralization of fossils and the gradual erosion of river valleys. Young-earth creation has instead highlighted evidence that these processes can all occur very quickly in certain situations.

Many fossil layers seem to have been laid down rapidly in a catastrophic event. Deep deposits of coal, trees buried upright and jumbled collections of large numbers of fossils in certain locations all point to instances of rapid deposition of thick layers of material. Fossilization can take place rapidly, as shown in the aftermath of the eruption of Mount St. Helens.[12] Rapid carving of a canyon through recently deposited sediments when a natural dam burst was observed after the Mount St. Helens event as well and is cited in support of the YEC position that the Grand Canyon was carved rapidly following the breaching of a dam left by the flood (Austin, 1995; Morris & Austin, 2003). None of the evidence for *catastrophism is disputed by other scientists, but little of the evidence has made its way into lower-level textbooks. Young-earth creation supporters who make the public aware of it claim it is being suppressed because it challenges *uniformitarianism.[13]

7.3 What Does Each Need to Address?

We will now turn to the greatest question that each group of models needs to answer. In this case the main division is between the three models on the left end of the spectrum and the three on the right. The former group claims science must follow methodological naturalism (MN); the latter challenge that definition. The former claim science will

---

[12]Rapid fossilization due to volcanic activity has long been known, for example in Pompeii. This is a separate issue from the rate of fossilization due to burial by sedimentation in the absence of volcanic activity, which represents the majority of the fossils.

[13]There are at least two forms of uniformitarianism. One claims that the rates of processes in the past were the same as they are at present. The second claims that past processes followed the same basic laws of nature that we observe at the present, although the rates may differ. The latter is preferred by almost all scientists today.

be able to fully explain everything after the origin of the universe based on natural causes; the latter say MN, by looking only for natural causes, makes it impossible to find the truth if God acted historically in a way that differs from the way he is acting now. In spite of the differences, the ultimate problem for both groups, for which neither has a good *scientific* explanation, is the origin of life.

Overcoming the odds. As we saw in chapter three, the three models on the left—naturalistic, nonteleological and planned evolution—all claim that we will ultimately be able to explain the origin of life on the basis of natural laws, possibly with some involvement of *stochastic, random events that happened to occur at just the right time and place to make life possible without divine intervention or direction. Whether this is due to the lack of anything supernatural (NE), the lack of involvement of the supernatural with the natural after the moment of creation (NTE) or the perfect planning of the Creator (PE), all of the events leading up to the origin of life are thought to have occurred naturally. The problem with this scenario is that there is no viable hypothesis of how life could have arisen; no deterministic processes have been found that would inevitably lead to life, and the probability that the complexity of life arose by chance is extremely low.

Once again, we need to stop to define terms. The ideas of probability and chance are difficult for many people to understand, and there are differences between common and scientific uses of many terms.[14] *Chance* can mean both that events are *random*, in the sense that various possible outcomes are equally likely, and *undirected*, that no intelligent agent influenced the outcome. In this section I will use *chance* to convey both random and undirected, and will use either random or undirected if I mean only one.

It is also important to revisit the idea of natural laws, since some laws are essentially deterministic, in which each outcome is predictable, while others are probabilistic, in which the overall pattern is predictable, although the outcome of a particular event is not. A game of cards can illustrate the difference. If you deal a playing card, it will fall toward the

---

[14]In the language of statistics there is even a difference between probability and likelihood, two words used interchangeably in common speech (Sober, 2008: 35).

table 100% of the time. The law of gravity determines the outcome. In a fair deal, however, a probabilistic law determines the outcome. The chance of being dealt a spade as the first card is 1 in 4, as is the probability of being dealt any other suit.

Whether an event is deterministic or probabilistic is not the only factor that affects our ability to make an accurate prediction; the number of factors involved and the number of events observed also have an influence. Roulette is somewhat different from cards, because the bounces of the ball are completely determined by the laws of physics. If you could calculate the exact speed of the wheel and the ball, the incident angle and position, the elasticity of the collisions, and various other factors, it would be theoretically possible to predict the outcome every time. But limitations on both our knowledge of initial conditions and processing speed make the outcome unpredictable. Going back to the cards, while the laws of probability accurately predict the chance of getting any particular card, the result of any particular draw is not predictable. Large numbers of repetitions are necessary to observe the patterns expected by probability.

These four situations are illustrated in figure 7.1. The law of gravity is predictable and deterministic. The probability of being dealt a spade is predictable but probabilistic. The spin of a roulette wheel is unpredictable because of the complexity. Whether you will get an ace on any particular draw is unpredictable because it is stochastic.

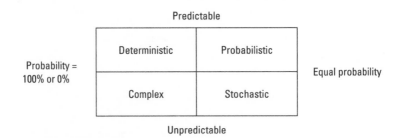

Figure 7.1. Probability and predictability of events

So what does all this have to do with the origin of life? The ID movement claims there are only two alternatives to design, chance or necessity, representing probabilistic and deterministic processes, respectively. Neo-Darwinists reply that this is a false dichotomy because there is another factor, natural selection, that acts to select favorable combinations in the same way a player selects which cards to keep or discard to increase his chance of winning. What ID is talking about, however, is the mechanism that generates material for natural selection to work on. Following this line of thought, a difference appears between origin of the large-scale features of the universe and the origin of life.

If we start with big bang cosmology, it is possible to explain the origin of most aspects of the current universe, from the origin of various elements to galaxies to star types and planets.[15] As we saw in chapter three, this is not the same as saying the universe could have come into being without the action of God, because we still need an explanation of why the basic physical constants are all set at levels appropriate for life to exist. Nevertheless, given that they are, most of the physical features of the universe could have developed without further intervention, based on a combination of deterministic and probabilistic laws. No selection is necessary, and many different types of stars and galaxies are observed to have formed, depending on initial conditions that arose by chance.

For a long time it was thought that life was fairly simple, so it would be easy for life to arise from nonlife. Thus representatives of evolutionary models thought and taught that time and chance plus natural selection explained everything. Given enough time life would be inevitable. Much has changed in our understanding of the cell, however. Only fifty years ago we thought cells were basically bags of protoplasm with a few organelles floating around inside. Now we know that the whole cell is filled with trackways, gated channels and molecules interacting in extremely complex patterns. Chance, by itself, is looking less and less probable as a way of generating the necessary complexity.

To overcome this low probability, these models are pinning their hope on finding a combination of deterministic and probabilistic mechanisms, aided by natural selection for types that are more advantageous. In other words, they are betting that life is not ultimately stochastic but

---

[15]With the acceptance of several hypothetical entities that have not yet been detected, including dark matter, dark energy and inflation.

fits instead in the category of complexity. They expect that underlying principles will be discovered, principles that may not be totally deterministic, being dependent on extremely small differences in starting conditions but nonetheless sufficient to make life inevitable. There is, however, one more glitch, the question of information. Many of the objections to neo-Darwinism can ultimately be reduced to the question of the origin of information, something found in living things but not physical entities like stars.

In the laboratory we can generate *monomers, subunits of various macromolecules. So it is fairly easy to speculate how natural processes might generate the "letters" of life. What is missing is a way to combine those letters in a way that makes sense. As proponents of ID have claimed, if those letters are combined by any sort of a stochastic process, the probability that they will provide any useful information, particularly in the amount necessary to create a functional cell, is vanishingly small. On the other hand, deterministic processes do not create the type and amount of diversity present in the order of bases in the DNA. Invoking selection does not solve the problem, because for selection to work there must be at least partial function, which requires assembly of large numbers of subunits.[16]

The question of information extends to other areas as well. The origin of new types of organisms requires new information. For minor changes of form, between closely related species, this might come from modification by mutation. But ultimately every gene contains information. How many separate and distinct genes exist in all of the millions of species of organisms in the world? How much information does this represent? How and when did all that information originate?[17]

Even the argument made by YEC that evolution violates the second law of thermodynamics comes down to a question of information. Op-

---

[16]Here I obviously differ from proponents of these models, who claim that invoking selection is sufficient to produce function. Most models that claim to do this select toward a preset target, but how does the prebiotic assemblage of molecules know what the target is?

[17]There is increasing evidence that functional proteins can be assembled from basic components (domains) coded for by DNA found in various parts of the genome (Shapiro, 2011: 95-98), and that most if not all of these basic components can be found in prokaryotes. Two questions remain: how the cell "knows" what components to assemble for a particular purpose and how those domains originated.

ponents often misstate the YEC argument in this area, saying that they ignore the fact that the earth is not a closed system but receives input of energy from the sun, thus the reduction of entropy does not violate the second law. But the YEC argument (simply put) is that input of energy by itself, in the absence of an organizing factor, does not reduce the entropy of a system, which is true.[18] Photosynthesis and various chemosynthetic mechanisms currently provide the organizing principle, but again the question reverts to what organizing principle allowed these mechanisms to form in the first place. Any organizing principle, like the organized structures it produces, is inherently related to information.

To reiterate, the ultimate question that noninterventionist models need to address is how the complexity of life, with all of its encoded information, could have arisen. Currently there is no proposed mechanism that would overcome the low probability of it arising by chance or, on the other hand, make it inevitable. Going back to our analogy, natural selection can select the cards, but the question remains, where did the cards come from in the first place?

Providing a mechanism. The second group of models—directed evolution, old-earth and young-earth creation—is more diverse, but has some similarity with regard to this key area of the origin of life. The appeal to God's involvement answers the question of source of information, but none of the models have proposed a scientific mechanism for creation, and two of the models do not seem to think this is a valid question.

Directed evolution has been identified as a separate model from PE on the basis of an underlying philosophical commitment to the idea that God could and probably did continue to interact with creation, rather than creating the world perfectly so that no intervention was needed. As discussed earlier, proponents of this model have written primarily to address certain issues, problems they see with either the creation models on one side or neo-Darwinian models on the other. No writer from this model has written specifically on origin of life, to my knowledge. This will be an important area for this model to address.

---

[18]This has been the YEC argument for years (Morris & Parker, 1987: 205-6).

What form would God's interaction take, and would it be detectable scientifically? Various answers to those questions could be proposed that would be logically consistent with the overall model, including directed assembly of the first cells by control of low probability events (which might be scientifically undetectable) or an immediate origin of at least the first cells (similar to the creation models, which might be detectable as a gap that natural processes could never explain), followed by evolutionary change in form.[19]

The two creationary models simply say God created, without specifying a mechanism. Theologically, this is called primary causation, referring to the direct action of God outside of natural processes, as opposed to secondary causation, where God uses natural processes to accomplish his purposes. Even though the method God used is outside of our normal experience, it would be possible to form a hypothesis of how God could have created. In fact different Hebrew words used in Genesis to describe God's action hint at different possible scientific explanations.

God could have created truly ex nihilo, that is, bringing the very atoms comprising the organisms into existence, already fully connected in the form of whatever was being created. This would supposedly involve somehow displacing the matter already in existence in the place the new creature would fill. This is similar to the meaning of the Hebrew word transliterated *bārā'*, a creative act that only God could do. On the other hand, God could have created matter first, then used the matter present to form new organisms. This is more similar to the Hebrew words *ʿāśāh* and *yāṣar*, the latter used when God formed Adam out of the dust of the earth. In practice, and perhaps in part because all three terms are used in Genesis, neither OEC nor YEC attempt to specify *how* God created. That being the case, it is hard to see how "God created" qualifies as a scientific explanation.

Creation supporters might say that it is a miracle, and therefore it is neither possible nor necessary to provide a scientific mechanism. Yet YEC views the biblical flood as a miracle, and extensive work has been

---

[19]In a book published as this one was in the final revision, Poe & Davis (2012) argue that God could interact with creation in ways that would be undetectable to science through the uncertainty in quantum and chaotic systems.

undertaken to demonstrate a possible method whereby God could have caused a flood of that proportion. Similarly, OEC accepts the big bang as the mechanism God used to create the universe, while YEC has offered an alternate scientific mechanism, white-hole cosmology. Why should the origin of life be any different?

Lacking such a hypothetical mechanism, it would be better for YEC and OEC to admit that they have no scientific explanation of mechanism *for that part* of the process. That does not automatically mean that the whole model is nonscientific. In fact, it places them in exactly the same position as the evolutionary models, which do not have a viable hypothesis for the origin of life either. Supporters of evolution will undoubtedly disagree with that statement, claiming that they have at least the framework of a hypothesis. Nevertheless, I contend that until the gap between monomers and cells is significantly reduced, there is no viable scientific explanation for the beginning of life from a naturalistic perspective, and that "God did it" and "Nature did it" (*Nature* capitalized to show its deification) are equally religious explanations.

There are a number of other questions that YEC in particular needs to address in order to be taken seriously by the broader scientific community.[20] According to modern YEC teaching, essentially all of the fossil-bearing sedimentary rock on earth was laid down during the global flood. Given that pollen is carried worldwide, being found in deep ocean sediment cores and polar ice cores, it seems that it should be found in all of the flood-deposited sediments, even if other fossils were indeed sorted in some way, yet no pollen is found in any rocks before the Mesozoic (age of the dinosaurs). All YEC would need to prove flood geology would be to demonstrate the regular occurrence of even small amounts of pollen in every layer.[21] Similarly, in several places around the

---

[20]YEC feels it has addressed these issues, and answers are given on various YEC websites, but personally I find the answers insufficient or inaccurate. A detailed analysis is not possible here.

[21]YEC groups say pollen has been found in pre-Cambrian rocks (e.g., Emil Silvestru and Carl Wieland, "Pollen paradox," *Creation Ministries*, http://creation.com/pollen-paradox). The usual reference cited is R. M. Stainforth (1966), "Occurrence of pollen and spores in the Roraima Formation of Venezuela and British Guiana," *Nature* 210 (1966): 292-94. This fits in the category of an anomaly, one datum for which there is not a good explanation. But the point is that if all the sediments were laid down in the flood, we would expect pollen to be ubiquitous in just about every sedimentary layer all around the world, as it is in sediments today.

world there is a thin layer containing iridium, soot and shocked quartz at a boundary marking the end of the age of the dinosaurs. Even if larger living things were sorted by the action of the flood, there is currently no explanation of how these microscopic markers could have been laid down in a single layer in so many different places. Also, following the flood, according to YEC, there was rapid plate tectonic movement, followed by an ice age and the migration and speciation of all creatures. All this must have happened within a few thousand years, including all the genetic changes that separate species within kinds, which would require a rate of change even higher than that required by evolution.[22]

To reiterate, science frequently begins with description of a phenomenon but then seeks to move beyond that to determine mechanism and causation. Therefore the lack of such a proposed mechanism for one part of the process does not necessarily disqualify these models from being scientific, but it does point to the direction they must move to remain in contention in the origins debate.

7.4 SEEING THE BIG PICTURE

We live in an age of specialists. Scientists do not have time to read extensively in areas of science outside their specialty, let alone in philosophy or theology. The same could be said for philosophers and theologians, who can become very adept in a certain subfield of their discipline but only dabble in other areas. But the study of origins touches on many areas of science and theology, as well as philosophical questions about the nature of science. Somehow, we have to find a way to work together to get the big picture.

Poles apart. It could be said that NE and YEC are poles apart, and the analogy is fitting. If an observer were to look at the earth from a position in space above the North Pole, he or she would see lots of land, covering almost 50% of the area, with ice-covered ocean in the middle and ocean primarily along one side. The globe would appear to be turning counterclockwise. In contrast, an observer above the South Pole

---

[22]If Noah lived about 1,650 years after a 4000 B.C. creation event, according to traditional YEC chronology, there would be only 350 years between the flood and the beginning of written records in China about 2000 B.C.

would see mostly ocean, with an ice-covered landmass in the center and a little more land around the very edges. The globe would be turning clockwise. If the two were to admit that they each have access to only part of the information, and were willing to share, it would be possible to come up with a fairly complete picture. Unfortunately, in the study of origins, that has not been the case.

There are also observers in intermediate positions, able to see some but not all of the evidence from both hemispheres. These observers too have the option of declaring that their position is the only correct one, that they are able to see everything, or on the other hand admitting the limitations of their perspective and seeking to contribute to the knowledge of the whole.

Certainly this illustration is too simplistic. The primary problem is that it implies that all the evidence is already on the table, visible to one position or another, and that all that is necessary is to put it together. If it were that easy, we might actually be able to do it. The problem is that we are tied to the globe, or maybe flying in a plane, but not high above it, and so our perspective is far more limited than we imagine.[23] We talk to those near us, and thus we get a pretty good picture of the area we inhabit. We may even talk to those in neighboring areas and have some idea of what their sector is like. But communication between one pole and the other is nearly impossible, for various reasons ranging from lack of communications links to use of different language, and many sections of the origins globe remain unexplored or even undiscovered.

Even if the problems of communication links and language were solved, there would still be a fundamental dilemma. The two hemispheres have a different notion of which end of the globe ought to be considered the top, and each is actively lobbying for their position, rather than working together to put the puzzle together first, then deciding based on the finished product which way is up.

Removing the blinders. Our personal philosophies act as blinders,

---

[23]Even if we were to say the observers were at the height of the international space station, the highest semi-permanent human observation point, they would only be able to see about 25° away from the point directly beneath them, about the same as the Arctic or Antarctic circle. What is visible of earth within the polar circles is not representative even of the hemisphere they are in, let alone the whole world.

allowing us to see clearly what is right before our eyes but restricting our vision so that certain evidence or lines of argument are not even visible. These blinders can also cause us to focus on the worst arguments of the opposition rather than the best. Blinders benefit the person controlling a horse, reducing distractions that might make control more difficult in a race or on city streets, but they do not benefit a horse trying to safely negotiate treacherous ground or find a new trail through uncharted and constantly varying terrain. Beyond our philosophical presuppositions, there are other personal and societal blinders we need to be aware of as well.

At a personal level, perhaps it is inevitable that each scientist has an incomplete picture. The problem in origins mirrors that found in science as a whole. Given the great volume of literature in any field, we become selective readers. Groups and individuals that we agree with and have found useful we read more and in more detail. Those we disagree with we skim over quickly, looking for faults in their arguments, points to attack. Our lack of time sets blinders on our reading.

Similarly, we judge other research by what we know and trust. The conflict between viewpoints is not restricted to the area of origins or to topics that have eternal ramifications. In every field of science there are research groups working on the same topic from different perspectives, and in many cases there is some degree of animosity between these groups, each claiming to have a better method. Each group often centers on a key individual who is able to write successful grants, attracting funding and graduate students, and thus produce both large volumes of work and large numbers of supporters in the peer-review process. Continuation of funding for successful ongoing projects from respected institutions is almost automatic. Blind review does not work because there are always enough hints to allow anyone familiar with the field to tell which research group a proposal is from. Funding for innovative projects from young researchers with new ideas that challenge the current paradigm is extremely limited.[24] Our experience sets

---

[24]As one of the reviewers noted, there is funding for innovative research, but this is a very small amount of the total funding, and it still must meet the goals of the funding agency. So I believe my description is accurate.

blinders on the options we are willing to consider.

Science is not the totally objective, dispassionate search for truth that some believe it to be. As a social institution it is directed toward specific goals set by the funding agencies. Much good research is not funded because it does not meet those criteria, and researchers who present results at odds with the viewpoint of the funding institution are not likely to get funded again. Thus it is not surprising that research funded by the current science establishment finds little fault with evolutionary thought, or that research funded by YEC organizations concludes the earth is young. Our funding system sets blinders on our research.

Is there any solution to this problem? We cannot make progress toward resolving this issue as long as we work only with the puzzle pieces in our own hands. The issue is just too large, and no group has all the pieces. But to work together we must examine the *best* evidence, examples and arguments used by the opposition, not the weakest. We must not denounce them based on their model or the underlying worldview, or focus on old arguments they have already abandoned. This requires actually reading what they write rather than looking for points to attack, participating in dialogue rather than debate, looking at the actual evidence, not secondary descriptions of it.[25] It requires more work, but is the only way to reach the desired end.

In every position, there are two tiers of research and writing, the popular level and the research level. The popular level is easy to attack, and often worthy of being debunked. Many of the "Icons of Evolution" (Wells, 2000) found in textbooks were worthy of attack. As mentioned in chapter five, some have been dropped as arguments, dropped out of textbooks, and others deserve to be. On the other hand, creation supporters have also dropped or changed certain arguments, a fact opponents sometimes ignore. But for every position there is another tier. Many Christians who are scientists adhere to an evolutionary position because they have examined evidence too technical for the general public to understand and find it convincing. On the other hand, there is now a generation of Christians who are getting advanced degrees in

---

[25]As another author has said on the same subject, "And maybe the various sides should talk. Not debate—talk" (Ratzsch, 1996: 198).

appropriate fields of science who are seeking to develop scientifically rigorous alternate explanations from a YEC position (Ratzsch, 1996: 82). That they have not succeeded yet is not surprising, given that it has taken one hundred fifty years to develop the evolutionary model to its current state, whereas the modern YEC movement is only about fifty years old. The same could be said for the ID movement (twenty years old) and non-Darwinian models of evolution.

Just as some of the greatest advances in science now are coming from cross-disciplinary studies, bringing together fields that previously had no interaction, so too the greatest advances in origins research will likely come from those willing to take the time and effort to combine the best work from all sides of the debate, and respond thoughtfully to opponents, rather than brushing them off as worthless.

The Definition at
the Heart of the Debate

• • •

Throughout this book our focus has been on the scientific aspect of the
origins debate, but every scientific debate is carried out in a social
context, which cannot be ignored. The definition of science, like any
definition, is a social construct, which changes over time. It is not based
on empirical evidence, and therefore cannot be decided using the
methods of science. Currently, this definition has become a central battleground in the origins debate, by which certain models are excluded
from science education. But just as our judgment of the strength or
weakness of various inferences is affected by our philosophical presuppositions, so is our judgment of the validity of different definitions. In
this chapter, as in the rest of the book, I will try to demonstrate the logic
of each position, to help the reader understand the debate, rather than
arguing for a particular definition.

For at least twenty years, science education standards in the United
States have stressed the importance of teaching the nature of science,
and have specifically linked it with the teaching of origins (AAAS, 1993;
NAS, 1998; NRC, 1996). But those same standards also make it clear that
science is very hard to define. In the first chapter of this book I adopted
Gauch's PEL (presuppositions, evidence, logic) model as a working

definition of science. In subsequent chapters I have shown how six different models of origins make different logical inferences, leading to different interpretations of the same evidence, based on different philosophical presuppositions that are outside the realm of science. It is now time to wrap up the discussion, by showing how the definition of science itself is at the heart of the debate and likewise dictated by our philosophical presuppositions. That being the case, the question becomes, whose definition of science do we use and why?

8.1 WHOSE DEFINITION OF SCIENCE?

Baby boomers were raised in a day when science was viewed as objective truth, based firmly on empirical evidence and therefore absolutely certain, the legacy of Francis Bacon and logical empiricism. Many teachers continue to promote this definition of science, even though both scientists and philosophers of science have gradually accepted that the human and subjective element cannot be eliminated from science and is in fact an integral and important part of it. It takes a long time for social customs to change, unless a revolution (physical or ideological) overthrows the established order. Old ideas, like those who hold them, do not easily cede their influence to the younger generation. But the definition is changing, and we need to understand why.

We will now turn our attention to four deep questions about science, all related to its definition: Is empirical knowledge inherently superior to other knowledge? Is there a universal definition of science? Would it be theoretically possible for science to detect supernatural intervention? Finally, to what degree can either science or our definition of science be objective?

The inadequacy of empiricism. Some, usually atheists speaking from a position of philosophical naturalism, assert science is the only way of knowing, an attitude known as scientism. But scientism quickly runs into a fatal philosophical flaw.

There are many areas of science that appear to give universal, unquestionable results. Laws of physics are the same regardless of who performs the experiment. But even in physics, if the object under study is very large or very small, complex or far away, there is almost always more than one possible interpretation of the data. Whenever there is interpretation, the background knowledge and assumptions of the researcher, including his or her philosophical assumptions, play a role, as is nearly universally recognized by modern philosophers of science.

Even though it is now realized that science is not completely empirical, there are many who claim it is still superior to other types of knowledge because it is based on empirical evidence. Yet this argument itself has a fatal flaw, because the claim that empirical evidence is somehow superior to reasoning is itself a nonempirical statement, with no empirical evidence to back it up. If then this foundational claim is itself nonempirical, the primacy of the empirical is undermined and collapses.[1]

It is impossible to do science without a foundation of underlying philosophical presuppositions. At the root of the origins debate is the question of which presuppositions, which principles, should guide scientific inquiry in our generation, a debate that cannot be settled based on the empirical evidence.

Different definitions of science. If science is not the only way of knowing, it becomes important to come up with a working definition of what distinguishes science from other ways of knowing, even if the demarcation is not absolute. For this book I have adopted Gauch's definition of science as a working definition, but many definitions have been proposed.

Like any other social institution, science is constantly changing, both reflecting and influencing the course of the society, so it is impossible to define prescriptively; science is not the same at every time in every society. While scientists themselves may decide what they consider to be good technique at a particular time in each particular discipline, it is the philosophers and historians of science who have a broader view of what defines science, and what they tell us is that the definition of science is constantly shifting.[2]

Over the course of the twentieth century alone, four different para-

---

[1]Many other authors have cited this same argument and explained it in more depth (e.g., Ratzsch, 1996).

[2]For a good summary of both historical and modern ideas of science, and mistakes both creation and evolution make in talking about the nature of science, see Ratzsch (1996: chap. 8-11) and Ratzsch (2000).

digms of science waxed and waned in popularity: inductivism, hypo-thetico-deductivism, falsificationism and postempiricism (Ratzsch, 1996: chap. 8). All have been shown by philosophers of science to be inadequate, yet components of each are still promoted by one group or another as *the* test of whether something is scientific.

Young-earth creation literature often gives the impression that past events cannot be studied scientifically, that only experimental science is true science.[3] This definition seems to be based on old textbook defini-tions of "the scientific method," which persist in spite of the fact that it has been known for decades that there is no such thing as a universal method followed by all scientists, only general principles of inquiry.[4] In addition to experiment, science frequently utilizes observation, since many phenomena are too large or too small, too slow or too fast, to modify some variable and do a replicated experiment. This includes whole fields of science, including astronomy, meteorology and clima-tology on one end and particle physics and quantum physics on the other, along with fields like epidemiology, where there are moral constraints on experimentation. There are also many historical sciences that study unique past events. It is impossible to say the study of evolution is not science without at the same time cutting off archaeology, whose results are cited by YEC as evidence of the historical veracity of the Bible.

On the other end, evolutionary models often claim that creationary models are not science because they make no testable predictions, are not falsifiable and do not adhere to the principle of methodological naturalism. Both prediction (related to the hypothetico-deductive method) and falsifiability have been shown to be inadequate defini-tions of science (Gauch, 2003: chap. 3), so neither of these are strong arguments. The question of whether science must follow MN, looking

---

[3] YEC supporters may deny this, but it is common in YEC writings to find a distinction between experimental science, which is trusted, and historical, which is not. For example, "However, these teachings are *not* science in the empirical (repeatable, testable) sense. Scientists have only the pres-ent to work with. To connect the present to the past involves interpretations based on unprovable assumptions" (Ham, 2006: 50).

[4] The typical textbook presentation of the scientific method started with asking a question, forming a hypothesis, then doing an experiment to either confirm or reject the hypothesis. While poten-tially useful for school science, it is seriously deficient as a description of how science is actually done.

only for natural explanations for natural phenomena, requires more careful attention.

Evolutionary and creationary positions agree that the proper realm for science is the investigation of the natural world and empirical phenomena, but they disagree on whether supernatural explanations should be automatically excluded. As with most other issues in the debate, it comes from looking at the question from two different perspectives. Three models (NE, NTE, PE) claim that science is the search for *natural causes and explanations of phenomena and empirical data*, whereas the other three (DE, OEC, YEC) claim that science is the search for *causes and explanations of natural phenomena and empirical data*. Notice how much difference the placement of one word makes. The first group, models that accept methodological naturalism, restrict science to the search for natural *explanations*, whereas the models that reject MN extend science to the search for explanations of natural *phenomena*.

The different definitions of science are closely related to the philosophical presuppositions of the two groups. Naturalistic evolution claims that science is the only valid way of knowing because there is no supernatural. Nonteleological and planned evolution, based on a complementary model of knowledge, place a firm divide between science and other ways of knowing: both the evidence and the explanation must lie in the natural realm to qualify as science. Directed evolution and old-earth creation, based on an interacting model of knowledge, reject this firm divide, saying that interactions between the two realms are expected, so science must seek explanations of empirical data, whether those explanations are found in the realm of the natural or the supernatural, or the interaction between the two. Young-earth creation claims that in Scripture God revealed some things about creation that cannot be discovered by science alone. Thus the latter three models claim, as stated by Alvin Plantinga (2006), "If you exclude the supernatural from science, then if the world or some phenomena within it are supernaturally caused—as most of the world's people believe—you won't be able to reach that truth scientifically."[5]

---

[5]This quote is widely cited, usually without proper citation. The journal it was published in is no longer in print, but the article is archived at www.discovery.org/a/3331.

These two definitions of science rest on different philosophical foundations, but is there a way to decide which is a better definition? To answer this question we must revisit our definition of science and the role of presuppositions in science.

Presuppositions and the definition of science. According to Gauch's PEL model, any scientific claim is based on presuppositions, evidence and logic (Gauch, 2003: 128). Importantly, he says that the presuppositions must be drawn from the various hypotheses under consideration, and must be "non-differential regarding the credibilities of the individual hypotheses" (127). He says further, "Too many presuppositions will wed science to one worldview, while divorcing it from others, and thereby obliterate science's objectivity" (113).[6] It is therefore imperative to consider what level of presuppositions is appropriate, to avoid wedding science to a particular philosophical perspective. In particular, is it valid to presuppose that the supernatural does not interact with natural processes?

Scientists are in full agreement that the natural world exists. Moreover, scientists in five of the six models are convinced that something supernatural exists as well. Gauch demonstrates, based on pure logic, that if the natural (N) and supernatural (S) both exist, there could possibly be an interaction between the two (S x N), and if it does exist, it is a valid area of investigation by science because it involves a natural component. He notes, "Consequently, only if there are no interactions between supernatural and natural entities can it be presumed that no observations by scientific methods of natural entities could occur that would have supernatural explanations and worldview import" (Gauch, 2003: 372).

He goes on:

> Furthermore, to preserve science's status as a public institution, its presuppositions must suit a worldview forum that includes all worldviews (except radical skepticism). . . . If the world is as some worldviews would have it, then no traces of supernatural activity will be found in scientific observations. But if the world is as some other worldviews would have it,

---

[6]Gauch does not define *worldview* or separate its cultural and personal elements, as I am doing in this book. In most cases his worldview is equivalent to what I am calling a "personal philosophy."

then some scientific or physical observations that require supernatural explanations are to be expected. And if the world is as still other worldviews would have it, there may be no clear expectation either for or against observable S x N interactions. In any case, the important point from a methodological perspective is that precisely because hypotheses about physical reality interacting or not interacting with nonphysical reality are not among science's (legitimate) presuppositions, such hypotheses retain eligibility to be considered in light of the data if admissible and relevant data can be identified and collected. (2003: 372)

If Gauch is correct, it is an improper use of presuppositions to exclude a hypothesis just because it includes recourse to an interaction between the supernatural and the natural as part of the explanation. On the other hand, it is a valid question to ask whether there is evidence for such an interaction. The three models that favor restricting science to natural explanations think there is no evidence of such an interaction, while the two creationary models think such evidence exists. Directed evolution is split on this issue between those who think God's intervention is detectable scientifically and those who think it is not.

While it is easy to see why NE would want to restrict science to natural causes, since it claims nothing exists apart from the natural world, it is harder for those from a creationary perspective to understand why PE would accept this restriction. Proponents of this model accept that the Son of God took on human form, was raised from the dead and in many cases also affirm other miracles in the Bible, all of which seem to point to events that natural causation cannot explain, places where God did intervene in the course of history after the moment of creation. But PE proponents also make the theological claim that there is a difference between the way God works in redemptive history and the way he works in natural or formative history. They further say that extending the definition of science would play into the hands of scientism, by extending the reach of science, rather than reserving a realm for theology that science cannot encroach on.

Proponents of ID and the creationary models, on the other hand, claim that while it is reasonable for science to continue to search for secondary mechanisms God may have used, Christians should leave open the possibility that there could be times not specifically mentioned in Scripture that God used primary causation. On this basis they seek and claim to have found evidence of God's intervention.

It is important to note again that for both sides the claim of how God works guides scientific study, rather than being a conclusion arising from the data. This raises again the essential question of whether it is ultimately possible to agree on a definition of science that is truly objective with regard to philosophical presuppositions.

The objectivity of science. Gauch claims that science is and should be objective, echoing the claim of major science organizations, that its strength lies in the fact that its claims are nearly independent of philosophical presuppositions, the only exception being radical skepticism, which denies the reality of the natural world. But should science be objective, and is the *definition* of science itself objective? The answer given to these questions again depends on our philosophical presuppositions.

Evolutionary models claim that the strength of the evolutionary interpretation is that the same basic explanation fits the data independent of philosophy, whereas the creation explanation is explicitly tied to one philosophical and theological position. On the other hand, many of those who promote creationary models (YEC, OEC) claim that science, the study of the creation, will reveal not only that there *is* a Creator, but something about the *identity* of that Creator. According to this view, science is *not* objective but will demonstrate the veracity of the Bible and the Christian worldview. A third approach is taken by ID, which basically asserts that S x N interactions are detectable and give indication of design, without revealing the specific identity of the supernatural, which can only be studied by theology.

Thus the question of whether science is objective is closely wedded to theological ideas, as well as philosophical. The models on the left end of the spectrum state science must be objective, giving results largely independent of worldview, because science and religion address separate questions. Many of those on the right end of the spectrum feel it is impossible to do science from an objective perspective, because they believe the study of creation will reveal the Creator, and that the general and special revelation of God cannot be separated into different compartments.

Similarly, the definition of science currently employed by many science and science-teaching organizations says creationary models are not scientific, because they are wedded to a particular religious belief and therefore are not objective. On the other hand, if that same definition excludes a view held by half of the population of America because of their religious beliefs, can it truly be said to be objective?[7] It may be possible for a definition to be independent of religion, in the sense that many different religions could agree on one definition (as long as that definition keeps science and religion in separate compartments), but it is hard to see how there could be any single definition of science that would be independent of philosophical presuppositions, since some draw a firm line between science and religion as distinct ways of knowing, and others do not.

8.2 THE HEART OF THE DEBATE

In the previous section we saw how the very definition of science is at the heart of the origins debate. In this last section we will examine how the origins debate is itself a matter of the heart. We may hear the arguments of different models, but when a conflict arises between the mind and the heart, the heart often wins.[8] While we may have a rational explanation or defense for our beliefs, our personal philosophical and religious choices are largely independent of the scientific evidence, and if we are convinced that those choices are good, we naturally want to pass them on to others.

In addition to our individual philosophical position, there is a dominant worldview in the society, and that worldview has a strong effect on the next generation.[9] Thus the battle of how to define science and teach

---

[7]Note we are talking here about whether a definition of science can be objective with regard to various underlying philosophical presuppositions, not whether a certain model is true, which is a separate issue. Ultimately, only one of the six models can be true, in the sense of being the correct interpretation of what happened. The question here is whether the six can all be called possible *scientific* explanations.

[8]Naturalism, of course, claims that both mind and heart are merely projections invented by the brain.

[9]Dominance of a worldview in society cannot be measured by sheer numbers, but is measured also

origins is a battle for the hearts of the next generation. Even those who argue that science teaching should be neutral with regard to religion differ in how they think that should be accomplished. We will conclude by considering how we should treat our Christian brethren who have a different definition of science and a different understanding of how God created than we do.

The battle for America's youth. Beyond the scientific debate itself, the societal aspect of the origins debate is in large measure a battle for the hearts of the children, a battle about how the topic of origins is taught in the schools, and the definition of science plays a major role in that debate. Many evolution proponents are perfectly willing to allow creation proponents to present their case, as long as it is called a religious argument and not science. But creation proponents insist their model is scientific, based on a different definition, one based on a philosophy that does not draw a strict line between science and religion. As I said in chapter two, it is possible to teach origins without reference to a particular religion, but not without implicit acceptance of one philosophical position. To understand how educational policy got to the current point, we will very briefly review the history of the public debate in America.

Less than one hundred years ago, creation was still taught in the schools, and the teaching of evolution was forbidden. It was not until 1947 that the phrase "separation of church and state" became established in jurisprudence (Everson v. Board of Education, 330 U.S. 1). Prior to World War II, the vast majority of the population agreed with the Christian teaching that God created the world. The manner of creation was not a major societal issue, and textbooks did not usually address the question one way or the other. In the wave of educational reforms instigated by the Cold War, textbooks like the Biological Sciences Curriculum Study (BSCS, inaugurated in 1958), placed evolution in the center of the biology curriculum. Education, once largely a local affair reflecting the values of a relatively homogeneous local community, became increasingly regulated by state and national policies. With increasing restrictions of the role of the church in education, a state law

---

by the power and influence of those who hold different worldviews.

prohibiting the teaching of human evolution was declared invalid in 1968. An important part of this ruling was a definition of science that restricted science to natural explanations (Epperson v. Arkansas, 393 U.S. 97).[10]

But what is decided in the courts does not control public opinion, and often a large proportion of the people, even a majority, will not agree with the decision of the court.[11] In response to the increasing secularization of education and promotion of evolution, the publication of *The Genesis Flood* in 1961 became a rallying point for many conservative churches and initiated the modern YEC movement. The battle lines of the current conflict began to be drawn.

With the new curriculum, theistic evolutionists had to decide where their loyalties lay, with other evolutionists or with their ecclesiastical brethren. Since the question dealt with science education, they cast their lot with the scientific interpretation they favored. On the other side of the conflict for many years was the creation alliance. There has always been a somewhat tenuous alliance between young-earth and old-earth creation positions. While the two are allied against evolution, the fact that they adhere to different interpretations relative to dating has limited their cooperation. More recently, a new alliance has formed under the banner of ID. While similar to the creation alliance in its opposition to Darwinian evolution and the current definition of science, this is a more centrist alliance and has not won the support of the majority of the creation block, the YEC supporters.

The strength of the evolutionary alliance is that according to their definition, science can be done independent of religious beliefs. The strength of the ID alliance is that because they refuse to endorse any particular model, it is currently the only forum where Christians from evolutionary, old-earth creation and young-earth creation perspectives can all discuss their interpretations freely.

---

[10]The definition of science used, frequently cited in subsequent court cases, was based on testimony by Michael Ruse that for a theory to be scientific it must be (1) guided by natural law, (2) explanatory by natural law, (3) testable against the empirical world, (4) tentative in its conclusions, and (5) falsifiable. Scholars from many fields have subsequently challenged various aspects of this definition, but it has not been replaced in jurisprudence.

[11]Particularly where the decision turns on a definition, as in the definition of "sexual activity" in the trial of President Clinton, or the definition of punch types and valid votes in the reelection of President Bush.

As public policy changed, so did the burden of proof. At the Scopes trial in 1925 the burden of proof was on the evolutionists to show that there was merit to their case, and on the atheists to show that there was no God. Since then the influence of religion on society has ebbed, society has become more diverse, and now the burden of proof is on the theist to prove that God exists, that there is a Creator or that there are problems with evolution.

It is inevitable that the burden of proof must rest on one party. Many court cases are decided on circumstantial evidence, evidence that can be interpreted in different ways, and a decision must be made ahead of time which way the case will go if it ends up deadlocked. The fact that a person is released if the charges against him or her cannot be proven by the prosecution does not mean that the evidence has proven this person innocent. It means that society has determined, apart from the evidence, that it is better to allow a guilty person to go free than to place an innocent person behind bars. Similarly, the fact that creation, at the moment, cannot prove its case against evolution, and so evolution walks free in the land, does not mean that evolution is without fault. The case is deadlocked, the jury divided along ideological lines, but society has determined that something must be taught in the schools about origins, and it currently feels that it is better to teach a model that is neutral toward the idea of God than one that requires the existence of God.

We might dream of a perfect world where there was no burden of proof. If everyone, including the defendant, told the whole truth every time, trials would be very short and outcomes always just. Yet in spite of the oath, it is quite obvious that people seek their own interest in the outcome of a trial, and even if they tell nothing but the truth, it may not always be the whole truth. This situation as well is mirrored in trials about how to teach origins, with each side seeking to win the case, rather than admitting the areas of strength and weakness in their argument.[12] There is too much at risk; the right to influence the next generation, the desire to promote a particular ideology, a particular philosophy, may trump the desire for full disclosure, especially when they firmly believe

---

[12]Whether this happens as well in scientific debate is a separate issue.

they know the truth, the proper interpretation of the evidence.

Leveling the playing field. Switching to another analogy, sportsmanship requires that all teams be allowed to play on a level field. But in debates about origins those with the home field advantage often emerge the apparent victor. In large part this is because the home field defines what definitions are accepted by the majority of the audience. Since the time of Darwin, the playing field has been tipped, first one way, then the other. When the weight was on the two ends, this was nearly inevitable, with each side trying to tip the field in its favor. But as time has gone on, positions toward the middle of the spectrum have become more vocal, and some are now trying to level the playing field, although they still differ on the best way to do that.

In the spring of 2010 a debate was held at Wheaton College between Stephen Barr and Michael Behe on whether ID should be taught as science. Barr, a physicist, holds a position that would be classified as PE in the framework of this book. Behe, a biochemist and advocate of intelligent design, would fit within the DE model. Although the two hold adjacent positions in the middle of the spectrum, their different philosophical commitments ensured they would not see eye to eye. In the end, as often happens in a debate, it seemed that the two largely talked past each other, trying to convince the audience without addressing the root issue separating them.

Both in essence promoted a level playing field, but Barr said this should be done by removing philosophy from science, while Behe supported allowing different philosophies equal access. According to Barr, since ID is philosophy, not science, it should not be taught as science, but by the same token, atheism is also a philosophy, and should be banned from science education. Behe took the other approach, saying that since philosophical naturalism is effectively promoted in many science textbooks, ID should be allowed to present its case as well.

The underlying question neither debater addressed directly is whether science can be done and taught without implicit acceptance and promotion of some philosophy. The central goal of the ID movement is promotion of a philosophy of science at odds with the currently reigning paradigm of science, challenging the way science is currently defined (which is not the same as challenging the way science is actually practiced on a day-to-day basis). Those who oppose it often implicitly recognize this fact, by saying ID is not science. While it is true that ID is not science as science is currently defined by the evolutionary alliance, that does not address the main underlying question—is it possible to do science from a different philosophical framework? It is certainly not possible to do science without reference to an underlying, often implicit, philosophical framework.

What can we conclude? As we reach the conclusion of this book, what can we conclude? For each of us, there are things we take to be self-evident truths that are neither self-evident nor considered truths by others. We each believe things to be true that are neither contrary to the evidence, nor determined by it. This is the case for theists and nontheists alike, and for all varieties of Christian belief. How then should we act toward those who hold different interpretations of both the documentary evidence of Scripture and the empirical evidence of science?

In the final analysis all of us believe in something we cannot see or evaluate scientifically. Atheists accept an infinite eternal multiverse for which there is no scientific evidence, in the same way that theists accept an infinite eternal God. Many scientists believe in things that cannot be seen or detected, because theory and the available evidence require it. One prime example is dark matter. No one has ever seen dark matter or detected it with any scientific instrument, but most scientists believe it exists. There is not enough matter in galaxies to explain their apparent gravitational attraction, measured by their shapes or ability to bend beams of light.[13] Dark matter has been proposed to supply the additional mass, which is not an insignificant amount. Current estimates say that there should be five times as much dark matter as there is normal matter, of which everything we see is made. This is not so different from the fact that Christians believe in God, although no one has ever seen him. We are convinced that the evidence we have seen in our own lives, as well as the historical evidence of Jesus Christ, are sufficient to demonstrate that he exists.

---

[13]This ability was predicted by relativity and is seen as strong evidence for that theory.

Vern Poythress states an idea that others have traced back to the church fathers,

> In the case of apparent discrepancies between the Bible and science, we must therefore be ready to reexamine both our thinking about the Bible and our thinking about science. . . . But the Bible is always right, and should be trusted on that account. Likewise, God's word concerning providence is always right and trustworthy. But modern science, as a human interpretation of God's providence, may make mistakes. Our interpretation of providence may need revision. And our interpretation of the Bible may need revision. (2006: 43-44)

The problem is that each of the six models of origins presented here is intimately wedded to a certain theological interpretation of Scripture, so the model and the theology rise or fall together. Since we each have a faith commitment to a certain theology, we also have a faith commitment to a corresponding model. To change our model we also need to change our theology and admit that what we believed is incorrect. This is something few are willing to do, and so the conflict will continue.

There is a war going on, but it is not a war between science and religion. Rather, it is a war about what science is, a war that is philosophical more than religious, although the different camps tend to line up along religious lines as well, and sometimes state their arguments in religious terms. Hopefully this book has helped you understand what the various positions are and why their ideas are mutually irreconcilable and thus will continue to be at war. The debate centers on two ultimate questions: is there a God, and if so how does he interact with his creation? Pursuant to that is the question of whether knowledge questions can be clearly divided into empirical and nonempirical domains, with no overlap and no interaction, or whether the two are inseparable, or whether knowledge from one trumps the other.

On these questions rest the eternal debate that has been with us for centuries and will continue to be for the rest of the history of humankind, in varying guises, the debate about how we got here, and thus our relation to the Creator and the rest of creation. It is not a black and white question, but one with many fine shadings of hue that appear differently when viewed from different perspectives. I have attempted to map out the various positions in a way that will promote mutual understanding and thus honest communication about the underlying issues with less animosity.

Wars are costly and take resources away from other things the time and money and lives could be better spent on, whether those wars are for control of physical territory or the hearts and minds of the next generation. Unfortunately, they seem to be inevitable, a result of our sinful hubris that leads us to believe that we are right and others are wrong, rather than admitting that the truth is beyond our ability to grasp. Doubtless in the end the whole truth will prove far more complex than we can conceive at the moment, in the same way that what we know of genetics and inheritance today was totally unimaginable a century ago. In the face of that knowledge, let us strive for humility and charity in our dealings with our brothers and sisters (and even those we do not consider family) who hold a different understanding of the issue than we do, realizing that we all see as "through a glass, darkly" (1 Cor 13:12 KJV) until we see face to face.

Epilogue

• • •

It is impossible for anyone to write from a totally objective position. An author will always leave clues about his or her own position. From the choice of words to the order of topics to the underlying philosophy, the clues are there for all to read if they can.

So where do I stand? I will only say that as far as I know, no one has yet written a comprehensive justification of the model I support, from a theological and scientific perspective. Perhaps now that this book is done, I can consider attempting that.

At the beginning of the book I said I would not try to convince anyone to change his or her position. That is because I believe the literature on conceptual change. There is a substantial body of literature on this subject, including a seminal article written by Kenneth Strike and George Posner in 1992.[1] As stated therein, there is substantial agreement that for conceptual change to take place, four factors must be present:

1. There must be dissatisfaction with current conceptions.

2. A new conception must be intelligible.

3. A new conception must appear initially plausible.

4. A new conception should suggest the possibility of a fruitful research program.

---

[1] K. A. Strike & G. J. Posner (1992), "A revisionist theory of conceptual change," in *Cognitive models of science*, ed. R. N. Giere (Minneapolis: University of Minnesota Press), pp. 147-76.

Most people are not dissatisfied with their current conception, and therefore any attempt by others to change their mind is doomed to failure. On the other hand, if for whatever reason you are dissatisfied with what you formerly heard and believed, I hope I have helped you understand the logic, plausibility and potential of other models, and provided enough references to allow you to take the next step, to begin to see the world from a wider, and perhaps eventually different, perspective.

Appendix 1

Tables Comparing
Six Models of Origins

. . .

Table A1.1. Six Models of Origins

Names

Used in this book	Naturalistic Evolution (NE)	Nonteleological Evolution (NTE)	Planned Evolution (PE)	Directed Evolution (DE)	Old-Earth Creation (OEC)	Young-Earth Creation (YEC)
General	materialistic evolution	theistic evolution	theistic evolution	theistic evolution	progressive creation	recent creation
Used by proponents (submodels)	modern synthesis, punctuated equilibrium		evolutionary creation		day-age creation, gap model	scientific creation
Used by opponents[1]	Darwinism	Darwinism, deistic evolution			creationism	creationism
Basic Propositions						
Scientific process	random, spontaneous natural processes	universe created, then undirected natural processes	universe created perfectly, no subsequent intervention	intervention by direction of natural processes	major body plans created separately	each kind created separately
Interpretation of Genesis account	ancient myth, no God	ancient myth, God exists	nonconcordist,[2] Adam and Eve not individuals	nonconcordist, Adam and Eve are individuals	concordist, days extended	concordist, days literal

[1]This highlights the dichotomy in the public debate. The two middle positions are more recent (both popularized since 1995). Each has been classified by opponents with the extremes (Darwinism or creationism), but there are significant differences, as shown by comparing the following distinguishing features.

[2]See appendix 2 for a comparison of concordist and nonconcordist positions. Interpretations of Adam and Eve tend to follow this pattern, but there are exceptions.

Distinguishing Features

Theology?	no supernatural	Creator	Creator	Creator	Creator	Creator
Teleology?	no purpose	no purpose	purpose	purpose	purpose	purpose
Intervention?	no intervention	no intervention	no intervention	intervention	intervention	intervention
Genealogy?	common descent	common descent	common descent	common descent	de novo creation	de novo creation
Cosmology?	old universe	old universe	old universe	old universe	old universe	recent creation

Underlying Philosophy

Theology	atheistic, agnostic[3]	monotheistic, deistic, other[4]	monotheistic	monotheistic	monotheistic	monotheistic, other
Relationship between science and religion[5]	overlapping or complementary domains:[6] religion inferior	complementary domains: equal	complementary domains: each superior in its area	interacting domains: each superior in its area	interacting domains: equal	overlapping or interacting domains:[7] religion superior
Methodology of science	naturalism: only natural causes	methodological naturalism: only natural causes	methodological naturalism: only natural causes	open inquiry: best natural or supernatural cause	open inquiry: best natural or supernatural cause	imperfect inquiry: secondary to perfect revelation

[3]Many adherents of NE are secular humanists, an atheistic religion that is essentially existentialist.

[4]Traditional polytheistic religions rarely try to harmonize their creation story with science. Thus they effectively mirror NTE or YEC positions: either the two represent different realms, answering different questions (as NTE) or the religious teaching is held to be correct based on its inherent merit (as YEC). Many other religions, including Eastern pantheism and New Age, reach the same conclusions but for a different reason, contending that the physical is illusory. Since they do not normally attempt to explain the scientific evidence in light of their religious beliefs, they are not part of the debate and thus are not included here, but logically would present arguments mirroring one of these two positions.

[5]Overlapping means the whole truth can be known by either empirical (scientific) or nonempirical (religious) methods. If this is the case, one must provide a better explanation, eclipsing the other. Diagrammatically, this could be shown as the overlap of two full circles. Complementary means that each tells us about something different, using different methodologies to answer different questions; the perceived relative importance of each differs among models. Diagrammatically, this could be shown as two half circles. Interacting means that although each is primarily responsible for one area, the other still has something important to contribute to that area. Diagrammatically, this could be illustrated by a symbol shaped like the yin/yang.

[6]Overlapping = atheism; complementary = agnosticism.

[7]Overlapping = do not support ID; interacting = support ID.

Table A1.2. Origin of the Universe

	Naturalistic Evolution (NE)	Nonteleological Evolution (NTE)	Planned Evolution (PE)	Directed Evolution (DE)	Old-Earth Creation (OEC)	Young-Earth Creation (YEC)
Explanation	apparent beginning	in the beginning				apparent age
Mechanism	big bang, multiple universes	big bang, singularity as moment of creation				white hole, direct creation of components
Contention	conditions and physical constants are suitable for development of life by chance	conditions and physical constants were established at values suitable for development of life				universe was created essentially as it is now, with apparent age
Changing Universe						
Evidence	red shift	light from distant galaxies is shifted toward the red end of the spectrum				
Interpretations	expanding universe					apparent age
Evidence	cosmic microwave background radiation (CMBR)	background temperature of intergalactic space fits predictions based on cooling rate				
Interpretations	universe ~13.8b years old					apparent age
Evidence	relative abundance of light elements and isotopes (H, H-2, He, Li)	ratios are as predicted by big bang and stellar nucleosynthesis theories				
Interpretations	rapid cooling after big bang due to expansion of universe					created as is

Evidence	agreement with theory predictions based on big bang theory have been confirmed observationally		
Interpretations	big bang model is best explanation of observed values		created as is
Fine-Tuned Universe			
Evidence	physical constants perfectly balanced if constants were slightly different, elements and galaxies would not exist		
Interpretations	chance	created perfectly for life to develop	created as is
Evidence	universe ideal for life if conditions were slightly different, universe would not support chemistry necessary for life		
Interpretations	chance	created perfectly for life to develop	created as is
Evidence	solar system ideal for advanced life if conditions were slightly different, earth could not sustain life		
Interpretations	chance	created perfectly for life to develop	created as is

Table A1.3. Origin of Life

	Naturalistic Evolution (NE)	Nonteleological Evolution (NTE)	Planned Evolution (PE)	Directed Evolution (DE)	Old-Earth Creation (OEC)	Young-Earth Creation (YEC)
Explanation	inevitability			purposeful direction	immediate appearance	
Mechanism	natural law-like processes in combination with random occurrences and selection			direction of low probability events	direct creation of complete organisms	
Contention	no supernatural intervention after creation			agents create by assembly	systems are too complex to have been developed stepwise	
Life from Nonlife						
Evidence	organic precursors	can be formed from inorganics in the lab, under highly constrained conditions that differ for each molecule				
Interpretations	conditions could have occurred				conditions carefully designed and controlled	
Evidence	random reactions	in the absence of a living system, reactions yield random products, racemic mixtures				
Interpretations	some unknown mechanism determined or selected			order does not naturally arise from disorder		
Evidence	coacervates; simple bubbles of lipid can enclose organics					
Interpretations	could have protected and facilitated reactions			very different from cell membrane		
Evidence	cells; simplest cells are extremely complex					
Interpretations	stepwise process will be found			directed	too complex for stepwise process	

Information			
Evidence	nearly universal and ideal code the genetic code is nearly universal, efficient, and minimizes errors in translation		
Interpretations	selected by prebiotic evolution, common descent	planned	common design
Evidence	independence of carrier origin of random DNA is not the same as DNA that carries information to code for cell products and functions		
Interpretations	effective messages selected by pre-biotic evolution	constructed	created as part of functional cell
Evidence	specified complexity in everyday experience, information both complex and specific is associated with intelligence		
Interpretations	useful DNA sequences selected, modified naturally	best explained by intelligent agent	
Evidence	irreducible complexity if any part from many molecular systems are removed, they would not work at all		
Interpretations	exaptation and spandrels modify simpler systems	directed	too complex for stepwise process

Table A1.4. Origin of Species

	Naturalistic Evolution (NE)	Nonteleological Evolution (NTE)	Planned Evolution (PE)	Directed Evolution (DE)	Old-Earth Creation (OEC)	Young-Earth Creation (YEC)
Explanation	neo-Darwinian synthesis			non-Darwinian evolution[1]	creation	
Mechanism	natural selection acting on random mutations, in conjunction with random events, reproductive isolation and other natural mechanisms			direction of low probability processes	direct creation of body plans (phyla)	direct creation of kinds (genera or families)
Contention	speciation is gradual, with continuity of all life forms			agents modify teleologically	periods of creative activity	creation week
Fossils						
Evidence	sorting different types of fossils found in each layer, with index fossils in the same relative sequence					
Interpretations	appearance and extinction of species over long time periods					global flood
Evidence	dating rocks lower in a stratigraphic column are usually radiometrically older than rocks above them					
Interpretations	superposition and other natural processes					inaccurate
Evidence	stasis and saltation species appear and disappear abruptly, remaining unchanged for long periods, few intermediate at higher taxa					
Interpretations	incomplete record, relatively rapid change				creative periods	global flood
Evidence	extinctions and explosions several times, almost the entire biota present in one layer is replaced by a totally different one in the next					
Interpretations	mass extinctions followed by adaptive radiation to new niches				creative periods	global flood

[1]A small minority of scientists within NE, NTE and PE also favor a non-Darwinian evolutionary model. Their arguments for the degree of involvement of God would differ from the ones shown for DE, although the scientific mechanism would be similar (see chap. 5).

Evidence	geographical distribution mammals are continent specific, but most earlier fossils are not		
Interpretations	plate tectonics separated, allopatric speciation		separate creations, rarely discussed
Genetics			
Evidence	selection selection within a population has its limits, and stabilizing dominates in stable environments		
Interpretations	gradual changes in new environments	additional mechanisms needed	
Evidence	population genetics gene frequencies change slowly in populations in absence of strong selection pressure		
Interpretations	many generations or strong selection	directed	microevolution
Evidence	mutations most mutations have small effects or are deleterious		
Interpretations	rare advantageous selected	teleological	mutations neutral or deleterious
Evidence	homeotic genes genes similar between species direct overall development		
Interpretations	similar by descent, lead to rapid changes in organism	teleological	similar by design
Evidence	genome complexity many closely related species cannot interbreed due to differences in chromosome number or structure		
Interpretations	isolating mechanism	directed	created with differences

Table A1.4. Origin of Species (continued)

	Naturalistic Evolution (NE)	Nonteleological Evolution (NTE)	Planned Evolution (PE)	Directed Evolution (DE)	Old-Earth Creation (OEC)	Young-Earth Creation (YEC)
Similarities						
Evidence	embryological	similar forms can arise from different processes, or dissimilar forms from similar processes				
Interpretations	common descent, with variation				created differently	
Evidence	vestigial structures	many structures once thought to be vestigial have been shown to have function				
Interpretations	formation and reabsorption of primordia shows common descent				all created with function	
Evidence	noncoding DNA	much DNA once thought to be junk has been shown to have a function				
Interpretations	common descent transmits nonfunctional			function will be found for most if not all		
Evidence	gene order	similar genes are in a similar order on the chromosomes across a broad range of species				
Interpretations	common descent transmits same order			both	functional purpose	
Evidence	molecular sequences	differences in DNA sequence can be mapped into trees, but trees are not the same for each gene				
Interpretations	patterns are similar, differences will be resolved			directed	similar by design	
Evidence	symbiosis	mitochondria and chloroplasts contain DNA and are structurally similar to prokaryotes				
Interpretations	endosymbiosis				similar by design	

Table A1.5. Origin of Humans

	Naturalistic Evolution (NE)	Nonteleological Evolution (NTE)	Planned Evolution (PE)	Directed Evolution (DE)	Old-Earth Creation (OEC)	Young-Earth Creation (YEC)
Explanation	sentient animal	special animal		special purpose	special creation	
Mechanism	undirected evolution of human form and brain	universe created so sentience was inevitable result of evolution, group became human gradually		direction of form, impartation of spirit	separate de novo creation of human form and spirit at the same time	
Contention	mind is only a projection of the brain, there is no separate soul	sentience allows for development of moral capacity, an essential component of the image of god; interpretations of soul vary		first progenitors given spirit	Adam and Eve were two individuals created in the image of god, body and spirit at the same time	

Hominoids, Hominids or Hominins

	Naturalistic Evolution (NE)	Nonteleological Evolution (NTE)	Planned Evolution (PE)	Directed Evolution (DE)	Old-Earth Creation (OEC)	Young-Earth Creation (YEC)
Evidence	fossils					
	fossils exist that have some ape-like and some human-like traits, with intermediate brain size					
Interpretations	at least some of the fossils are human ancestors, linked evolutionarily				fossils are either apes or human	
Evidence	artifacts					
	artifacts have been dated as old as 2.5 million years, with the earliest *Homo* fossils, changing over time					
Interpretations	gradual development of use of tools, rapid change with modern humans				*Homo* human	dates inaccurate

	Naturalistic Evolution (NE)	Nontelelogical Evolution (NTE)	Planned Evolution (PE)	Directed Evolution (DE)	Old-Earth Creation (OEC)	Young-Earth Creation (YEC)
Chimps Versus Humans						
Evidence	chromosome 2 one human chromosome appears to be a fusion of two ape chromosomes					
Interpretations	evidence of common descent				similar by common design	
Evidence	DNA sequence 35 million nucleotide substitutions (1.23%), 5 million indels (10% difference in genome size)					
Interpretations	stress similarity (highlighting percent substitutions)			stress differences (highlighting numbers)		
Evidence	molecular clock differences in polymorphisms can be analyzed to give dates of separation of lineages, minimum population size					
Interpretations	accept inferred dates and population sizes as accurate			varied	question assumptions of method	

Table A1.6. Modern Proponents of Each Model

	Naturalistic Evolution (NE)	Nonteleological Evolution (NTE)	Planned Evolution (PE)	Directed Evolution (DE)	Old-Earth Creation (OEC)	Young-Earth Creation (YEC)	
Authors[1]	Dawkins Dennett Gould Mayr Scott Wilson	Barbour de Duve Haught	Collins Falk Lamoureux Miller Van Till	Behe Haarsma Schaefer	Kenyon Meyer Newman Ross	Austin Bergman Brown Ham Humphreys Morris	Nelson Oard Reynolds Sanford Sarfati Wise
Organizations[2]	Berkeley ENSI NCSE TalkOrigins		BioLogos		RTB	AIG CMI CRS ICR	

	Intelligent Design (ID)[3]	
Multiple-Model Position		
Authors	Dembski Johnson O'Leary Wells Woodward	
Organizations	ARN DICSC IDN ISCID	

[1]This list is by no means complete, but will serve as a starting place to identify some of the more prolific or better-known authors.

[2]Organizations: NE: Understanding Evolution (Berkeley), Evolution and the Nature of Science Institutes, National Center for Science Education, Talk Origins Archive; PE: BioLogos Institute; OEC: Reasons to Believe; YEC: Answers in Genesis, Creation Ministries International, Creation Research Society, Institute for Creation Research; ID: Discovery Institute Center for Science and Culture, Intelligent Design Network, Access Research Network, International Society for Complexity Information and Design.

[3]These authors promote intelligent design, which is compatible with any of the last three models, rather than a specific scientific model. Some authors who do take a position on a particular model (Behe, Kenyon, Meyer) also support ID. Not all those in either DE or YEC would support ID. See chap. 2, sec. 2.2.4 for further explanation.

Comparison of Various Interpretations of Genesis 1

• • •

SYMBOLIC (HELD BY EVOLUTIONARY MODELS NE AND NTE)

Basic idea: The story overall is largely symbolic.

Variations:

1. Religious only. The Bible only teaches religious truths, with no relation to science.
2. Revelatory day. God gave the revelation to the writer of Genesis on six different days. (Now rare)[1]

NONCONCORDIST (HELD BY EVOLUTIONARY MODELS DE AND PE)

Basic idea: The days are not sequential, but tell us something about God's relation to the world.

Variations:

1. Framework (Lamoureux, 2008). In the beginning, the earth was formless and void, so God gave form and filled the void. The framework tells us what happened, but nothing about the length or order of the creative acts.

---

[1]For more information on and evaluation of each of these various interpretations, see Poythress (2006), who claims the basic categories have changed little for over fifty years.

Forming	Filling
1. Separated light and dark	4. Populated light and dark (sun and moon/stars)
2. Separated water and sky[a]	5. Populated water and sky (fish and birds)
3. Separated land (from water)	6. Populated land (animals and humans)

[a]Two words in this passage are very difficult to translate into English. The first, the space created between the waters, is variously translated "firmament," "expanse," "vault" and "space." This space is then called either "sky" or "heaven." There is no good single English word to convey the meanings of either Hebrew word.

2. Analogical day (Poythress, 2006). God creates for six days and rests for one, analogous to our six days of work and one of rest.

3. Cosmic temple (Walton, 2009). God establishes the whole earth as his temple and takes up his residence there on day seven, similar to stories of the establishment of the temple in other ancient literature. Thus he gives creation function, rather than creating the form.[2]

CONCORDIST (HELD BY CREATION MODELS YEC AND OEC)

Basic idea: God created the world in six successive days.

Day	1	2	3	4	5	6
Created	dark light	water sky	land plants	sun moon stars	fish birds	animals humans

Variations:

1. Gap (OEC): There is a gap between the original creation in Genesis 1:1 and the recreation of the world in six days after it "became" without form and void in Genesis 1:2. Fossils are part of the old creation. (Now rare)

2. Intermittent day (OEC): Each day of creation was twenty-four hours long, but separated by long periods in which there was no creative work. (Now rare)

---

[2]These interpretations would be logically compatible with *de novo* creation over a long period of time, but since they do not require or expect the order things were created in to follow the order specified in Genesis, they are not compatible with current OEC models. Similarly, each of the three nonconcordist models is logically compatible with various views of Adam, including continuity or discontinuity with other life at both a biological and spiritual level, so there will be various opinions about this among proponents of any one of these interpretations of Genesis.

3. Progressive or day-age creation (OEC): Each day was a long period of time. The luminaries were created in day one but only became visible in day four, perhaps due to clearing of the atmosphere.

4. Twenty-four-hour day (YEC): each day was twenty-four hours long. This is usually connected in modern YEC with flood geology (fossil bearing strata were laid down in the global flood) and mature creation (apparent age).[3]

---

[3]OEC views are sometimes called "outside in" because evidence outside the Bible is used to guide our interpretation of what is in the Bible. YEC, in contrast, is called "inside out," because what is in the Bible is taken as the starting point, and external (scientific) evidence interpreted based on that (Walton, personal communication).

Glossary

• • •

The brief definitions below express the way these terms are used in this book. They may not reflect the way they are used in other fields of study.

abiogenesis. The origin of life from nonliving matter.

agnosticism. A system of belief characterized by the proposition that ultimate reality, including the existence of a deity, is unknown and probably unknowable.

allele. One form of a gene; different alleles arise from changes in the DNA, which may result in changes in the gene products formed.

Alu element. A type of transposable element only found in primates, the most common mobile genetic element in the human genome.

analogy. Similar traits that are thought not to be the result of descent from a common ancestor, such as the streamlined shape of many water-dwelling animals.

anthropic principle. The proposition that since sentient beings exist, the universe must have suitable conditions for our existence, therefore it is unremarkable that it in fact does have those properties.

atheism. A system of belief characterized by the proposition that there is no deity and therefore no Creator.

autotroph. An organism that can produce its own energy source from inorganic components, often by photosynthesis.

base pair. A pair of chemical rings that bond together to form the "rungs" of the "ladder" of DNA, either A:T or C:G, the order of which determines the order of amino acids in a protein produced from that section of DNA, according to the genetic code; the number of base pairs is used to designate how long a section of DNA is, for example there are approximately three billion base pairs in the human genome.

big bang. A model of expansion of the universe in which the universe expands from an initial singularity, implying it had a starting point; the currently dominant cosmological model.

Cambrian explosion. A relatively brief period of geological time during which the majority of animal phyla appear in the fossil record.

catastrophism. The proposition that at certain times in the history of earth major cataclysmic events have rapidly changed the ecosystem, whether an asteroid strike or a global flood.

centromere. The middle part of a chromosome, where replicated copies of chromosomes are held together until they separate into two daughter cells during cell division.

coacervate. A bubble of lipid (fat-related) molecules that forms in water, sometimes enclosing a small amount of water or other chemicals inside.

common descent. The proposition that organisms descended with change from a common ancestor, a central tenet of both neo-Darwinian and non-Darwinian evolution.

complementary (domains of knowledge). The philosophical proposition that empirical and nonempirical ways of knowing answer different questions, with no overlap. *See* interacting; overlapping.

concordist. A framework for biblical interpretation based on God revealing the order of events of creation in the book of Genesis. *See* appendix two.

convergence. The process of producing analogous traits in different evolutionary lines as a result of similar selection pressure.

copy number variation. Variation in the number of times a recognizable sequence of DNA is present in different organisms of the same or closely related species.

cosmic microwave background radiation (CMBR). The observation that in spaces between stars there is radiation of a particular wavelength, in the microwave region of the spectrum.

cosmology. The study of the origin and structure of the universe.

creationary. A collective term for models (OEC, YEC) that propose limited common descent from a large number of kinds that were separately created. *See* evolutionary.

dark energy. A theoretical entity required by big bang cosmology to explain the rate of expansion of the universe, a force countering the effect of gravity.

dark matter. A theoretical entity that cannot be detected because it interacts so weakly with normal matter and energy; required by current theory to explain why the apparent gravitational attraction of galaxies far exceeds what would be expected by the amount of matter visible.

deism. A system of belief characterized by the proposition that the Creator has no goal for the universe and does not interact with the universe after creation.

deletion. The removal of one or more base pairs from a DNA sequence.

directed evolution (DE). A model of origins based on the premise that the Creator continues to be active, working primarily through secondary causes to bring about his goals.

DNA. Deoxyribonucleic acid, the double stranded helical molecule that is responsible for heritable characteristics, either as a result of the genetic content of the DNA or the epigenetic elements associated with it.

documentary evidence. Something recorded in texts, either historical or religious, that documents what others observed or thought.

domain. (1) A sequence of amino acids with a particular function, such as binding to another molecule or holding a protein in a particular orientation in a membrane; each exon often produces one domain, with different domains connected to form the final protein. (2) A taxonomic unit larger than kingdom; currently three domains are widely recognized, archaea, eubacteria and eukarya, the first two being prokaryotes, the latter including all eukaryotes.

empirical evidence. Something that can be observed by our five senses, with or without assistance of a tool to extend or quantify our senses.

endosymbiosis. The proposition that eukaryotic mitochondria and chloroplasts are the result of prokaryotes once living in symbiotic relationship with a host cell that gradually became more and more interdependent until neither could live independently.

enzyme. A protein that facilitates chemical reactions, increasing reaction rate by decreasing the amount of energy necessary to start the reaction.

epigenetics. Heritable changes resulting from changes to a chromosome that do not change the DNA sequence; for example, binding various molecules to the DNA, different packing density or position within the nucleus.

eukaryote. An organism with a membrane-enclosed nucleus and other intracellular structures; includes plants, animals and fungi.

evidence. Something that gives an indication whether a proposition is true or false. *See* empirical evidence, documentary evidence.

evo-devo. Evolutionary developmental biology, which studies developmental processes with the goal of elucidating possible mechanisms for evolution based on changes in embryonic development.

evolutionary. A collective term for models (NE, NTE, PE, DE) that propose common descent of all living things from one or a few ancestors. *See* creationary.

exon. A section of DNA that codes for part of a protein; exons within a gene may be separated by introns.

experimental science. Study of a repeatable phenomenon by manipulating a variable to determine its effect, while holding other conditions constant; includes prototypical laboratory science, but is also used in field settings.

extrapolate. To extend or project results outside the range of available data, an inherently risky procedure.

falsificationism. A philosophical position based on the proposition that a theory cannot be considered scientific unless it is potentially falsifiable based on empirical data, associated with Karl Popper.

family. The level of taxonomic classification above genus. Members of one family often have recognizable similarities, but with various sizes and forms, for example the cat family.

gene expression. A measure of gene activity that can be turned on and off by a combination of epigenetic marks and regulatory molecules.

gene. Originally, a section of the DNA that codes for one protein; now, a recognizable DNA sequence in a definite location on the chromosome, with a particular function.

genetic code. The correspondence between three bases (a triplet) in the messenger RNA and the amino acid they code for, nearly universal across all species.

genome. The complete genetic information of a species, as contained in the DNA of one set of chromosomes.

genus (pl. genera). The level of taxonomic classification just above species. Members of one genus may not normally mate due to geographical isolation or differences in appearance, mating time or mating rituals, but often can produce fertile offspring if forced to mate.

germ-line cell. A cell in the reproductive organs destined to produce egg or sperm (gametes).

gradualism. One of the basic propositions of neo-Darwinism, that changes in species are the result of the accumulation of many small mutations, and therefore change from one species to another should be gradual.

heterochromatin. Sections of chromosomes that remain tightly coiled after cell division, when the rest of the DNA spreads out.

heterotroph. An organism that must ingest energy rich organic molecules produced by some other organism.

historical science. Study of unique phenomena that are historically contingent, based on empirical traces or modeling; includes ancient history such as paleontology and recent history such as forensics.

homeotic gene. A gene that controls early stages of development of an organism, resulting in a major change in the embryo, including overall body structure.

hominan. The newest term for humans and fossils identified as being in the human lineage, introduced when hominin was extended to include chimps.

hominid. Originally humans and fossils identified as being in the human lineage, but now includes all human-like organisms, including apes.

hominin. A term for humans and fossils identified as being in the human lineage, introduced when hominid was extended to include apes.

hominoid. All human-like organisms and fossils, including humans, apes and their ancestors.

homology. Similar traits that are thought to be due to descent from a common ancestor, such as the similar bone structure of vertebrate forelimbs.

horizontal gene transfer (HGT). The proposition that certain sections of DNA have been transferred from organism to organism not through normal (vertical) inheritance but by transfer between totally different types of organisms, by ingestion, infection, symbiosis or other processes.

hypothesis. A proposed explanation that can be tested by some scientific method.

hypothetico-deductivism. A philosophical position based on the proposition that science entails deduction and must describe theories that are tested by predictions; perhaps the dominant view of science today, found in many college biology textbooks.

igneous. Rocks formed by the solidification of molten rock either on the surface of the earth (lava) or under the surface (magma).

inductivism. A philosophical position based on the proposition that science entails induction, reasoning from specific observations to general conclusions or laws, associated with Francis Bacon.

inference. A logical conclusion, either inductive or deductive, based on the evidence, often incorporating some degree of spoken or unspoken background knowledge or assumptions.

inflationary period. In big bang cosmology, a theoretical time early in the history of the universe during which the universe expanded very rapidly due to a phase shift, as water does when it turns into water vapor.

insertion. The addition of one or more base pairs to a DNA sequence.

intelligent design (ID). The philosophical contention that design in nature is empirically detectable, or the social movement dedicated to that contention and thus opposed to methodological naturalism.

interacting (domains of knowledge). The philosophical proposition that at least some questions can be approached from both empirical and nonempirical perspectives, so the two realms cannot be completely separated. *See* complementary; overlapping.

intron. A section of DNA between the exons of a gene; introns are copied into RNA, but the section of RNA is cut out before protein production takes place.

inversion. A section of DNA that is reversed end to end and reinserted in the same location from which it was cut.

irreducible complexity. The proposition that some complex structures could not have arisen in a gradual stepwise manner with each stage having a selective advantage.

isotope. Different forms of an element, containing the same number of protons, but different numbers of neutrons.

kind. A term used by creationary models for the level of organisms that were created separately, from which all modern species descended by limited common descent.

law. A pattern in the data, often expressed mathematically, that may be able to predict what happens, but not why it happens.

logical empiricism. A philosophical position based on the proposition that all true knowledge comes from logical inferences drawn on empirical evidence, associated with the Vienna Circle.

mass extinction. One of five periods of geological history where large numbers of species went extinct at the same time in the fossil record, apparently as a result of some cataclysmic change affecting earth and its ecosystems.

materialism. A philosophical position that the material world is the only thing that exists.

mechanistic. A view of the world as a machine, which can be described by its component parts and mechanism of operation; it is the dominant metaphor of the world employed by science in modern society, as opposed to organic or magical views prevalent in other cultures or times.

methodological naturalism (MN). The philosophical claim that although God created the cosmos, he does not normally intervene in its function, and therefore science can seek and ultimately find a natural cause for all natural phenomena after the point of creation.

micro-RNA. A very short section of RNA that is able to bind to longer sections of RNA and thereby control gene expression by inhibiting the production of protein.

model. An idealized and often simplified representation of a situation or phenomenon that tells us something about how the real thing works or why it works.

molecular clock. An estimate of how long it has been since two evolutionary lineages diverged, based on the number of molecular differences between the two and an estimate of the average mutation rate.

monomer. A subunit that can bind together in long chains to form a macromolecule; for example, amino acids form proteins and nucleotides form nucleic acids (DNA and RNA); in inorganic chemistry monomers are identical, so order is unimportant, but in organic chemistry the monomers vary, so order is crucial.

morphology. The basic physical structure of a species, based on average size and shape, either of the whole individual or certain parts.

multiverse. A theoretical entity to explain the existence of our universe in the absence of a Creator, according to which our universe is only one of many universes; currently the most common nontheistic explanation.

natural selection. The process whereby organisms better adapted to a particular environment are more likely to produce higher numbers of offspring, resulting in an increase in certain traits; the main mechanism for evolution, according to neo-Darwinism.

naturalism. A philosophical position that everything in the world can be explained by natural causation.

naturalistic evolution (NE). A model of origins based on the premise that there is no supernatural, thus no Creator, so everything can be explained by natural causes.

nature of science. A term used in science education to refer to the history and philosophy of science; an understanding of what science is, its practices and limitations.

Neanderthal. A group of human-like fossils, very similar to humans and coexistent with them, which disappear from the fossil record about forty thousand years ago.

neo-Darwinian evolution. A model of the origin of species based on the gradual descent of all life from a common ancestor, under the direction of natural selection.

neutral mutation. A mutation that does not affect fitness, either because it makes no change or minimal change in the gene product or because it is in a section of DNA that does not make a gene product.

nonconcordist. A framework for biblical interpretation based on Genesis not revealing the order of events of creation, but only God as Creator. *See* appendix two.

nonoverlapping magisteria (NOMA). The proposition that science and religion answer different questions, using different methods, with no overlap; a name given to the idea of complementary domains of knowledge.

nonteleological evolution (NTE). A model of origins based on the premise that the Creator did not interfere with natural causation after the point of creation and had no specific goals for creation.

nucleus. (1) The central region of every atom, containing the protons and neutrons. *See* orbital. (2) The central dark-staining portion of a eukaryote cell, containing the DNA and associated molecules that form the chromosomes.

observational science. Study of naturally occurring situations, often used for phenomena where manipulation of conditions is not feasible; includes much of what used to be called natural history, and the study of living organisms *in situ*.

old-earth creation (OEC). A model of origins based on the premise that the Creator acted sequentially in creation, according to the order referred to in Genesis, over a long period of time.

orbital. The region outside the nucleus of an atom where electrons are found, although their exact path and position cannot be measured at the same time; two electrons can occupy each orbital, with different orbitals at different energy levels.

overlapping (domains of knowledge). The philosophical proposition that either science or religion can fully explain the origin of the universe. *See* complementary; interacting.

parthenogenesis. Production of an individual from an unfertilized egg, which occurs frequently in certain types of insects and plants but rarely in other organisms.

phylogenetic tree. A branching diagram indicating the proposed evolutionary relationships between different species or groups, based on morphological or molecular similarities.

phylum (pl. phyla). The level of taxonomic classification below kingdom. Members of a phylum typically share a basic body plan that is different from other phyla, for example the jointed exoskeleton of arthropods (including insects and crustaceans).

physical constants. One of approximately twenty-six independent numbers that determine the physical characteristics of the universe, including the four basic forces, the speed of light and the masses of the subatomic particles.

planned evolution (PE). A model of origins based on the premise that the Creator formed the creation such that no intervention was necessary after creation to bring about his goals.

plate tectonic theory. The theory that the rigid surface of the earth is broken into a number of plates that are gradually moving as a result of production of new crust at spreading plate boundaries (such as the middle of the Atlantic Ocean) and subduction and melting at colliding plate boundaries (such as the rim of the Pacific Ocean).

polymorphism. The presence of more than one form of a DNA sequence in a population, particularly neutral mutations.

postempiricism. A philosophical position based on the proposition that scientists normally work within a paradigm that shapes their research, associated with Thomas Kuhn.

prebiotic evolution. The proposition that organic molecules could theoretically be selected by natural selection for functionality, in the same way species are selected for adaptation.

presupposition. An assumption necessary to carry out scientific research; includes general assumptions necessary for science as a whole and specific assumptions adopted by particular fields.

prokaryote. An organism lacking a membrane-enclosed nucleus and other membrane-bound intracellular structures; includes eubacteria and archaebacteria.

pseudogene. A section of DNA with a sequence similar to a gene that produces a protein, but that does not itself produce a protein; many pseudogenes produce RNA, which may play a regulatory role in the cell.

punctuated equilibrium. The proposition that the observations of stasis and saltation are not a result of the imperfection of the fossil record but reveal rapid change of organisms at certain times.

racemic. Chemical term for an equal mix of right and left handed (*d* and *l*) forms of a molecule that has two mirror image (enantiomeric) arrangements.

radiometric dating. A method of dating materials based on their content of certain isotopes that are unstable and decay at constant rates under all conditions that have been measured.

reading frame. One of three possible ways of dividing a sequence of RNA bases into triplet codes; each frame would result in a totally different string of amino acids.

red shift. The observation that the farther away a star is, the more the light from it is shifted toward the red end of the spectrum.

RNA. Ribonucleic acid, a usually single-stranded molecule encoded by the DNA with many functions in the cell, including production of protein and regulation of gene expression.

saltation. The observation that fossil forms change relatively quickly at certain points in the fossil record, with some forms disappearing and others appearing.

science. The pursuit of understanding the natural world; a way of knowing characterized by logical inferences based on empirical evidence and necessary presuppositions; includes experimental, observational, historical and theoretical methodologies.

sedimentary. Rocks formed by the solidification of sediments deposited by water or, less frequently, wind.

selective advantage. A characteristic that allows an organism to survive and reproduce better in a certain environment than organisms of the same species lacking that characteristic.

single nucleotide substitution. The exchange of one DNA base for another, without changing the length of the DNA sequence.

singularity. According to big bang cosmology, the original state of the universe before it expanded, when the universe was condensed to zero or near zero volume, containing not only all matter and energy, but also all time and space.

somatic cell. A body cell, anything other than a germ-line cell.

species. The lowest level of taxonomic classification; many methods have been used to distinguish species, including reproductive isolation (biology) and disparate morphology (paleontology), but none work in every situation.

specified complexity. Characteristic of structures that are both non-repetitive (specified) and complex, which therefore require a large amount of information to produce.

stasis. The observation that fossils remain relatively unchanged for long periods of time in the fossil record.

steady state. A model of expansion of the universe in which matter is created as the universe expands, allowing it to be infinite in time and space; a cosmological model that now has few supporters.

stellar nucleosynthesis theory. A theoretical stepwise progression for production of all the elements under conditions inferred to exist in different kinds of stars.

stochastic. Random processes, where the overall pattern may be predictable but the result of any particular event is not.

superposition. The principle that new layers of sediment, which may become sedimentary rocks, are normally deposited on top of existing materials.

symbiosis. A lasting association between two organisms that benefits at least one, often to the point that it could not live without the other.

taxon (pl. taxa). A level of the taxonomic system used to classify different types of organisms, including domain, kingdom, phylum, class, order, family, genus and species.

taxonomy. The study of classification of organisms, initially based on morphological similarity, now increasingly based on molecular similarity and putative evolutionary relationships.

teleology. The study of design in nature, or the idea that nature is directed toward a goal by the Creator.

telomere. A specific DNA sequence at the end of chromosomes that both protects the ends from damage and prevents uncontrolled replication of the chromosome.

theism. A system of belief characterized by the proposition that there is a personal Creator who is both transcendent of creation and immanent in creation.

theoretical science. Study of phenomena that have not yet been observed but can be predicted based on mathematical modeling; includes many subfields within physics and cosmology.

theory. A widely accepted explanation for which there is considerable empirical or mathematical support.

transposable element. A short section of DNA that is able to move from one place to another within the genome, sometimes interrupting genes when it does so, including Alu elements.

uniformitarianism. The proposition that past processes that cannot be observed directly can be understood with reference to present processes because they were similar in type, if not necessarily in magnitude.

white hole. A model of expansion of the universe proposed to explain how the stars could be billions of years old, but the earth only thousands of years old; a cosmological model proposed by YEC.

young-earth creation (YEC). A model of origins based on the premise that the Creator finished creation in a period of six twenty-four-hour days, in the order listed in Genesis, within the past ten thousand years.

Bibliography

...

American Association for the Advancement of Science. 1993. *Benchmarks for science literacy*. Washington, DC: American Association for the Advancement of Science.

Austin, Steven A. 1995. *Grand Canyon: Monument to catastrophe*. Institute for Creation Research.

Barbour, Ian G. 2000. *When science meets religion: Enemies, strangers, or partners?* San Francisco: Harper.

Beckwith, Francis J. 2003. *Law, Darwinism, and public education: The establisment clause and the challenge of intelligent design*. Lanham, MD: Rowman & Littlefield.

Behe, Michael J. 1996. *Darwin's black box: The biochemical challenge to evolution*. New York: Touchstone.

_____. 2004. "Irreducible complexity: Obstacle to Darwinian evolution." In *Debating design: From Darwin to DNA*. Edited by William A. Dembski & Michael Ruse, 352-70. Cambridge: Cambridge University Press.

———. 2007. *The edge of evolution: The search for the limits of Darwinism*. New York: Free Press.

Berkman, M. B., Pacheco, J. S., & Plutzer, E. 2008. "Evolution and creationism in America's classrooms: A national portrait." *PLOS Biology* 6(5): e124.

Biello, David. 2009, August 19. "The origin of oxygen in earth's atmosphere." *Scientific American*, www.scientificamerican.com/article.cfm?id=origin-of-oxygen-in-atmosphere.

Biémont, Christian. 2010. "A brief history of the status of transposable elements: From junk DNA to major players in evolution." *Genetics* 186, 1085-93.

BioLogos Foundation. 2011. "At what point in the evolutionary process did humans attain the 'Image of God'?" *BioLogos*, http://biologos.org/questions/image-of-god.

Bradley, Walter L. 2004. "Information, entropy, and the origin of life." In *Debating Design: From Darwin to DNA*. Edited by William A. Dembski & Michael Ruse, 331-51. Cambridge: Cambridge University Press.

Brinster, R. L., Allen, J. M., Behringer, R. R., Gelinas, R. E., & Palmiter, R. D. 1988. "Introns increase transcriptional efficiency in transgenic mice." *Proceedings of the National Academy of Sciences USA* 85: 836-40.

Brown, J. R. 2003. "Ancient horizontal gene transfer." *Nature Reviews Genetics* 4: 121-32.

Brown, Walt. 2001. *In the beginning: Compelling evidence for creation and the flood.* 7th ed. Phoenix: Center for Scientific Creation.

Campbell, Neil J., & Reese, Jane. 2005. *Biology.* 7th ed. Upper Saddle River, NJ: Pearson, Benjamin Cummings.

Carleson, Richard F., & Longman, Tremper, III. 2010. *Science, creation and the Bible: Reconciling rival theories of origins.* Downers Grove, IL: InterVarsity Press.

Chapman, Bruce. 1998. "Postscript: The 21st century has arrived." In *Mere creation: Science, faith & intelligent design.* Edited by William A. Dembski, 454-59. Downers Grove, IL: InterVarsity Press.

Chimpanzee Sequencing and Analysis Consortium. 2005. "Initial sequence of the chimpanzee genome and comparison with the human genome." *Nature* 437: 69-87.

Cleland, Carol E. 2002. "Methodological and epistemic differences between historical science and experimental science." *Philosophy of Science* 69(3): 447-51.

Coles, Peter. 2001. *Cosmology: A very short introduction.* Oxford: Oxford University Press.

Collins, Francis S. 2006. *The language of God: A scientist presents evidence for belief.* New York: Free Press.

Conway Morris, Simon. 2003. *Life's solution: Inevitable humans in a lonely universe.* Cambridge: Cambridge University Press.

Cornell, James, ed. 1989. *Bubbles, voids and bumps in time: The New Cosmology.* Cambridge: Cambridge University Press.

Crick, F. H. C., & Orgel, L. E. 1973. "Directed panspermia." *Icarus* 19: 341.

Darwin, Charles. 1859. *On the origin of species.* In *The Complete Work of Charles Darwin Online,* http://darwin-online.org.uk.

Dawkins, Richard. 1996. *The blind watchmaker: Why the evidence of evolution reveals a universe without design.* New York: W. W. Norton.

———. 2006. *The God delusion.* Boston: Houghton Mifflin.

de Duve, Christian. 1995. *Vital dust: The origin and evolution of life on earth.* New York: Basic Books.

de Jong, W. W. 1998. "Molecules remodel the mammalian tree." *TREE* 13(7): 270-75.

Dembski, William A. 1999. *Intelligent design: The bridge between science and theology.* Downers Grove, IL: InterVarsity Press.

———. 2004. *The design revolution: Answering the toughest questions about intelligent design.* Downers Grove, IL: InterVarsity Press.

Dembski, William A., ed. 1998. *Mere creation: Science, faith & intelligent design.* Downers Grove, IL: InterVarsity Press.

Dennett, Daniel C. 1995. *Darwin's dangerous idea: Evolution and the meanings of life.* New York: Simon & Schuster.

Denton, Michael. 1985. *Evolution: A theory in crisis.* Bethesda, MD: Adler & Adler.

DeYoung, Don. 2005. *Thousands . . . not billions: Challenging an icon of evolution, questioning the age of the earth.* Green Forest, AR: Master Books.

Dorus, S., et al. 2004. "Accelerated evolution of nervous system genes in the origin of Homo sapiens." *Cell* 119: 1027-40.

Duschl, Richard, & Grandy, Richard. 2008. "Reconsidering the character and role of inquiry in school science: Framing the debates." In *Teaching Scientific Inquiry: Recommendations for Research and Implementation.* Edited by Richard A. Duschl & Richard E. Grandy, 1-37. Rotterdam: Sense Publishers.

Edwards, Rem B. 2001. *What caused the big bang?* New York: RodOpi.

European Molecular Biology Laboratory. 2009, November 27. "First-ever blueprint of 'minimal cell' is more complex than expected." *ScienceDaily,* www.sciencedaily.com/releases/2009/11/091126173027.htm.

Falk, Darrel R. 2004. *Coming to peace with science: Bridging the worlds between science and faith.* Downers Grove, IL: InterVarsity Press.

Ferrier, D. E. K., & Holland P. W. H. 2001. "Ancient origin of the Hox gene cluster." *Nature Reviews Genetics* 2: 33-38.

"The fickle Y chromosome." 2010. *Nature* 463: 149.

Forster, A. C., & Church, G. M. 2006. "Toward synthesis of a minimal cell." *Molecular Systems Biology* 2: 45.

Fowler, Thomas B., & Kuebler, Daniel. 2007. *The evolution controversy: A survey of competing theories.* Grand Rapids: Baker Academic.

Futuyma, Douglas J. 2006. *Evolutionary biology.* 3rd ed. Sunderland, MA: Sinauer.

Gauch, Hugh G., Jr. 2003. *Scientific method in practice.* Cambridge: Cambridge University Press.

Giberson, Karl W., & Yerxa, Donald A. 2002. *Species of origins: America's search for a creation story.* Lanham, MD: Rowman & Littlefield.

Gibbs, W. Wayt. 2003. "The unseen genome: Gems among the junk." *Scientific American* 289(5): 26-33.

Gilbert, Steven W., & Ireton, Shirley Watt. 2003. *Understanding models in earth and space science.* Arlington, VA: NSTA Press.

Gonzalez, Guillermo, & Richards, Jay W. 2004. *The privileged planet: How our place in the cosmos is designed for discovery.* Washington, DC: Regnery.

Gould, Steven Jay. 1999. *Rocks of ages: Science and religion in the fullness of life.* New York: Ballantine.

————. 2002. *The structure of evolutionary theory.* Cambridge, MA: Belknap Press of Harvard University Press.

Gould, Steven Jay, & Lewontin, R. C. 1979. "The spandrels of San Marco and the Panglossian paradigm: A critique of the adaptationist programme." *Proceedings of the Royal Society London B.* 205: 581-98.

Haarsma, Deborah B., & Haarsma, Loren D. 2007. *Origins: A reformed look at creation, design, & evolution.* Grand Rapids: Faith Alive.

Halvorson, Hans, & Kragh, Helge. 2011. "Cosmology and theology," in *Stanford Encyclopedia of Philosophy.* Edited by Edward N. Zalta. http:\\plato .stanford.edu/entries/cosmology-theology.

Ham, Ken, ed. 2006. *The new answers book 1.* Green Forest, AR: Master Books.

Hartwig-Scherer, Sigrid. 1998. "Apes or ancestors?" In *Mere creation: Science, faith & intelligent design.* Edited by William A. Dembski, 212-35. Downers Grove, IL: InterVarsity Press.

Haught, John F. 2010. *Making sense of evolution: Darwin, God, and the drama of life.* Louisville: Westminster John Knox Press.

Hooper, Judith. 2002. *Of moths and men: An evolutionary tale.* New York: Norton.

Howell, Kenneth J. 2003. *God's two books: Copernican cosmology and biblical interpretation in early modern science.* Notre Dame, IN: University of Notre Dame Press.

Hughes, J. F., et al. 2010. "Chimpanzee and human Y chromosomes are remarkably divergent in structure and gene content." *Nature* 463: 536-39.

Hui, Jerome, Peter, H. L., Holland, W. H., & Ferrier, David E. K. 2008. "Do cnidarians have a ParaHox cluster? Analysis of synteny around a Nematostella homeobox gene cluster." *Evolution & Development* 10(6): 725-30.

Johnson, Phillip E. 1991. *Darwin on trial.* Downers Grove, IL: InterVarsity Press.

———. 1995. *Reason in the balance: The case against naturalism in science, law & education.* Downers Grove, IL: InterVarsity Press.

———. 1997. *Defeating Darwinism by opening minds.* Downers Grove, IL: InterVarsity Press.

Kapranov, Philipp, Willingham, Aarron T., & Gingeras, Thomas R. 2007. "Genome-wide transcription and the implications for genomic organization." *Nature Reviews Genetics* 8: 1-11.

Keeling, P. J., & Palmer, J. D. 2008. "Horizontal gene transfer in eukaryotic evolution." *Nature Reviews Genetics* 9: 605-18.

Kuhn, Thomas S. 1996. *The structure of scientific revolutions.* 3rd ed. Chicago: University of Chicago Press.

Lamoureux, Denis O. 2008. *Evolutionary creation: A Christian approach to evolution.* Eugene, OR: Wipf & Stock.

Le Hir, H., Nott, A., & Moore, M. J. 2003. "How introns influence and enhance eukaryotic gene expression." *Trends in Biochemical Sciences* 28(4): 215-20.

Lederman, N. G. 2006. "Syntax of nature of science within inquiry and science instruction." In *Scientific inquiry and nature of science: Implications for teaching, learning, and teacher education.* Edited by L. B. Flick & N. G. Lederman, 301-18. Dordrecht: Springer.

Lewis, C. S. 1938. *Out of the silent planet.* New York: Scribner.

Livingstone, David N. 1984. *Darwin's forgotten defenders: The encounter between evangelical theology and evangelical thought.* Vancouver: Regent College Publishing.

Martin, W., Baross, J., Kelley, D., & Russell, M. J. 2008. "Hydrothermal vents and the origin of life." *Nature Reviews Microbiology* 6: 805-14.

Mayr, Ernst. 2001. *What evolution is.* New York: Basic Books.

McComas, William F. 1998. "The principal elements of the nature of science: Dispelling the myths." In *The nature of science in science education: Rationales and strategies.* Vol. 5. Edited by William F. McComas. Boston: Science & Technology Education Library, Kluwer Academic.

Meyer, Stephen C. 2009. *Signature in the cell: DNA and the evidence for intelligent design.* New York: Harper One.

————. 1994. "The methodological equivalence of design & descent." In *The creation hypothesis: Scientific evidence for an intelligent designer.* Edited by J. P. Moreland, 67-112. Downers Grove, IL: InterVarsity Press.

Meyer, Stephen C., & Keas, Michael Newton. 2003. "The meanings of evolution." In *Darwinism, design, and public education.* Edited by John Angus Campbell & Stephen C. Meyer, 135-56. East Lansing: Michigan State University Press.

Meyer, Stephen C., Ross, Marcus, Nelson, Paul, & Chien, Paul. 2003. "The Cambrian explosion: Biology's Big Bang." In *Darwinism, design, and public education.* Edited by John Angus Campbell & Stephen C. Meyer, 323-402. East Lansing: Michigan State University Press.

Miller, Kenneth R. 1999. *Finding Darwin's God: A scientist's search for common ground between God and evolution.* New York: Cliff Street Books.

————. 2004. "The flagellum unspun: The collapse of 'irreducible complexity.'" In *Debating design: From Darwin to DNA.* Edited by William A. Dembski & Michael Ruse, 81-97. Cambridge: Cambridge University Press.

Milton, Richard. 1997. *Shattering the myths of Darwinism.* Rochester, VT: Park Street Press.

Moreland, J. P., & Reynolds, John Mark. 1999. "Introduction." In *Three Views on Creation and Evolution.* Edited by J. P. Moreland & John Mark Reynolds, 7-38. Grand Rapids: Zondervan.

Morris, Henry M., & Parker, Gary E. 1987. *What is creation science?* Green Forest, AR: Master Books.

Morris, John, & Austin, Steve. 2003. *Footprints in the ash: The explosive story of Mount St. Helens.* Green Forest, AR: Master Books.

National Academy of Science. 1998. *Teaching about evolution and the nature of science.* Washington, DC: National Academy Press.

National Research Council. 1996. *National science education standards.* Washington, DC: National Academies Press.

————. 2012. *A framework for K-12 science education: Practices, crosscutting concepts, and core ideas.* Washington, DC: National Academies Press.

Nord, Warren A. 2003. "Intelligent design theory, religion, and the science curriculum." In *Darwinism, design, and public education.* Edited by John Angus Campbell & Stephen C. Meyer, 46-58. East Lansing: Michigan State University Press.

Numbers, Ronald L. 1992. *The creationists: The evolution of scientific creationism.* Berkeley: University of California Press.

Numbers, Ronald L. , ed. 2010. *Galileo goes to jail and other myths about science and religion.* Cambridge, MA: Harvard University Press.

Oard, Michael. 1990. *An ice age caused by the Genesis flood.* Dallas: Institute for Creation Research.

Orr, H. Allen. 2009. "Testing natural selection." *Scientific American* 300(1): 44-50.

Pearcey, Nancy R., & Thaxton, Charles B. 1994. *The soul of science: Christian faith and natural philosophy.* Wheaton, IL: Crossway Books.

Plantinga, Alvin. 2006, March 7. "Whether ID is science isn't semantics." *Science & Theology News.* Archived at www.discovery.org/a/3331.

Poe, Harry Lee, & Davis, Jimmy H. 2012. *God and the cosmos: divine activity in space, time and history.* Downers Grove, IL: IVP Academic.

Poythress, Vern S. 2006. *Redeeming science: A God-centered approach.* Wheaton, IL: Crossway Books.

Quintana, Elisa V., & Lissauer, Jack J. 2010. "Terrestrial planet formation in binary star systems." In *Planets in binary star systems.* Edited by Nader Haghighipour. New York: Springer. Abstract at http://arxiv.org/abs/0705.3444.

Rana, Fazale R. 2010. "Chromosome 2: The best evidence for human evolution?" *New Reasons to Believe,* 6-7.

Ratzsch, Del. 1996. *The battle of beginnings: Why neither side is winning the creation-evolution debate.* Downers Grove, IL: IVP Academic.

———. 2000. *Science and its limits: The natural sciences in Christian perspective.* Downers Grove, IL: IVP Academic.

Ross, Hugh. 1991. *The fingerprint of God.* 2nd ed. Orange, CA: Promise Publishing.

———. 1993. *The Creator and the cosmos: How the greatest scientific discoveries of the century reveal God.* Colorado Springs, CO: NavPress.

———. 2004. *A matter of days: Resolving a creation controversy.* Colorado Springs, CO: NavPress.

———. 2009. *More than a theory: Revealing a testable model for creation.* Grand Rapids: Baker Books.

Ross, Marcus R. 2005. "Who believes what? Clearing up confusion over intelligent design and young-earth creationism." *Journal of Geoscience Education* 53(3): 319-23.

Ruse, Michael. 2004. "The argument from design: A brief history." In *Debating design: From Darwin to DNA.* Edited by William A. Dembski & Michael

Ruse, 13-31. Cambridge: Cambridge University Press.

Ryan, Frank. 2002. *Darwin's blind spot.* Boston: Houghton Mifflin.

Sanford, John C. 2008. *Genetic entropy & the mystery of the genome.* 3rd ed. Waterloo, NY: FMS Publications.

Schaefer, Henry F. 2003. *Science and Christianity: Conflict or coherence?* Athens: University of Georgia Printing.

Scherer, Siegfried. 1998. "Basic types of life." In *Mere Creation: Science, Faith and Intelligent Design.* Edited by William A. Dembski, 195-211. Downers Grove, IL: InterVarsity Press.

Schwartz, Jeffrey H. 1999. *Sudden origins: Fossils, genes, and the emergence of species.* New York: John Wiley.

Schweitzer, M. H., Whittmeyer, J. L., Horner, J. R., & Toporski, J. K. 2005. "Soft-tissue vessels and cellular preservation in Tyrannosaurus rex." *Science* 307(5717): 1952-55.

Scott, E. C. 1999. "The creation/evolution continuum." *NCSE Reports* 19(4): 16-17, 23-25.

Shapiro, James A. 2011. *Evolution: A view from the 21st century.* Upper Saddle River, NJ: FT Press Science.

Sire, James W. 2004. *Naming the elephant: Worldview as a concept.* Downers Grove, IL: InterVarsity Press.

Smoot, George, & Davidson, Keay. 1993. *Wrinkles in time.* New York: Avon Books.

Snelling, Andrew A. 2009. *Earth's catastrophic past: Geology, creation & the flood.* Dallas: Institute for Creation Research.

Sober, Elliott. 2008. *Evidence and evolution: The logic behind the science.* Cambridge: Cambridge University Press.

Tenesa, A., et al. 2007. "Recent human effective population size estimated from linkage disequilibrium." *Genome Research* 17: 520-26.

Thaxton, Charles B., Bradley, Walter L., & Olsen, Roger L. 1984. *The mystery of life's origin: Reassessing current theories.* Dallas: Lewis & Stanley.

Tompkins, Jeffrey P. 2011. "Genome-wide DNA alignment similarity (identity) for 40,000 chimpanzee DNA sequences queried against the human genome is 86–89%." *Answers Research Journal* 4: 233-41.

Van Till, Howard J. 1999. "The fully gifted creation ('theistic evolution')." In *Three views on creation and evolution.* Edited by J. P. Moreland & John Mark Reynolds, 159-218. Grand Rapids: Zondervan.

Vardiman, Larry, & Humphreys, D. R. 2011. "A new creationist cosmology: In no time at all, part 3." *Acts & Facts* 40(2): 12-14. www.icr.org/article/5870.

Vardiman, Larry, Snelling, Andrew A., & Chaffin, Eugene F. 2005. *Radioisotopes and the age of the earth.* Vol. 2. Dallas: Institute for Creation Research.

Venema, Dennis R. 2010. "Genesis and the genome: Genomics evidence for human-ape common ancestry and ancestral hominid population sizes." *Perspectives on Science and Christian Faith* 62(3): 166-78.

Vlcek, S., Dechat, T., & Foisner, R. 2001. "Nuclear envelope and nuclear matrix: Interactions and dynamics." *Cellular and Molecular Life Sciences* 58: 1758-65.

Walton, John H. 2009. *The lost world of Genesis one: Ancient cosmology and the origins debate.* Downers Grove, IL: IVP Academic.

Weart, Spencer. 2011, January. "Discovery of global warming: Rapid climate change." *American Institute of Physics,* www.aip.org/history/climate/rapid.htm.

Weissenbach, Jean. 2004. "Differences with the relatives." *Nature* 429: 353-55.

Wells, Jonathan. 2000. *Icons of evolution: Science or myth?* Washington, DC: Regnery.

———. 2003. "Second thoughts about peppered moths." In *Darwinism, design, and public education.* Edited by John Angus Campbell & Stephen C. Meyer, 187-92. East Lansing: Michigan State University Press.

———. 2011. *The Myth of Junk DNA.* Seattle: Discovery Institute Press.

Whitcomb, John C., & Morris, Henry M. 1961. *The Genesis flood: The biblical record and its scientific implications.* Phillipsburg, NJ: P & R.

Wilson, Edward O. 1998. *Consilience: The unity of knowledge.* New York: Vintage Books.

Windschitl, M., & Thompson, J. 2006. "Transcending simple forms of school science investigation: The impact of preservice instruction on teachers' understandings of model-based inquiry." *American Educational Research Journal* 43(4): 783-835.

Wise, K. P. 2002. *Faith, form, and time: What the Bible teaches and science confirms about creation and the age of the universe.* Nashville: Broadman & Holman.

Young, Davis A., & Stearley, Ralph F. 2008. *The Bible, rocks and time: Geological evidence for the age of the earth.* Downers Grove, IL: IVP Academic.

Subject Index

abiogenesis, 40, 64, 82, 193
Adam and Eve, 45-46, 51, 140-42, 145-50,
  168
agnosticism, 42, 55, 193
Alu elements, 139, 193
amino acids, 84, 86-87, 90-91, 111, 118,
  139-40, 194-95, 197, 200, 204
anthropic principle, 78, 95, 160, 193
antibiotic resistance, 109
apparent age, 78-80
astrobiology, 80, 85
atheism, 22, 42-43, 46, 56, 77, 176, 186-88,
  193
Australopithecus sp., 133-36
biblical interpretation, 23, 37-38, 40,
  45-46, 49-52, 74-75, 78-79, 98, 127, 143,
  148-49, 151, 189
big bang cosmology, 58, 63-66, 71, 74, 76,
  78, 157, 165, 169, 194
biogeography, 106-7
burden of proof, 186
Cambrian explosion, 56, 106, 127, 128, 160,
  194
chimpanzees, 131-33, 137-40, 146-47
chromosomes, 88, 100, 110, 112-13, 117, 123,
  138-40
    chromosome 2, 137-38, 144, 148
    Y Chromosome, 140, 142, 144
classification, 39-40, 118, 130-31, 135
coacervates, 87-88, 194
common descent, 41, 96, 119, 121-23, 126,
  128, 148, 156, 158, 194
complexity theory, 59, 92, 121
concordist, 75, 194, 201
consistency, 21, 28, 30, 36, 57, 65-66, 104
convergence, 113, 194
cosmic microwave background radiation,
  63-64, 65, 71, 157, 195
cosmological models. *See* big bang;
  steady state; white hole
creation
    old-earth (OEC), 38, 41, 48-50, 53-55,
      58, 66, 74-76, 97-98, 124-27, 143,
      147-48, 150, 158, 159-61, 168-69, 179,
      182, 185, 195, 202

young-earth (YEC), 36, 38, 41, 43, 48,
  49, 50-52, 53-55, 56, 71, 78-80, 85,
  97-98, 104, 124-27, 133, 136, 140, 143,
  147-48, 148-50, 157-58, 161-62, 166-67,
  168-70, 174, 178-79, 182, 185, 195, 206
dark energy, 66, 165, 195
dark matter, 66, 165, 188, 195
Darwinism. *See* evolution, neo-
  Darwinian
dating, 126, 137, 147, 185
    radiometric, 83, 103-4, 127, 161, 204
    relative, 103
definitions, 21, 32-35, 56, 84, 97, 131, 163,
  175, 185, 187
    of evolution. *See* evolution,
      definitions of
    of science. *See* science, definitions of
    of species. *See* species, definitions of
deism, 38, 43, 80, 195
deoxyribonucleic acid (DNA), 85, 87-91,
  96, 107, 110-13, 118, 119, 137-38, 166,
  193-204
    mitochondrial, 144
    noncoding ("junk"), 116-17
    sequencing, 119, 122, 138-42
design, 73-74, 76-77
    common, 126, 148
    constraints, 116
    detection of, 47, 53, 182
    intelligent. *See* intelligent design
directed evolution. *See* evolution,
  directed
directed panspermia, 96
domains of knowledge
    complementary, 42, 44, 46-47, 50, 55,
      179, 194
    interacting, 47, 49, 55, 143, 179, 199
    overlapping, 50-51, 55, 202
embryology, 114
enantiomers, 86-88, 96, 111, 196
endosymbiosis, 119, 121, 159, 196
enzymes, 86-88
epigenetics, 111, 116, 124, 128, 158, 196
evidence, 20, 23-24, 28, 30, 38, 57-58, 60,
  102, 154, 156, 173, 186, 188, 195, 196

anomalies, 102, 104, 122, 126, 169
empirical, 23-24, 28, 53-55, 176-77
indirect, 60-61, 83-84
evo-devo, 114-15, 196
evolution
definitions of, 40, 110, 119-20
directed (DE), 39, 40, 41, 46-48, 49,
53-55, 74-76, 98-99, 122-24, 143,
145-48, 158-59, 167-68, 179, 181, 187,
195
macro-, microevolution, 119, 125, 128
naturalistic (NE), 36, 38-43, 46, 50-51,
53-55, 66, 76-78, 80, 95-98, 119,
120-22, 143-44, 148, 156-58, 163, 170,
179, 181, 201
neo-Darwinian, 120-22, 156-58
non-Darwinian, 122-24, 158-59
nonteleological (NTE), 39, 41, 43-44,
46, 53-55, 58, 74-76, 95-97, 98, 120-22,
143-45, 156-58, 163, 179, 201
planned (PE), 39-41, 45-46, 49, 53-55,
74-76, 95-98, 120-22, 143-45, 156-58,
163, 167, 179, 181, 187, 203
prebiotic, 82, 93, 96, 166, 203
theistic, 37-39, 44, 54, 148, 185
exaptation, 96, 121
extinctions, 106, 200
extrapolation, 109, 125, 197
falisification, 178, 197
fine tuning, 58, 66-73, 76-77, 160
flood, 51, 127, 149, 161-62, 168-70, 185
fossils, 35, 49, 83, 102-7, 121-22, 123, 126-27,
130-37, 141, 146, 147, 157-58, 160, 161-62, 169
index (indicator), 103
paraconformities, 104, 106
soft tissue in, 104
transitional, 35, 105-6, 122, 127, 147, 157
fruit flies, 111-12, 117
Galapagos finches, 109, 125
gap model, 49, 127
gene, 89, 100, 107-13, 115-18, 126, 138-41,
144, 147, 158-59, 166, 197
expression, 88, 113, 115, 122, 197
Genesis, 23, 36-37, 45-46, 49, 74-76, 78,
125-27, 143, 148-50, 168
genetics, 102, 107-13, 116-18, 121-22, 123-24,
128, 190

geocentric model, 34, 61
God of the gaps, 97
God's action in creation, 30, 45-49, 51-52,
55, 74-76, 78-80, 94, 97-99, 122-23, 125,
143, 145-47, 163, 167-69, 181-82, 189
gradualism, 56, 105, 119, 121-23, 126, 128,
145, 156, 158, 160, 197
Hardy-Weinberg equilibrium, 109
heliocentric model, 34, 61
homeotic genes, 111-12, 117, 126, 159, 198
hominids, 130-37, 144, 198
Homo sp., 133-35
homology, 113, 160, 198
horizontal gene transfer (HGT), 122, 126,
198
Hubble's law, 62
hypothesis, 26, 32-33, 178, 181, 198
hypothetico-deductivism, 178
inductivism, 178
inference, 24-25, 30, 38, 60, 101, 137,
175-76, 199
abductive, 25
deductive, 24-25
inductive, 24-25
inflation, 66, 71, 165, 199
information, 24, 74, 83, 87, 89-94, 160-61,
166-67
intelligent design (ID), 33, 47, 52-56, 89,
93, 146, 152, 159-61, 164-66, 174, 181-82,
185, 187-88, 199
introns, 116, 199
irreducible complexity, 56, 90, 93-94,
96-97, 99, 126, 160, 199
kinds, 41, 52, 125, 157-58, 170, 199
law, 33-34, 44, 46, 47, 60, 62, 69, 75, 77, 98,
163-67, 185, 199
materialism, 42
mathematics, 24-25, 27, 33-34, 59-60,
89-90, 92, 109
mechanism, 40, 61, 88, 99-100, 124, 128,
158-59
lacking, 54, 65, 82, 94, 98, 99, 125-26,
159, 165, 167-70
philosophical assertions about, 46-48,
55, 98-99, 181
mechanistic model, 27, 200
Miller-Urey experiment, 84-85

minimal cell, 88-89
miracles, 48, 75, 168, 181
model, 31-34
molecular clock, 140-42, 144-45, 147-148,
    200
morphology, 102, 118, 200
multiverse, 76-77, 188, 201
mutation, 53, 109-12, 116, 121-22, 142, 148,
    157, 158-59, 166
    deleterious, 110, 111, 122, 158
    neutral, 121, 139, 141, 144, 201
natural selection, 96, 102, 108, 110-11, 116,
    119, 121-23, 126, 128, 146, 158, 165, 167, 201
    selective advantage, 93-94, 110, 204
naturalism
    methodological, 54-56, 98, 121, 162,
        178-79, 200
    philosophical, 42, 53-54, 58, 97, 98, 121,
        150, 176, 183, 187, 201
naturalistic evolution. *See* evolution,
    naturalistic
neo-Darwinian synthesis. *See* evolution,
    Darwinian
nonempirical, 28, 55-56, 154, 177, 189
nonoverlapping magisteria (NOMA),
    42, 46, 201
nonteleological evolution. *See* evolution,
    nonteleological
old-earth creation. *See* creation,
    old-earth
oxygen, 69, 85, 87
parthenogenesis, 113, 202
peppered moth, 108-9, 160
philosophy, 19, 56
    of science, 24-28, 34, 53-56, 125, 161,
        170, 176-80, 182, 184, 187-88
    personal, 20-22, 27, 30, 34, 36-39, 74,
        82, 92-93, 124, 130, 148, 151, 155, 171-72,
        175-76, 180, 182-83
    underlying models of origins, 30-31,
        95, 98-99, 167
phylogenetic trees, 118, 122, 202
physical constants, 66-69, 77-78, 165, 202
planned evolution. *See* evolution,
    planned
plate tectonic theory, 107, 161, 170, 203
pollen, 104, 107, 169

polymorphisms, 141-42, 157-58, 203
postempiricism, 178, 203
prediction, 24-25, 33, 49, 59-60, 66, 99,
    157-58, 164, 178, 198
presuppositions, 11, 19, 21, 23, 25-27, 30,
    36-38, 82, 91, 93, 98, 153, 172, 175-77,
    179-83, 203
    of author, 20, 27, 58
probability, 24, 47-48, 59, 77-78, 80, 92-93,
    95, 97-99, 124, 141, 163-68
pseudogenes, 116, 203
punctuated equilibrium, 105, 121, 160, 203
quantum events, 48, 59, 65, 124, 168, 178
racemic, 86, 203
reading frame, 113, 204
red shift, 62-63, 204
reducing atmosphere, 85
religion, 21, 27, 42-44, 46-47, 49, 51, 55-56,
    143, 182-83
revelation, 42, 49, 150, 183
rhetoric, 25, 32, 40, 45, 50
ribonucleic acid (RNA), 87, 90-91, 100,
    116, 200, 204
saltation, 104-6, 121-23, 126, 136, 146-47,
    158, 204
science
    definitions of, 23, 31, 44, 56, 96-98, 125,
        162, 170, 175-85, 188
    experimental, 23, 26, 34, 84, 92, 178,
        196
    historical, 24, 26, 59, 92, 133, 178, 198
    nature of, 24, 32, 170, 175, 177, 201
    objectivity of, 26, 173, 176, 180, 182-83
    observational, 24, 60, 178, 202
    social, 27, 130
    teaching, 44, 50, 56, 63, 82, 147, 175-76,
        183-86
    textbooks, 32-33, 38, 43, 50, 84, 87, 101,
        108-16, 121, 134, 138, 152, 156, 160-62,
        173, 178, 184, 187
    theoretical, 24, 206
scientism, 51, 176, 181
similarities, 113-19
singularity, 64, 66, 71, 73-74, 76, 204
social Darwinism, 151
spandrels, 96
species, definitions of, 37, 125, 132, 205

specified complexity, 91-93, 96-97, 99,
    160, 205
stasis, 104-6, 136, 205
steady state cosmology, 64-65, 76, 205
stellar nucleosynthesis theory, 65, 69-70,
    205
superposition, 103-4, 205
symbiosis, 118-19, 121, 123, 126, 158-59, 205
teleology, 44, 45, 52-53, 121, 124, 160, 205
theology, 39, 40, 42, 45-47, 53, 81, 129,
    148-50, 154, 170, 181, 189
    natural, 52, 55
theory, 26, 33-34, 51, 53, 59-60, 62, 64, 206
thermodynamics, second law of, 166-67

tool use, 135-36
transposable elements, 104, 117, 123, 193,
    206
truth, 22, 38, 173, 176, 179, 186, 188, 190
uniformitarianism, 162, 206
universe, expansion of, 61-66, 70-71, 73,
    76, 79
vestigial structures, 115, 160
white hole cosmology, 79-80, 157, 169,
    206
worldview, 20-22, 34, 37, 75, 151, 180-84
young-earth creation. *See* creation,
    young-earth

Person and Organization Index

Answers in Genesis, 51, 161
Austin, Steven, 51, 162
Barbour, Ian, 39, 44
Barr, Stephen, 187
Behe, Michael, 48, 56, 93-94, 146, 187
Biologos Institute, 45, 145
Brown, Walt, 51, 161
Center for Scientific Creation, 51
Collins, Francis, 45
Conway Morris, Simon, 73, 82, 84-86, 95
Creation Ministries International, 51,
    120, 169
Crick, Francis, 95-96
Darwin, Charles, 95, 102, 104-105, 107-9,
    114, 119, 121, 128
Dawkins, Richard, 42, 51
de Duve, Christian, 44
Dembski, William, 47, 53-54, 56, 98, 116
Dennett, Daniel, 42
Denton, Michael, 123
Discovery Institute, 49, 51-52, 55
Einstein, Albert, 61-62
Galilei, Galileo, 61
Gauch, Hugh, 23, 25-27, 175, 178, 180-82
Goldschmidt, Richard, 124
Gould, Steven Jay, 42, 50, 96, 105, 116, 121,
    128
Haarsma, Deborah & Loren, 24, 48
Haeckel, Ernst, 114
Ham, Ken, 50-51, 78, 161, 178
Haught, John, 44
Hubble, Edwin, 62
Humphreys, D. Russell, 51, 79, 157
Johnson, Phillip, 52, 56

Lamoureux, Denis O., 40, 44, 53, 75,
    145-47
Maxwell, James Clerk, 63
Mayr, Ernst, 43, 95, 106, 113-15, 120-21,
    134-36, 147
Meyer, Stephen, 49, 53, 56, 106, 120, 125
Miller, Kenneth, 46, 94, 104
Miller, Stanley, 84
Milton, Richard, 118, 123, 126
Nelson, Paul, 51
Newton, Isaac, 61
Planck, Max, 120
Plantinga, Alvin, 179
Poythress, Vern S., 23, 80, 189
Ratzsch, Del, 20, 34, 124, 155, 173-74, 177,
    178
Reynolds, John Mark, 47, 51
Ross, Hugh, 49, 64, 72-73, 75-76, 80
Ross, Marcus R., 37, 40
Ruse, Michael, 52, 185
Ryan, Frank, 119, 123, 126
Sanford, John, 51, 110
Schwartz, Jeffrey H., 90, 109, 123-24,
    134-35
Scott, Eugenie, 37, 43
Shapiro, James A., 123-24, 166
Sire, James, 21
Sober, Elliot, 30, 113, 121, 163
Thaxton, Charles, 52, 56, 85
Urey, Harold, 84
van Till, Howard, 45
Vardiman, Larry, 79, 104, 157
Wells, Jonathan, 56, 108-9, 111, 114-16, 173
Wilson, Edward O., 27, 43, 50, 59